Vṛndāvana
in
Vaiṣṇava Literature

Reconstructing Indian History & Culture

ISSN 0971-3824

1. Society in Ancient India / Sures Chandra Banerji
   (ISBN 81-246-0000-7)

2. Political Thought in Ancient India / G.P. Singh
   (ISBN 81-246-0001-5)

3. Early Indian Historical Tradition and Archaeology / G.P. Singh
   (ISBN 81-246-0005-8)

4. *Vasantotsava*: The Spring Festivals of India / Leona M. Anderson
   (ISBN 81-246-0011-2)

5. Ecological Readings in the Veda / M. Vannucci
   (ISBN 81-246-0009-0)

Reconstructing Indian History & Culture, no. 6

Vṛndāvana in Vaiṣṇava Literature

History — Mythology — Symbolism

by

Maura Corcoran

Vrindaban Research Institute, Vrindaban

D. K. Printworld (P) Ltd., New Delhi

Cataloging in Publication Data — DK

Corcoran, Maura.
Vṛndāvana in Vaiṣṇava Literature.
(Reconstructing Indian history & culture; no. 6).
Includes bibliographical references (p.).
Including index.

1. Vrindavan, India in literature. 2. Vaishnava literature.
3. Krishna (Hindu deity) I. Title. II. Series: Reconstructing
Indian history & culture; no. 6.

ISBN 81-246-0024-4

First Published in India in 1995

Published by Vrindaban Research Institute, Vrindaban in association with
D.K. Printworld (P) Ltd., *Regd. office* : F-52, Bali Nagar, New Delhi - 110015
(*Phone* : 011-546-6019; *Fax* : 011-546-5926).

Foreword

VṚNDĀVANA is held in high esteem by the Hindu devotees and particularly the followers of the Vaiṣṇava sect. The perennial stream of devotional literature has been describing the holy place with great reverence since it was sanctified with the *līlās* (exploits) of Lord Kṛṣṇa in his boyhood days. What we see today is a township, the historicity of which can be traced back from the 16th century. Lost in the ruins and forest, its rebirth is due to the transcendental vision of Sri Chaitanya haling from Eastern India. He and his followers conceived it at the supramundane plane, and they harmonised it with the earliest concept of a holy place emitting divine resplendence.

Vṛndāvana has, therefore, been visualised under different aspects, viz. historical, mythological, and symbolical. All these facets as handed down in literature have been amply analysed by Dr. Maura Corcoran in her work — *Vṛndāvana in Vaiṣṇava Literature.* She has comprehensively surveyed Brajabhāṣa literature and also peeped into the Vedic hymns, *Purāṇas, Līlās,* and philosophical texts; and secular or non-sectarian views have also been considered. She has, however, not highlighted the Buddhist antiquity of the place as evidenced by some remains now preserved in the Mathurā Museum. Beside taking into account various texts, she also had the opportunity to inspect a number of spots during her stay at the Vrindaban Research Institute for the pursuit of her research.

Dr. Corcoran is to be complimented on this important achievement, and I hope this will be well received by scholars and by admirers of Vṛndāvana. I add my own verse in praise of the holy place:

वृन्दावनमनुवसन् विरलाश्च सन्ता:
त्यक्त्वा समस्त भोगान् मनसो विकारान् ।
चित्ते निधाय युगल तत्वमनुस्मरन् च
आत्यन्त सौख्यविपुलमनुमन्ति नित्यम् ॥

Dr. R.C. Sharma
Director General
National Museum, New Delhi

Preface

As well as being one of the holiest places for all followers of Kṛṣṇa, Vṛndāvana forms a key concept involved in the crystallization of modern *Vaiṣṇava* Hinduism. Vṛndāvana is that sacred space within which the eternal divine play of Kṛṣna occurs. It is not, therefore, surprising that the study of this largely medieval and modern conception can be seen to have significant and potentially far-reaching implication for the development of Vaiṣṇavism in the prehistoric and classical periods. I would hope that the present work may clarify some aspects of the concept of Vṛndāvana, throwing further light on these important *Vaiṣṇava* texts.

In the absence of clear historical testimony as to the early history of the place and of the relevant texts, this investigation seeks to identify a notional sequence of ideas connected with Vṛndāvana: the description of (a) a mythic place; (b) a symbolic place. (c) the geographical town as a centre of pilgrimage. Modern sources have for the most part concentrated on Vṛndāvana as a geographical place and have failed to throw light on its symbolic and mythic significance

An examination of Hindu literature often shows the re-emergence of the most ancient concepts at a much later date, indicating an unexpected continuity of tradition. It would be easy to suppose, for example, that the Kṛṣṇa of Braj Hindi literature would bear no relationship to the Kṛṣṇa which occurs in Vedic literature. An examination of Vedic literature, however, indicates that the roots of both the 'mythic' and the 'symbolic' approaches relate to a Vṛndāvana prototype linked with the earliest attestations of Kṛṣṇa.

It is interesting to look at the concepts in clusters and see the repercussions of a change in one concept or the others in that particular cluster. Two concepts which link in this way both with each other and with Vṛndāvan are incarnation (*avatāra)* and divine sport *(līlā)* — two of the most fundamental concepts of devotional Hinduism underlying the entire understanding of the nature of the divine and the relation of the divine to the material world. An examination based on the concept of incarnation seeks to define the 'mythic' approach of the *Purāṇas,* where the treatment of Vṛndāvana is linked with the manifest Kṛṣṇa, as opposed to the unmanifest Viṣṇu. By contrast Braj Bhāṣā and sectarian commentatorial literature obviate the need for incarnation as an event by ignoring (Braj texts) or rejecting (Sanskrit sources) the doctrine of incarnation and the orthodox hierarchy that this entails.

The concept of divine sport is the basis of a further distinction between the *Purāṇas* and sectarian literature. The latter delimits the definition of *līlā* to cover only Kṛṣṇa's extra-terrestrial activity, so that Vṛndāvana is envisaged as a purely divine realm, entirely separate from the cosmos. In the *Purāṇas, līlā* encompasses indeed all divine activity, both creation and incarnation, but it, and associated aspects of Vṛndāvana, remain wholly within the confines of the manifest world.

The various approaches to the representation of Vṛndāvana are reflected in the imagery used in the texts to describe it. This ranges from the mythical images of tree, river and mountain to the symbolic forms of lotus petals and pericarp reminiscent of Tantric *yantras.*

Because Vṛndāvana is identified as a holy place, it is also a pilgrimage centre within the material world. The significance of the geographical site varies markedly depending on the genre and sectarian source of the text. In looking at the concept of Vṛndāvana, it is not really important whether or not the site "rediscovered" by the Gauḍiya Goswamis and today a major centre for all worshippers of Kṛṣṇa, is in historic fact identifiable with the mythic Vṛndāvana. What matters is the meaning it assumes in the texts and the way in which the geographical Vṛndāvana is totally identified with the divine realm which it symbolises. This has implications for the interpretation of pilgrimage in such texts, which is no longer a ritual movement from one holy site to another as a means of gaining merit, but instead total immersion of mind and body in one place in order to take part in the divine play.

This work would not have been possible without the help, criticism and support of many. In particular I must thank Dr. R.D. Gupta who was instrumental in inspiring me to undertake this research and is securing the means for its publication. Without the help of Professor J.C. Wright I would not have been able to begin to trace the roots of these concepts to the Vedic literature. Professor Wright's critical comments also helped me to formulate my ideas more clearly. The interest and encouragement of Dr. R.S. Macgregor gave me the confidence to see the research through. One of the most valuable sources, however, was my visit to Vrindaban itself, and I am particularly grateful to all those at the Vrindaban Research Institute who made my stay so worthwhile.

Contents

Abbreviations

Anukr.	*Anukramaṇikā*
BhP.	*Bhāgavata Purāṇa*
BSOAS	*Bulletin of the School of Oriental and African Studies*
BrSaṃ.	*Brahma-saṃhitā*
Hariv.	*Harivaṃśa*
JAOS	*Journal of the American Oriental Society Kapiṣṭhala-kaṭha-saṃhitā*
MahāT.	*Mahānirvāṇa-tantra*
Mbh.	*Mahābhārata*
PadP.	*Padma Purāṇa*
Rasakadaṃba	*Rasakadaṃbacūḍāmaṇi*
Rāsap.	*Rāsapañcādhyāyī*
RV.	*Ṛg Veda*
ŚBr.	*Śatapatha-brāhmaṇa*
Siddhāntap.	*Siddhāntapañcādhyāyī*
TantraT.	*Tantrarāja-tantra*
ViP.	*Viṣṇu Purāṇa*

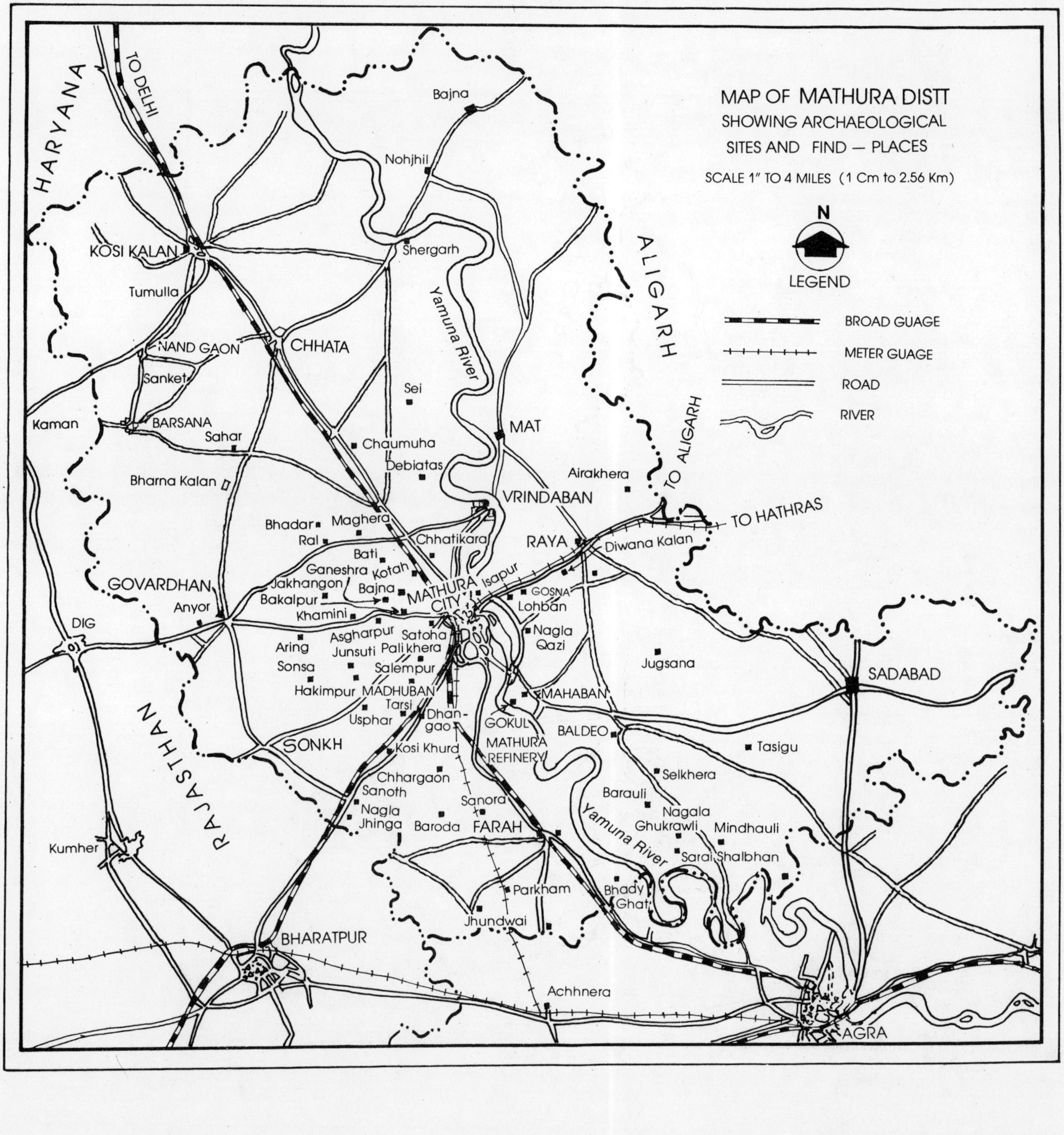

MAP OF MATHURA DISTT
SHOWING ARCHAEOLOGICAL
SITES AND FIND — PLACES
SCALE 1" TO 4 MILES (1 Cm to 2.56 Km)
N
LEGEND
BROAD GUAGE
METER GUAGE
ROAD
RIVER
HARYANA
TO DELHI
ALIGARH
TO ALIGARH
TO HATHRAS
RAJASTHAN
Bajna
Nohjhil
Shergarh
KOSI KALAN
Tumulla
NAND GAON
CHHATA
Yamuna River
Sanket
Sei
Kaman
BARSANA
Sahar
MAT
Chaumuha
Debiatas
Bharna Kalan
Airakhera
VRINDABAN
Bhadar
Maghera
Ral
Chhatikara
RAYA
Diwana Kalan
Bati
Ganeshra
Kotah
Jakhangon
Bajna
MATHURA CITY
Isapur
GOSNA
GOVARDHAN
Bakalpur
Lohban
Anyor
Khamini
DIG
Aring
Asgharpur
Satoha
Nagla Qazi
Junsuti
Pali khera
Sonsa
Salempur
Jugsana
Hakimpur
MADHUBAN
MAHABAN
SADABAD
Tarsi
Usphar
Dhan-gao
GOKUL
BALDEO
SONKH
Kosi Khurd
MATHURA REFINERY
Tasigu
Chhargaon
Selkhera
Sanoth
Sanora
Barauli
Nagla Jhinga
Baroda
FARAH
Nagala Ghukrawli
Mindhauli
Kumher
Yamuna River
Sarai Shalbhan
Parkham
Bhady Ghat
Jhundwai
BHARATPUR
Achhnera
AGRA

MAP OF VRINDABAN

1

Introduction

VṚNDĀVANA is a known geographical site — a major centre of Kṛṣṇa worship on the banks of the Yamunā, between Delhi and Agra. Its historical development from the 16th century onwards can be gathered from documents such as land-grants. However, in the devotional Sanksrit and Braj Bhāṣā literature another dimension of Vṛndāvana dominates the picture, i.e., its role as an expression of divine space. In fact, it is arguable that Vṛndāvana is firstly a mythic and symbolic concept, and that the identification with a specific geographical spot is a later development. This book intends, therefore, to look at Vṛndāvana as it is presented in the literature, taking into consideration related religious and philosophical concepts.

Primary Sources

Vṛndāvana is inseparable from Kṛṣṇa (particularly in his aspect as child and youth); consequently, any medieval texts mentioning Kṛṣṇa inevitably mention Vṛndāvana. To discuss every allusion to Vṛndāvana would entail including the entire immense corpus of Kṛṣṇa literature in these languages. As a result, the main issues would be clouded and considerable repetition would be unavoidable. It has been necessary, therefore, to choose representative texts of particular interest to the relevant concepts.

It will be seen how the genre to which a particular text may belong has an important bearing on its presentation of Vṛndāvana. These genres can be roughly divided into mythological, metaphysical, commentatorial and devotional, according to their emphasis.

The extent to which certain concepts are inherent in the very nature of Vṛndāvana and its association with Kṛṣṇa can be seen from the way in which motifs suggesting a Vṛndāvana-like place are to be found in Vedic literature associated with a Kṛṣṇa-entity. The Vedic approach is primarily metaphysical, though even here in certain contexts the process of mythologisation is discernible.

In order to illustrate the way in which the metaphysical contrast between the two aspects of the divine — transcendent and immanent — is transformed into mythology, the *Mahābhārata* and its portrayal of incarnation have been discussed. This is important because of the way in which the *Harivaṃśa* and *Viṣṇu Purāṇa* follow the same basic pattern and because of the implications this has in the portrayal of Vṛndāvana in these *Purāṇas*.

The *Harivaṃśa* (*Hariv.*) and *Viṣṇu Purāṇa* (*ViP.*) contain the earliest attested portrayal of Vṛndāvana in its basic form as it was to be depicted throughout the succeeding centuries. The exact date of these two texts, as of most of the texts under consideration, is impossible to determine, most secondary sources suggesting 100 to 300 B.C.[1] The relative position of the two texts is equally a matter of controversy. Hazra is of the opinion that the *ViP.* precedes the *Hariv.* His conclusion is based on the presence of the concept of *aṁśāvatāra* (not found in the *ViP.*) in the *Hariv.* as well as the more explicitly erotic nature of the *rāsa* in the *Hariv.*, both of which he identifies as later developments.[2] Neither of these arguments, however, is conclusive since the *aṃśāvatāra* concept is found in the *Mahābhārata* itself, while the less erotic nature of the *rāsa* in the *ViP.* could well be a result of what Ingalls calls the 'pietizing' of the *ViP.*[3]

Ingalls is of the opinion that the root of the tradition is the *Hariv.* His argument is that in the *Hariv.* the motives for the adventures of Kṛṣṇa are simpler and closer to a true folklore, less Brāhmanical-orthodox, showing the earlier nature of the *Hariv.*[4] Ingalls' position on this matter would seem to be more in accordance with the impression afforded by the limited sections of both texts relevant to Vṛndāvana discussed in this book. In the *Hariv.* the ambiguity between Vṛndāvana as a terrestrial and an extraterrestrial place is more complete and is thus closer to the spirit of the Vedic motifs. In the *ViP.*, on the other hand, the divinity of Kṛṣṇa is made more blatant, while at the same time the imagery used to describe Vṛndāvana loses its celestial connotations and becomes purely mundane. The greater use of alliteration in the *ViP.* may similarly suggest lateness.

The *Bhāgavata Purāṇa* (*BhP.*), dated between the 6th and 9th century A.D.,[5] though it incorporates the mythological framework of the *Hariv.* and *ViP.* basically belongs to a different genre. Whereas the *Hariv.* and *ViP.* have an epic approach, the focus of the *BhP.* is on the metaphysical implications and in this respect it reflects a re-emergence of the Vedic preoccupations. It is, however, more Upaniṣadic in its insistence on the unity of Kṛṣṇa, the immanent, and Viṣṇu, the transcendent.

The Gauḍīya texts appear to form a bridge between the above *Purāṇas* and the Braj Bhāṣā devotional poetry. They frequently give an impression of commenting on the *BhP.* in terms of concepts inherent in the Braj Bhāṣā texts and thus of formulating those concepts in theological language.

The text of the Gosvāmīs are ascribed to the end of the 16th century A.D.[6] and are thus roughly contemporaneous with the traditional dates assigned to the Braj Bhāṣā poets such as Sūradāsa, Nandadāsa and Hita Harivaṃśa. This lends all the more credence to the supposition that the originality found in the Gauḍīya Sanskrit texts *vis-à-vis* the *BhP.* owes a considerable debt to the vernacular tradition.

The main Gauḍīya texts used in this Book are the two so-called commentaries on the *BhP.* — the *Laghubhāgavatāmṛta* of Rūpa Gosvāmī and the *Bṛhadbhāgavatāmṛta* of Sanātana Gosvāmī. The *Laghubhāgavatāmṛta* is preoccupied with the nature of the divinity and its manifestations. For this reason it is of primary relevance to Chapter I of this Book. The *Bṛhadbhāgavatāmṛta,* on the other hand, focuses on the devotee and the nature of devotion and is therefore of interest in the context of Chapter 4.

The Braj Bhāṣā texts can be divided into two basic categories: (a) those which retain the mythological structure of the *BhP.*, in particular the concept of incarnation; and (b) those which reject that structure — the texts of the *rasikas* who proclaim the unceasing nature of the eternal sport (*nitya vihāra*).

The most important example of the first category is the *Sūrasāgara.* J.S. Hawley has shown that the text as it is found in later manuscripts and printed editions is much larger than the oldest collections.[7] Until more information is made available as to exactly which *padas* are found in the earliest manuscripts it is only possible to speak in general terms of the *Sūrasāgara* as a corpus representing one particular literary tradition.

Hawley has suggested that *padas* showing the influence of both the *BhP.* and Vallabhaite sectarian affiliations belong to a later stratum. As will be seen, the treatment of Vṛndāvana and related themes certainly suggests that sectarian considerations are decidedly less pronounced in the *Sūrasāgara* than in other Braj Bhāṣā texts.

The question of the role of the *BhP.* in the *Sūrasāgara* is rather more difficult. The theme of *viraha,* for example, which Hawley finds dominating the earliest collections[8] is also important in the *BhP.* but is totally foreign to the *rasika* poetry, while the Gauḍīyas take an intermediate stand, emphasizing the temporary nature of *viraha.* Moreover, Hawley mentions[9] that *pada* 622 is found in Bikaner Ms. 158, one of the earliest manuscripts dated 1641 A.D. (the earliest examined by him is 1598-1628 A.D.). This particular *pada* follows the *BhP.* account of the birth of Kṛṣṇa closely, showing that the incorporation of *BhP.* themes began early in the history of the *Sūrasāgara.* It suggests that even the earliest *padas* of the *Sūrasāgara* were seen as being compatible with the *BhP.* so that a certain continuity of tradition was maintained even in the *padas* added later.

The viewpoint of the second category — the *rasikas* — is presented most lucidly by the writings of Dhruvadāsa, of the Rādhāvallabha sect, and Bihārinadāsa of the Haridāsī sect. Both these poets can be regarded as essentially the first exponents of the principles of these two sects. The traditional founders — Hita Harivaṃśa of the Rādhāvallabha and Haridāsa of the sect named after him — were not only much less prolific but it is arguable that the distinctive doctrines of the sectarian viewpoint are much less pronounced in their works. The importance of living in Vṛndāvana, for example, which forms a central theme of the later Rādhāvallabha poetry goes unmentioned in the *Hitacaurāsī* of Harivaṃśa.

According to Snātaka in his study of the Rādhāvallabha sect, no other poet has given so complete an account of Rādhāvallabha sectarian doctrines as Dhruvadāsa.[10] There are forty-two short works ascribed to this poet. These include poems devoted to a description of the eternal sport of Rādhā and Kṛṣṇa as well as works such as the *Siddāntavicāra līlā*, which expound the principles of devotion. The two texts of most interest to this study are the *Vṛndāvana sata līlā*, a work of 116 verses in praise of Vṛndāvana, and the *Bṛhadbāvanapurāṇa bhāṣā līlā*. This last purports to be a translation of a Sanskrit text — the *Bṛhadvāmana Purāṇa* — which is untraceable today, though such a text is mentioned in the commentary of Jīva Gosvāmī on the *Brahma-saṃhitā*.[11] Because of the unavailability of the text it is impossible to assess the extent to which Dhruvadāsa actually made use of it. The reference by Jīva does suggest that the work was indeed concerned with the same basic story, i.e., the request by the Vedas to be born as *gopīs* and to see Kṛṣṇa in Vṛndāvana. This basic theme is found in a number of other sources, including the *Sūrasāgara*.[12] Dhruvadāsa's treatment, however, differs considerably from the others, and is completely in accord with concepts expressed in his other works. It is therefore likely that he modified the Sanskrit original substantially, even if such a source was used as a basis.

The date of Dhruvadāsa can be inferred from the colophons of a number of the works ascribed to him. Thus the *Vṛndāvana sata* gives the date *Saṃ*. 1686 (1629 A.D.);[13] the *Rasānanda līlā*, *Saṃ*. 1650 (1593 A.D.);[14] *Rahasyamañjarī Saṃ*. 1698 (1641 A.D.).[15] His works thus belong to the first half of the 17th century.

Bihārinadāsa has a position in the Haridāsī sect similar to that of Dhruvadāsa in the Rādhāvallabha. He is regarded as the second of the eight *ācāryas* of the sect[16] and is without question the most prolific. Traditionally he is known as Gurudeva[17] — a title indicating his position as expounder of sectarian principles.

Like those of Dhruvadāsa, the poems of Bihārinadāsa can be divided into two categories — principles (*siddhānta*) and description of divine sport (*rāsa*). All of his poetry consists entirely of single *padas* and *dohās*.

The only basis for dating Bihārinadāsa is tradition which places him towards the end of the 16th century. That he preceded Dhruvadāsa can be concluded from his mention in the *Bhaktanāmāvalī* (of Dhruva).[18]

Nandadāsa, whose date has been given roughly as 1530-85,[19] would seem to fall between the *Sūrasāgara* and the *rasika* tradition in his approach, and in this way comes closest to being a Braj Bhāṣā equivalent of the Gauḍīya standpoint. In both his main works, the *Rāsapañcādhyāyī* and the *Bhramaragīta*, he uses the basic structure of the *BhP*. However, a close examination of both texts shows many instances in which he makes changes which put his poetry more in accord with that of Dhruvadāsa or Bihārinadāsa. There is substantial evicence that Nandadāsa was a follower of the Vallabha sect and that he adhered to the principles of the sect in his presentation of the material. That he is at the same time so close to the Gauḍīya position would suggest the existence of considerable similarity between both so-called commentators on the *BhP.*, i.e., Vallabha and the Gauḍīya Gosvāmīs.

The above four poets have been primarily relied upon in this study. They are representative of the main sects in question — Rādhāvallabha, Haridāsī and Vallabha. At the same time they illustrate most clearly the trends in Braj Bhāṣā literature.

The other sect of the Vṛndāvana area, i.e., Nimbārkīya, has a much less extensive literature. One of the main poets — Harivyāsadeva — has been discussed, both in the context of incarnation (in this Chapter) and of the description of Vṛndāvana (Chapter 3). Basically his views appear to be in accord with those of Bihārinadāsa and Dhruvadāsa, though a more pronounced slant towards philosophy and ritual, rather than pure *rasa*, may be observed.

There is little scope for an examination of the concept of Vṛndāvana in the Braj Bhāṣā Gauḍīya texts. There are for the most part short poems describing the *līlā* of Rādhā and Kṛṣṇa which do not go into doctrinal discussion. Such doctrines are covered in much greater detail by the Sanskrit texts which will be discussed in this book.

Secondary Sources

The *Mathurá Memoir* (3rd edition 1883) by Growse[20] is the earliest comprehensive discussion of the Braj area. This work is mainly concerned with the geographical Mathurā and the surrounding area, including Vṛndāvana, as it was found at the time of the author — the temples, peoples, archaeological remains and geographical details. It is precisely this aspect of Vṛndāvana which is ignored by the texts under consideration and hence is irrelevant to this study.

Growse also looks at the political history of the area and its rulers, beginning with the sack of Mathurā in 1071 A.D. by Mahmud of Ghazni. As with the geography such historical facts have little bearing on the texts in question and moreover concern mainly Mathurā and Vṛndāvana only peripherally.

Growse's attempted etymology of the place-name Vṛndāvana is the point probably of most relevance to this study. He[21] derives it from the plant name *vṛndā*, identified with *tulasī*, the holy basil plant, and thus fitting in with his theory that all of the oldest place-names of the area are derived from physical features. He rejects summarily etymologies connecting it with Vṛndā as a female proper name denoting Rādhā, a goddess or a *sakhī*. Unfortunately for this theory, attestations of *vṛndā* as a synonym for *tulasī* are no more ancient or reliable than those of the proper name Vṛndā. This leaves *vṛnda*, 'group', as the most probable derivation (see Chapter 1, footnote 1), a possibility unmentioned by Growse.

The next study of the Braj area after Growse is that of K.D. Vājapeyī.[22] As its title — *Braja kā itihāsa* — suggests, this is mainly intended as a historical work. For the early period Vājapeyī relies heavily on Purāṇic sources which he regards as being based on historical fact and therefore of describing a historical Braj area. Such a position ignores the mythological character of the texts in question and so the metaphysical implications involved. The discussion of the later period is, on the other hand, like Growse, primarily concerned with political history and so equally irrelevant to this study.

One interesting reference to Vṛndāvana mentioned in the above work is that of Bilhaṇa in his *Vikramāṅkadevacarita*[23] where he describes how in his travels as a Paṇḍit he came and defeated in scholastic discussion the other scholars in Mathurā and then spend some time in Vṛndāvana. Though Bilhaṇa says nothing about Vṛndāvana being a pilgrimage centre, he certainly does associate it with the sport of Rādhā and Kṛṣṇa. This reference suggests, therefore, that Vṛndāvana was known both as a geographical place and the mythic site of Kṛṣna *līlā* even at the time of this text. The text itself is dated with considerable certitude — *c.* 1080 A.D.[24] — only a few hundred years after the date assigned to the *BhP.*

Snātaka's discussion on Vṛndāvana in his study of the Rādhāvallabha sect[25] is more along the lines of the present study insofar as it looks at Vṛndāvana through the religious texts. The basic point which Snātaka makes is that only Rādhāvallabha texts describe the earthly Vṛndāvana, while all other works — *Purāṇas*, Gauḍīya writings, etc. — deal with a divine Vṛndāvana.

In his discussion of non-Rādhāvallabha literature, Snātaka is extremely cursory and a closer examination reveals many distinctions which he ignores. For example, he lumps together the *BhP.* and the *Padma Purāṇa*, which are, as will be shown in this Book, very divergent in their approaches.

His exposition of the Gauḍīya standpoint is also lacking in clarity. He mentions that Prabodhānanda describes both the earthly and the unearthly Vṛndāvana but fails to indicate how he proposes to fit this fact into his general theory. He then goes on to quote a passage from the *Caitanyacaritāmṛta* in order to show how the Gauḍīyas dealt only with the divine Vṛndāvana and says nothing of their theory of two aspects of Vṛndāvana.

In his attempt to emphasize the unique nature of the Rādhāvallabha standpoint, Snātaka entirely ignores all other Braj Bhāṣā texts, particularly those of the Haridāsī sect. These are, as we shall see, in many ways similar to those of the Rādhāvallabha sect.

His analysis of the Rādhāvallabha standpoint itself is not entirely satisfactory. According to Snātaka, the Rādhāvallabha poets describe Vṛndāvana as it is on earth with all its physical features — trees, creepers, etc. However, the descriptions of Vṛndāvana are in fact singularly free from any features which would connect it with the geographical Vṛndāvana. It is only in the injunctions to make one's residence in Vṛndāvana that the connection with the earthly Vṛndāvana emerges. There is thus an identification between the divine Vṛndāvana which is described as the scene for the sport of Rādhā and Kṛṣṇa in the *rasa* verses and the physical Vṛndāvana where one is told by the *siddhānta* verses to live.

It is the identification between the divine Vṛndāvana and the physical Vṛndāvana as a symbol of the divine which Snātaka fails to explain satisfactorily. He says, for example, that a long passage from Dhruvadāsa which describes the importance of living in Vṛndāvana shows evidence of Rādhāvallabha sectarian considerations. He then quotes a further passage describing the divine nature of Vṛndāvana, and says that this shows how Dhruvadāsa also had in his imagination the eternal Vṛndāvana. Snātaka does not discuss how these two aspects are connected. He suggests, in fact, that they have their basis in two distinct influences — the sectarian and the traditional Purāṇic. Thus while there is a degree of truth in his statement regarding the importance of the physical Vṛndāvana in Rādhāvallabha doctrine, Snātaka is over-simplistic in his enunciation of its significance.

The major work on the Braj area after Growse is that of P.D. Mītala in three volumes — Vol. 1 on the cultural history of the area,[26] Vol. 2 on the history of the religious sects,[27] and Vol. 3 on the history of the arts.[28] In his volume on the cultural history, Mītala postulates five definitions for the Braj area:[29] (1) Political Braj which he identifies with the ancient Śūrasena, and which only became known as Braj under the Jāṭs in the 18th century. (2) Linguistic Braj, i.e., that area in which Braj Bhāṣā is spoken. (3) Cultural Braj which Mītala defines as being the results of the re-discovery by Rūpa and Sanātana. The borders of this area are based on the statements of Nārāyaṇa Bhaṭṭa in his *Brajabhaktivilāsa.* (4) Religious Braj which is again divided into two: (a) Sectarian Braj, i.e., the route of the *banayātrā* or *brajayātrā.* This *yātrā* begins and ends in Mathurā, but Mathurā is not situated in the centre of the area and neither is the area circular in shape. (b) Spiritual Braj — the imaginary spiritual form of Braj for worship and mental meditation. Mītala sees this form of Braj as being a symbol — *pratīka* — of Goloka. Here it is envisaged as a circular area with Mathurā in the centre.

Mītala's categories of sectarian and spiritual are to some extent in accordance with the findings of this Book — i.e., the division into a geographical and symbolic portrayal of Vṛndāvana. However Mītala has only mentioned these two aspects in passing and has not considered their full significance.

Ch. Vaudeville in her article 'Braj, lost and found'[30] has discussed the rediscovery of Vṛndāvana and has attempted to find lying behind many of the present Kṛṣṇaite religious sites a basis of primitive nature and goddess worship. She has therefore not looked at the concept of Vṛndāvana as it appears in the Sanskrit and Braj Bhāṣā texts themselves.

From this discussion of secondary sources dealing with Vṛndāvana it becomes apparent that Vṛndāvana has been dealt with primarily as a geographical and historical place. The concentration upon this aspect of Vṛndāvana, and the refusal to acknowledge the mythic and symbolic nature of Vṛndāvana has at times led to a misunderstanding of the nature of the texts in question. Where Vṛndāvana as a divine realm has been examined, it has been in insufficient depth an so has failed to elucidate the fundamental differences in approach between the classical and medieval texts. It is upon the nature of these differences that the present work intends to throw light.

References

1. Cf. D.H.H. Ingalls, 'The *Harivaṃśa* as *mahākāvya*', in *Mélanges d'Indianisme*, Paris, 1968, p. 394.
2. R.C. Hazra, *Studies in the Purāṇic records on Hindu rites and customs*, Dacca, 1940, p. 23.
3. Ingalls, *op. cit.*, p. 384.
4. *Ibid.*, p. 384.
5. Cf. T.J. Hopkins, 'The social teaching of the *Bhāgavata Purāṇa*', in *Krishna: myths, rites and attitudes*, Honolulu, 1966, p. 4.
6. S.K. De, *Early history of the Vaiṣṇava faith and movement in Bengal*, Calcutta, 1942, pp. 119-21.
7. J.S. Hawley, 'The early *Sūr Sāgar* and the growth of the Sūr tradition', *JAOS*, 99.1 (1979), p. 64.
8. *Ibid.*, p. 67.
9. *Ibid.*, p. 66.
10. V. Snātaka, *Rādhāvallabha saṃpradāya: siddhānta aur sāhitya*, Delhi, 1958, p. 426.
11. *Brahma-saṃhitā*, ed. Arthur Avalon, commentary by Jīva Gosvāmī, Calcutta, 1928, p. 9, v. 6.

    tathā ca śrīvṛhadvāmanapurāṇe
    śrībhagavatī śrutīnāṃ prārthanāpūrvakāṇi padyāni |
    ānandarūpam iti yad vidanti hi purāvidaḥ |
    tadrūpam darśayāsmākaṃ yadi deyo varo hi naḥ |
    śrutvaitad darśayāmāsa gokulaṃ prakṛteḥ param |
    kevalānubhavānanḍamātram akṣaramadhyagam |
    yatra vṛndāvanaṃ nāma vanaṃ kāmadugdhair drumair | *ityādi* |

    'As also in the *Vṛhadvāmana Purāṇa* (are found) the prayerful verses of the Vedas: "That blissful from which the knowers of the past seek, show us that form if you wish to bestow a boon upon us." Having heard this he showed them Gokula which is beyond Nature, formed purely from bliss arising from the experience of unity, existing in the indestructible region, where the wood called Vṛndāvana, with wish-yielding cows and trees . . . etc."
12. Sūradāsa, *Sūrasāgara*, ed. N. Vājapeyī, Kāśī, 1953, *pada* 1793.
13. Dhruvadāsa, *Vṛndāvana sata līlā*, in *Bayālīsa līlā*, Vṛndāvana, 1971, v. 115.

    solaha sai dhruva chyāsiya pūnyau agahana māsa |
    yaha prabandha pūrana bhayau sunata hota agha nāsa |

    'Dhruva completed this composition in 1686 in the holy month of Agahana; hearing it sins are destroyed.'
14. Dhruvadāsa, *Rasānanda līlā*, in *Bayālīsa līlā*, *op. cit.*, v. 184.
15. Dhruvadāsa, *Rahasyamañjarī*, in *Bayālīsa līlā*, *op. cit.*, v. 105.
16. P.D. Mītala, *Braja ke dharma saṃpradāyoṃ kā itihāsa*, Mathurā, 1968, p. 466.
17. *Ibid.*, p. 466.
18. Dhruvadāsa, *Bhaktanāmāvalī*, in *Bayālīsa līlā*, *op. cit.*, vv. 39-40.
19. R.S. McGregor, introduction to *Nanddas: the round dance of Krishna*, London, 1973, p. 34.

20. F.S. Growse, *Mathuá: a district memoir*, NWP and Oudh Government Press, 1883.
21. *Ibid.*, p. 173.
22. K.D. Vājapeyī, *Braja kā itihāsa*, Mathurā, 1955.
23. Bilhaṇa, *Vikramāṅkadevacaritam*, ed. G. Bühler, 1875, 18.87.
    dolāloladghana jaghanayā rādhayā yatra bhagnāḥ
    kṛṣṇakrīḍāṅgaṇaviṭapino nādhunāpy ucchvasanti |
    jalpakrīḍāmathitamathurāsūricakreṇa kecit
    tasmin vṛndāvanaparisare vāsarā yena nītāḥ |87|
    'Where the branches of the places of Kṛṣṇa's sport, broken by Rādhā with her heavy hips swinging in the swing, still have not recovered, in that area of Vṛndāvana he who had agitated the multitude of the scholars of Mathurā by the sport of his speech, passed some days.'
24. *Ibid.*, introduction, p. 20.
25. Snātaka, *op. cit.*, pp. 226-36.
26. P.D. Mītala, *Braja kā sāṃskṛtika itihāsa*, Delhi, 1966.
27. P.D. Mītala, *Braja ke dharma-sampradāyoṃ kā itihāsa*, Delhi, 1968.
28. P.D. Mītala, *Braja kī kalāoṃ kā itihāsa*, Mathurā, 1975.
29. P.D. Mītala, *Braja kā sāṃskṛtika itihāsa*, pp. 7-9.
30. Ch. Vaudeville, 'Braj, lost and found', *Indo-Iranian Journal*, 18 (1976), pp. 195-213.

[illegible]

[illegible] Journal [illegible] 1928

[illegible]

[illegible]

[illegible] by [illegible] with [illegible]

[illegible] pp. [illegible]

[illegible]

[illegible] 1956

[illegible]

[illegible]

[illegible]

[illegible] Journal, 15 (1964), pp. 171-173

2

Mythic Vṛndāvana as the Scene of Kṛṣṇa's Incarnation

THE prominence of mythic elements in depicting Vṛndāvana goes hand in hand with the mythological enunciation of the relationship between the two aspects of the divine — the unmanifest (Viṣṇu) and the manifest (Kṛṣṇa) — in terms of an event in the primordial past, i.e., incarnation. Vṛndāvana forms the mythic location for this event.

Sanskrit Sources

(a) Kṛṣṇa-Viṣṇu Motifs in Vedic Literature

Ostensibly, Vṛndāvana is a relatively late idea, and a contrast between a Kṛṣṇadhāman, Vṛndāvana, and a Viṣṇudhāman, Vaikuṇṭha, would seem to have been formed on the analogy of the fully developed relationship between Kṛṣṇa and Viṣṇu, e.g., as found in the *Purāṇas.* There may be a danger that, in arriving at this conclusion, too much reliance is being placed on the alleged chronology of ancient Indian literature. As a result too little allowance is made for the occasional substitution, throughout the history of the Indo-aryan language, of a different term for the same or similar concept. It is, in fact, feasible to suggest that a Vṛndāvana/Vaikuṇṭha prototype emerges simultaneously with the earliest attestations of Kṛṣṇa and Viṣṇu.

Even if the terms Vṛndāvana and Vaikuṇṭha do not appear in the most ancient literature, they must have an ancient etymology.[1] The fact that it is lost in the extant literature may indicate the limitations of the literary sources rather than be a proof of relative lateness.

Besides, there is no question but that the *trīṇi padāni* of Viṣṇu are one of the oldest concepts attested; and it is evident that the *parama* or highest of these is regarded as the abode of Viṣṇu,[2] in other words a prototype of 'Vaikuṇṭha'. It is the immediate purpose of this section to show that *Ṛg* Vedic mention both of the concrete, personified Kṛṣṇa (*kṛ́ṣṇaḥ*) and of the abstract, impersonal power (*kṛṣṇā́m*), does exist; and it is found in association with imagery suggesting a 'Vṛndāvana' prototype.

Preoccupation with the epic view of Kṛṣṇa's origins has led to disregard the relevance of the *Ṛg Veda* (*RV.*) attestations. The current standard view regarding the origins of Kṛṣṇa adopted in the secondary literature has been succinctly put by Gonda, who sees the development as that of a divinization of a historical Kṛṣṇa. He argues that Kṛṣṇa was a popular hero elevated to the status of a god; and that it can be supposed that this legendary person preached or reformed a religion, and then himself gradually received divine honours.[3] Because of this point of view, Gonda rigidly distinguishes the developed Kṛṣṇa figure from the Vedic Kṛṣṇa.

Regarding the connection between Kṛṣṇa and Viṣṇu, Gonda finds certain characteristics in the ancient Vedic Viṣṇu, such as his association with protection in his role as king, which would facilitate the assimilation of what he sees as basically later cult figures, such as Kṛṣṇa.[4] According to Gonda, this assimilation of Kṛṣṇa by Viṣṇu must have taken place in the interval which separated the *Bhagavadgīitā*, where Kṛṣṇa is not yet an *avatāra* of Viṣṇu, and the redaction of *Mbh.* 14, 53 where he appears as being this god.[5] In this way, Gonda sees the relation of Kṛṣṇa and Viṣṇu as a purely post-Vedic development, effecting an elevation in the status of Kṛṣṇa as a divinity, instead of being inherent in the basic functions of Kṛṣṇa and Viṣṇu even in the Vedic context.

A closer study of the *RV.* hymns, in fact, shows evidence that the metaphysical and mythic concepts embodied in the Purāṇic Kṛṣṇa do have counterparts in the *RV.* For example, Kṛṣṇa as the child demon-killer is reminiscent of Indra who performs heroic deeds as soon as he is born (cf. 8.96.16 discussed below, see Appendix A.5). Kṛṣṇa, the child in whom the divine becomes accessible to human beings, resembles Agni, whose birth is a major motif of the Vedic hymns, a fact which finds expression in the common epithet *yăviṣṭha*, 'youngest'.[6] Like Kṛṣṇa, Agni takes birth among mortals. He is born as the protector, *gopāḥ*, of the people.[7] Moreover, the hymns frequently address Agni as a relative,[8] denoting his accessibility, illustrated in the case of Kṛṣṇa by his relations with the people of Braj.

The concept of incarnation is similarly revealed in the Vedic myth of Purūravas. The essence of this myth lies in the relations between Purūravas and Urvaśī. Reference is made to the birth of a child in circumstances somewhat similar to Drapsá Kṛṣṇá (see below pp. 13-14), who is called *nárya*[9] (which may be taken to be an archaic version of *nārāyaṇa*). The distinction between father and son is never made explicit, thereby suggesting a process of incarnation.

Furthermore, the Purūravas myth contains two basic Kṛṣṇa motifs — birth in association with cow-women. In the *RV.* hymn, the child is said to be born specifically as a herdsman (*jajñisá itthā́ gopī́thyāya*).[10] Divine women (*gnā́*), identified as rivers (*nadyā́ḥ*), are said to have reared him[11] — a motif showing a marked likeness to the relation of Kṛṣṇa with the *gopīs.* The resemblance is further strengthened by the comparison of the water-women with cows (*gā́vo . . . dhenávo*)[12] while the image of Purūravas (or his son) drawing near them as they lay off their mantles — *jáhatīṣv átkam*[13] — is reminiscent of Kṛṣṇa stealing the clothes of the *gopīs* as they bathe.

In view of the connection between Agni and the concepts embodied by Kṛṣṇa (discussed above), it is interesting to note that in the *Kapiṣṭhala-kaṭha-saṃhitā*[14] and *Śatapatha-brāhmaṇa*[15] versions Purūravas receives fire together with a son. Significantly the son is called Āyu or Kumāra, epithets also of Agni. Thus once again the motifs of a new-born child and of Agni are linked.

(i) The term Kṛṣṇa as found in the *Ṛg Veda*: The actual term Kṛṣṇa appears in the *RV.* in two forms — the neuter *kṛṣṇám* and the masculine *kṛ́ṣṇaḥ;* as does *árjuna* with the accent unchanged. Similar pairs are not uncommon in the *RV.*, as, in particular, *mitrám* and *mitráḥ*, *indriyám* and *índraḥ*, *vṛtrám* and *vṛtráḥ*. The concepts of *kṛṣṇám* and *árjunam* represent basic mythic, metaphysical ideas, while the figures *kṛ́ṣṇaḥ* and *árjunaḥ* both occur as characters in an epic context, and appear to stem from 'personifications' which have lost much of their original significance.

The attestation of *kṛṣṇám áhar* and *árjunam áhar*, i.e., 'night' and 'day', at *RV.* vi. 9.1-3 (for a further discussion of this hymn see Appendix A.1) conforms to the pattern of other fundamental dualities such as Heaven and Earth, Mitra and Varuṇa, Iranian Good Mind and Bad Mind, etc. The alternation recurs in later Vaiṣṇava texts as the concepts of cosmic day and cosmic night. The idea, for example, is found of the day of Brahmā when creation is manifest and the night of Brahmā, which is the period following dissolution when creation remains unmanifest.[16] Analogous with this is the concept of creation latent in the sleeping Viṣṇu which becomes manifest on his awakening.[17] As in the Vedic texts these periods of manifestation and of dissolution follow one another in a cycle.

The 'personified' Ṛṣi Kṛṣṇa Āngirasa, father of Viśvaka Kārṣṇi, is postulated in *RV. Anukr.* as author of viii. 85 ff. (further discussion at Appendix A.2). This is evidently on the basis of an occurrence in this hymn of two characters (*jaritṛ*) Kṛṣṇa and Viśvaka.

The same Ṛṣi is listed also for x.42-44, which follows some material preoccupied with the ideas 'night' and 'day' (as *áhar*, though not explicitly *kṛṣṇá* or *árjuna*) and precedes some epic material ascribed in the *Anukr.* to Indra Vaikuṇṭha. If the *Anukr.*'s identification of the god as Vaikuṇṭha is a genuine key to the hymn, the point could perhaps lie in some inauspicious physical defect of the Indra in question. The epithet might have made its way to Viṣṇu (cf. Vāmana, etc.) at the same time as adjacent *kṛṣṇám áhar* material was becoming associated with Viṣṇu and Kṛṣṇa.

It does not seem possible to believe that mere juxtaposition has brought x.42-44 (further discussion at Appendix A.4 b-c) into association with the Ṛṣi Kṛṣṇa Āngirasa. In fact, the refrain of these three hymns (in each case vv.10-11) does seem to include features with Kṛṣṇa connotations. V.10 opens with *góbhiḥ* and *yávena*, thus incorporating the familiar cow motif, as well as the concept of plenty (cf. the green pastures of Vṛndāvana in the *Purāṇas*); and v.11 ends with the theme of making space for the allies — *sákhā sákhibhyo várivaḥ kṛṇotu*. It is possible that the reference to male *sákhīs* was seen as link with Kṛṣṇa, whose association in other contexts with female *sakhīs* was perhaps already developing. In any case the basic topic of the refrain is evidently the establishment of an earthly 'Vṛndāvana' and a heavenly 'Goloka'.

A further link in the chain of reasoning represented in the *Anukr.* is the linking of the name *rājno duhitā* Ghóṣā with Víśvaka Kṛṣṇiyá at i.117.7 and with Árjuna at i.122. 5 (for a discussion of the hymns attributed to Ghóṣā see Appendix A.3 a-c). In this way a connection is maintained at the 'personified' level as well as at the metaphysical *áhar* level between Kṛṣṇa and Arjuna.

A figure Kṛṣṇá Drapsá is the subject of the passage viii.96.13-15 (further discussion at Appendix A.5) describing an exploit of Indra. The position of the accent distinguishes this character from the Kṛ́ṣṇa of viii.85, who is connected with Víśvaka at i.117, and associates it more closely with the *kṛṣṇám áhar* and *árjunam áhar* of vi.9. It seems reasonable to infer that Kṛṣṇá Drapsá, a distinctly mythic notion of a 'black seed' which is to spring brilliantly to life in the waters of Aṃśumatī, belongs with *kṛṣṇám áhar*, the night that alternates with (and begets) day, as the basic conception, while the 'heroes' Kṛ́ṣṇa and Ārjuna are secondary, 'literary' constructions.

Three stages can, in fact, be postulated in the development of Kṛṣṇa as an entity:

(1) The first would be the basic unpersonified *kṛṣṇám* concept, quite possibly older in its origins than the *RV.* itself, which finds its expression in the *kṛṣṇám áhar* and *kṛṣṇáḥ drapsáḥ.*

(2) The second would be the transformation of this abstract concept into the deity Kṛṣṇa which finds its ultimate development in the *Purāṇas;* but which may be seen reflected to some extent even in the *kṛṣṇá drapsá* theme.

(3) The third would be the Kṛ́ṣṇa Āngrirasa Ṛṣi, connected with the compilation of the Śrauta texts and the increasing emphasis on elaborate sacrificial rules.

Presumably the second two stages were roughly parallel for a time; and epic and Purāṇic formations took shape while the Vedic material was gradually accumulating.

(ii) The relation between Kṛṣṇa and Viṣṇu: The other frequent assumption, i.e., that the relation between Kṛṣṇa and Viṣṇu is a late feature designed either to integrate two cults or to legitimize the late Kṛṣṇa cult, seems equally misplaced. The Kṛṣṇa-Viṣṇu dichotomy, in fact, appears basic to Vedic metaphysics. It can be seen basically as an expression of important motifs such as those of lower versus higher, dark versus light, immanent versus transcendent, manifest versus unmanifest.

In the *RV.* Agni and Viṣṇu form a pair similar in many respects to that of Kṛṣṇa and Viṣṇu found in the *Purāṇas.* The emphasis on the accessibility of Agni has already been discussed (see above p. 12). This is in contrast to Viṣṇu, who, in both Vedic and Purāṇic texts, remains on a much more purely celestial level. The contrast between the two roles is exemplified in the first verse of the *Aitareya-brāhmaṇa* which states:

> *agnir vai devānām avamo viṣṇuḥ paramas*।
> *tadantareṇa sarvā anyā devatāḥ* ।[18]

In other words, among expression of the divine, Agni is *avama*, i.e., the divine immanent, while Viṣṇu is *parama*, transcendent.

The dichotomy between 'higher' (*parà*) and 'lower' (*ávara*), as well as between light and darkness, is evident in vv.2-3 of vi.9, the *kṛṣṇám áhar* hymn. In fact, *kṛṣṇám áhar* versus *árjunam áhar* may be seen as forming a pair comparable to that of Viṣṇu-Kṛṣṇa.

A link between Kṛṣṇa and Viṣṇu is reflected in viii.96, the *Kṛṣṇá drapsá* hymn, in the form of two 'etymologies' of the name Viṣṇu, viz., *viviḍḍhi* (from the root *viṣ-*) and *víṣuṇe*. These are such as would be likely to accrue in any *RV.* hymn in association with the mention of a specific name (cf. 1.154 addressed to Viṣṇu which consists largely of 'etymology' — especially *vi-* but also *vīryà* and *vṛ́ṣan*).

It seems likely, therefore, that the *RV.* material already has in view a special relationship between Kṛṣṇa and Viṣṇu, and that the Purāṇic Viṣṇu and Kṛṣṇa had a parallel development.

(b) The Epic and Purāṇic Approach to the Relation between Kṛṣṇa and Viṣṇu

(i) The Distinctive Characteristics of Kṛṣṇa and Viṣṇu in the *Mahābhārata*: Basically, in the *Mahābhārata* (*Mbh.*) Kṛṣṇa is represented as a hero on earth (inmanent), while Viṣṇu is a divinity in heaven (transcendent). Apart from this difference their roles are similar, and earth is taken to be the scene for a re-enactment of the divine struggle between gods and demons.

There is an emphasis in the *Mbh.* on divine pairs showing a continuity with the *kṛṣṇám áhar-árjunam áhar* of the *RV.* In the heavenly struggle it is Nara and Nārāyaṇa who lead the gods.[19] Similarly, in the earthly struggle Kṛṣṇa and Arjuna, who are often identified with Nara and Nārāyaṇa, lead the Pāṇḍavas. Their power as a pair is expressed in the final verse of the *Bhagavadgītā*:

> *yatra yogeśvaraḥ kṛṣṇo yatra pārtho dhanurdharaḥ*।
> *tatra śrīr vijayo bhūtir dhruvā nītir matir mama*।[20]

(ii) The Relation between Kṛṣṇa and Viṣṇu—*aṃśāvatāra*: In the *Mbh.* the connection between Viṣṇu and Kṛṣṇa is expressed in terms of Kṛṣṇa as an incarnation in part (*aṃśāvatāra*) of Viṣṇu, i.e., Kṛṣṇa is subordinated to Viṣṇu. It is often alleged that the concept of *aṃśāvatāra* is a secondary interpolation, reflecting the incorporation of a

Kṛṣṇa cult into Vaiṣṇava religion. This suggestion is, of course, inevitable as the Vedic conception of Viṣṇu transcendent in *paramá vyòman* and Agni immanent in the *nā́bhi pṛthivyā́ḥ* yields to the historicizing tendency of the epic, where concepts must be expressed in terms of a sequence of events.

The process of partial incarnation is described in the *Mbh.* in terms which hardly depart in any essential respect from the preoccupations of the *RV.* Particularly striking is the imagery of the black and white hair which brings to mind the *kṛṣṇám áhar* and *árjunam áhar* of the *RV.* In this case the bright aspect is identified not with Arjuna but with Balarāma who takes the place of Arjuna as the companion of Kṛṣṇa in the Purāṇic descriptions of the youth of Kṛṣṇa. Kṛṣṇa and Balarāma are identified respectively with a black and a white hair of Viṣṇu, the context being that of the story of the five Indras who are born as the five Pāṇḍavas:

sa cāpi keśau harir udbabarha śulkam ekam aparaṃ cāpi kṛṣṇam |
tau cāpi keśau viśatām yadūnāṃ kule striyau rohiṇīṃ devakīṃ ca |
tayor eko baladevo babhūva kṛṣṇo dviīyaḥ keśavaḥ saṃbabhūva |21 |[21]

The main description of the process of partial incarnation occurs in the *Ādi Parvan* of the *Mbh.* An explanation for the parallel noted above between the earthly and the divine struggle emerges in this account of the descent of Viṣṇu as Kṛṣṇa. It is said that the demons who had been conquered in battle by the gods then took birth on earth:

ādityair hi tadā daityā bahuśo nirjitā yudhi |
aiśvaryād bhraṃśitās cāpi saṃbabhūvuḥ kṣitau iha |[22]

The earth, burdened by the these demons, seeks refuge with Brahmā, who orders the gods to be born in part;[23] whereupon the gods approach Nārāyaṇa. Indra requests Nārāyaṇa to descend in part and Nārāyaṇa agrees to this:

taṃ bhuvaḥ śodhanāyendra uvāca puruṣottamam |
aṃśenāvatarasveti tathety āha ca taṃ hariḥ |[24]

All of the gods are then said to descend from heaven to earth. Further on each of the characters in the *Mbh.* is identified with a god or demon, of whom he is an *aṃśa* (part), and Vāsudeva-Kṛṣṇa is identified as the *aṃśa* of Nārāyaṇa as he exists among men:

yas tu nārāyaṇo nāma devadevaḥ sanātanaḥ |
tasyāṃśo mānuṣeṣv āsīd vāsudevaḥ pratāpavān |90 |[25]

This process of *aṃśāvatāra* is remarkably similar to the account of creation as depicted in the *RV. Puruṣasūkta.*[26] In both there is a transformation of a portion of the divine, leaving the rest unchanged. In one case this leads to incarnation within the phenomenal universe; in the other to the creation of that universe itself.

(iii) Kṛṣṇa and Viṣṇu in the *Viṣṇu Purāṇa*: With regard to the relation of Kṛṣṇa with Viṣṇu as *aṃśāvatāra,* the *Viṣṇu Purāṇa* (*ViP.*) follows the *Mbh.* extremely closely, revealing the same process of historization. The *Mbh.* story of Kṛṣṇa and Balarāma as respectively a black and white hair of Viṣṇu is repeated in this text.[27] Moreover, in the first four verses of the fifth part of this *Purāṇa* in which the story of Kṛṣṇa is narrated, the concept of the descent in pat of Viṣṇu is expressed three times. Maitreya desires to hear at length about the incarnation in part, *aṃśāvatāra,* of Viṣṇu.[28] He then asks the sage to relate the deeds which the Lord performed having descended on earth through various parts-*aṃśāṃśenāvatīrya.*[29] Finally Parāśara replies with an admonition to listen to the account of the birth of the portion of a part of Viṣṇu:

maitreya śrūyatām etad yat pṛṣṭo 'ham idam tvayā |
viṣṇor amśāṃśasaṃbhūticaritam jagato hitam |4|[30]

The position of these verses in the beginning of this part of the *Purāṇa* indicates an attempt to place the account of Kṛṣṇa which follows in a relation to Viṣṇu.

(iv) Kṛṣṇa and Viṣṇu in the *Harivamśa*: Though the *Harivamśa* (*Hariv.*) attempts to establish a link with the *Mbh.* tradition, presenting itself as no more than an expansion of the account of the Vṛṣṇis and Andhakas only touched upon in the *Mbh.* itself,[31] its attitude to *avatāra* is different and arguably as archaic. As in the *Mbh.*, the process of historization is discernible in accordance with its claim to be an historical genealogy. However, if the *Mbh.-Vip.* idea of *amśāvatāra* can be seen as basically related to the Vedic Puruṣa concept, the *Hariv.* seems closer to the Purūravas and Drapsá concept wherein, through a process of incarnation one aspect of the divine is transformed into another — the father become the son.

As in the *Mbh.* the relation between Viṣṇu and Kṛṣṇa is explained by describing Kṛṣṇa as an incarnation of Viṣṇu. However, it may be noticed that the concept of *amśa* with regard to Kṛṣṇa is apparently disregarded. Though the other gods who descend with Viṣṇu are said to become incarnate in part,[32] such terms are not used with reference to Viṣṇu or Kṛṣṇa. The story of the black and white hair is omitted, and a statement regarding the incarnation of Viṣṇu simply says that Viṣṇu descended to earth and was born in the family of Vasudeva:

bhūyaḥ śṛṇu yathā viṣṇur avatīrṇo mahītalam |
prajānām vai hitārthāya prabhuḥ prāṇadhaneśvaraḥ |

yayātivaṁśajasyātha vasudevasya dhīmataḥ |
kule pūjye yaśaskāmo jajñe nārāyaṇaḥ prabhuḥ |[33]

Similarly in the words of Brahmā, Viṣṇu is asked to take incarnation not through his part (*aṁśa*), but instead through himself (*ātmanā*):

ātmānam ātmanā hi tvam avatārya mahītalam |
devakīm rohiṇīṃ caiva garbhābhyām paritoṣaya |[34]

Here instead of Kṛṣṇa being that part of Viṣṇu which performs certain actions, Viṣṇu becomes Kṛṣṇa in order to perform these actions.

(v) Kṛṣṇa and Viṣṇu in the *Bhāgavata Purāṇa*: Though the basic story as told in the *Bhāgavata Purāṇa* (*BhP.*) is very similar to that of the two *Purāṇas* discussed above, there is a distinct difference in the nature of this work. That is to say, unlike the other two texts, it does not aim to present a series of historical events, but takes place in a medium without reference to time or space; in this respect it resembles the *RV*.

The *BhP.* appears to be trying to demonstrate the essential identity of the divinity as immanent and transcendent. In other words, *kṛṣṇa* and *arjuna*, the manifest and the unmanifest, are essentially the same. It seeeks to demonstrate how in actuality, there is no difference between Viṣṇu *parama* and Agni *avama*.

With regard to the relation between *Kṛṣṇa* and *Viṣṇu*, it begins the Tenth book describing the life of Kṛṣṇa with words very similar to those of the *ViP:*

tatrāṁśenāvatīrṇasya viṣṇor vīryāṇi śaṁsa naḥ |[35]

Here the deeds of Kṛṣṇa are described as the heroic deeds of Viṣṇu when he became incarnate in part.

The concept of Kṛṣṇa as the expression of a part only of Viṣṇu is contradicted by a verse in the third chapter of Book I of this text. This particular chapter, coming as it does so near the beginning of the text, might be regarded as forming the foundation for the rest of the text. It starts with a description of how in the beginning the Lord assumes the Puruṣa form (elsewhere in the text identified with Viṣṇu) out of desire to create the world:

jagṛhe pauruṣam rūpam bhagavān mahadādibhiḥ |
sambhūtam ṣoḍaśakalam ādau lokasisṛkṣayā |1|[36]

This Puruṣa is said to be the source of various incarnations — *nānāvatārāṇām nidhānam* — and gods, men and animals are created through its various parts — *aṃśāṃśena*.[37] This is followed by an account of the various incarnations amongst which Kṛṣṇa is included. However, the account concludes by saying that while these are all portions and fractions of Puruṣa, Kṛṣṇa is the Lord himself:

> *ete cāṃśakalāḥ puṃsaḥ kṛṣṇas tu bhagavān svayam* |[38]

Here a distinction is drawn between the parts of the divine (*aṃśakalāḥ*) and divinity itself (*bhagavān svayam*), and Kṛṣṇa is identified with the divinity itself. In other words Kṛṣṇa equals Viṣṇu. The attempt to historicize and portray Kṛṣṇa in terms of an epic hero is disregarded and instead the metaphysical dimension is developed.

From the above discussion of *avatāra* and the relation between Kṛṣṇa and Viṣṇu, it seems possible to deduce three distinct approaches. In the first, that of the *Mbh.* and *ViP.*, the basic concept is that of the *Puruṣasūkta*. Parts of the deity perform certain functions and so constitute the immanent, while the deity as a whole remains transcendent. Kṛṣṇa is a portion of Viṣṇu as Agni is a portion of Puruṣa. Whereas in the *RV.* this is discussed in mythic terms, in the *Mbh.* and *ViP.* it is placed in an epic context.

The second, as evinced in the *Hariv.* is nearer to the concept represented by the Vedic myths of Purūravas and Drapsá. Here the transcendent becomes the immanent; the deity assumes a particular form in order to perform these functions. Viṣṇu becomes Kṛṣṇa. In the *Hariv.*, again as in the *Mbh.* and *ViP.*, the essential metaphysical concept is historicized.

The third, illustrated by the *BhP.*, is closest to the *kṛṣṇám áhar-árjunam áhar* concept of the *RV.* insofar as the metaphysical, cosmological dimension is retained, unclouded by historical preoccupations. There is no need for a subordination of the immanent to the transcendent, of Kṛṣṇa to Viṣṇu, because they are basically identical. Kṛṣṇa and Viṣṇu are one entity.

(c) Vṛndāvana Motifs in Vedic Literature

Not only does a similarity exist between the Purāṇic Kṛṣṇa and certain Vedic myths and concepts, but the mythological locations for these events involve some of the features found in the Purāṇic Vṛndāvana.

The Kṛṣṇá Drapsá myth, for example, takes place in the lap of a river. Moreover, this river is called Aṃśumatī, i.e., full of Soma plants; in this way the two motifs of plant and water are included. Such a juxtaposition of river and tree seems to be a basic environment for such birth myths (cf. the myth of Kārttikeya and the Kṛttikās[39]).

The Purūravas myth incorporates similar elements in its account of the place in which the dialogue between Purūravas and Urvaśī occurs. The location and characteristics of this place are portrayed in most detail in the *ŚBr.* version. It is described as *anyataḥplakṣeti bisavatī*,[40] that is, a lotus-lake with trees on one side. This imagery of water and tree is one which is equally an essential characteristic of Vṛndāvana. The nature of Vṛndāvana as a *vana* or forest in itself associates it with trees. Moreover, the Bhāṇḍīra tree on the bank of the Yamunā river, together with the Govardhana mountain, are the main recurrent elements in all descriptions of Vṛndāvana. In the *Hariv.*, for example, the description of the Bhāṇḍīra, Yamunā and Govardhana forms the basis for the account of Vṛndāvana which will be examined later. Similarly in the *BhP.* Vṛndāvana, Govardhana and Yamunā are conspicuously grouped together, as in a verse describing how Kṛṣṇa and Balarāma are exceedingly pleased to see Vṛndāvana, Govardhana and the banks of the Yamunā:

> *vṛndāvanam govardhanam yamunāpulināni ca* |
> *vīkṣyāsīd uttamā prīti rāmamādhavayor nṛpa* |36|[41]

Such an imagery of water and tree would appear to have both cosmological and paradisal connotations, insofar as a distinction can be drawn between these two aspects. In the cosmological sense, water can be understood as the water of creation, the source of existence, and the principle of that which is formless and potential. It is the source of life, the primeval waters, the watery chaos.[42] By paradisal is meant the concept of the 'living waters' which is often said to exist in the heavenly region.[43]

Similarly in the case of the tree, the concept of the cosmic tree is found in which the tree is an image of the cosmos.[44] Unlike the waters which represent the unformed chaotic source of the cosmos, the cosmic tree expresses the manifestation of the cosmos, the appearance of form. On another level, the tree can be seen as the tree of life, which like the waters of life, stands in paradise.[45]

The association of the two, water and tree, is not uncommon.[46] In the *Kauṣītaki-upaniṣad,* for example, a passage describes how the path of the gods (*devayānam panthānam*) passes through the spheres of Agni, Vāyu, etc. and at last reaches the region of Brahma which is described as containing the river Vijarā and the tree Ilya.[47] The name of the river, *vijarā,* means 'not growing old'[48] and at the end of the verse comes the statement, ' He has reached the river Vijarā; he will not grow old',[49] thus showing a connection with the river of life. The etymology of *ilya,* the name of the tree is more difficult to establish. A commentator, Śaṅkarānanda, has glossed it as:

> *ilā pṛthivī tadrūpatvena ilya iti nāma taruḥ* |[50]

That is to say: *ilā* is a term for the earth; because it has the same form (as the earth), the tree is called *ilya.* If such an etymology were correct it would connect this tree with the cosmic tree, though a more probable derivation is *irā,* 'fluid'.

In the *KKS*[51] and *ŚBr.*[52] account of the Purūravas myth there is an apparent opposition between the Vṛndāvana-like forest place and the inhabited *grāma.* A similar opposition can be found in the *Purāṇas* between the forest Vṛndāvana, where the cows are taken to graze, and the *vraja* (*gokula, goṣṭha,* etc.), the cowherd dwelling place.

Apparently, though Vṛndāvana derives from the idea of manifest creation or cosmos as opposed to unmanifest chaos, it is still not the material world of the *grāma* or *vraja.* Vṛndāvana, in fact, would seem to incorporate two aspects which are not differentiated in the Vedic texts, but are in quasi-historical Epic-Purāṇic literature. The first aspect is that of Eden — the cosmos immediately after or during creation, which has not yet evolved into an entirely material condition. This would fit in with the concept of the cosmic tree and cosmic water. The second is that of heaven, the divine realm; which would be supported by its apparent connection with the Devas in *KKS* and the Gandharvas in *ŚBr.* In this case the tree and water would represent the tree of life and the water of life. In the Vedic texts, the first stage of creation is identical with the divine realm, i.e., Eden is identical with Devaloka.

(d) The Nature of Vṛndāvana — Celestial and Terrestrial — In the *Purāṇas*

(i) The *Harivaṃśa*: In the portrayal of Vṛndāvana as found in the *Hariv.,* the basic concept of a divine region has been transferred to a historico-geographical setting. This can be compared with the treatment of Kṛṣṇa as an epic hero, while the cosmogonic-mythic concept of Kṛṣṇa was retained unchanged. It can best be illustrated by a study of a few passages from the text describing Vṛndāvana.

The first passage from the *Hariv.* — 53.32-34 — illustrates the main motifs characterizing Vṛndāvana. These motifs are mythic and indicate basically a divine realm, but can also be interpreted in historico-geographical terms.

In the first verse of this passage a connection is established between Kṛṣṇa tending cows and Vṛndāvana:

> *pūrvam eva tu kṛṣṇena gavām vai hitakāriṇā*[a]|
> *śivena manasā dṛṣṭam tad vanam vanacāriṇā*|32|[53]

The relation between a Kṛṣṇa-like entity and cows, or cow-maidens, in a 'Vṛndāvana' has already been shown to be a fundamental one (see above); therefore the picture conjured up here is compatible with that of a divine realm or Eden.

At the same time, the concept of the descent of a deity into the material world, i.e., *avatāra,* is also implied in this passage. This emerges from the use of the term *hitakārin,* which has connotations of 'furthering the interests of'[54] since the welfare (*hita*) of living beings is frequently given as one of the chief motives for incarnation.

The ambiguity between the extraterrestrial and the mundane is maintained in the second verse which introduces the motif of Vṛndāvana as an ever-green pasture:

paścime tu tato rūkṣe gharme māse[a] nirāmaye|
varṣatīvāmṛtaṃ deve tṛṇaṃ tatra vyavardhata|33|[55]

Here Vṛndāvana is envisaged as a place having supernatural attributes — grass grows even in the hottest months — which identify it with a heavenly pasture. The extraterrestrial impression is reinforced by the use of the terms *amṛtam* and *deve*, both words with divine connotations.

However, the phrase *varṣatīvāmṛtaṃ deve* can also be understood in a purely mundane sense of 'as in the rains'. Furthermore, the unseasonable growth of grass is presented as part of a sequence. Kṛṣṇa looks favourably on the wood and as a result the grass grows. It is an event, not a continuous state. This, again, is in accord with the *avatāra* theory; the earth flourishes through the grace of Kṛṣṇa.

The third, and final, verse sums up and expresses more explicitly the ideas inherent in the two previous verses. The broader implications of the cow imagery is indicated here by the inclusion with cows of 'other people', i.e., all living beings, who are benefited by the presence of Kṛṣṇa:

na tatra vatsāḥ sīdanti na gāvo netare janāḥ|
yatra tiṣṭhati lokānām bhavāya madhusūdanaḥ.|34|[56]

The ambiguity in this passage hinges on the term *bhava. Bhava*, derived from *bhū-*, 'to become', can have the sense 'being, existence', and be used as a term for the world itself.[57]

Used in this sense, the verse would mean 'where Madhusūdana remains for the existence of the worlds'. This interpretation evokes the idea of the descent of the divine for the preservation of the material universe.

On the other hand, *bhava* can be understood as heavenly existence and so salvation. According to this definition the presence of Kṛṣṇa ensures the salvation of the worlds; and the three verses are not about Kṛṣṇa's activity within the material world but on an extraterrestrial plane.

Leading up to these three verses, the *Hariv.* contains another longer passage in which the historico-geographical setting is even more pronounced. It can be seen as forming a commentary or elaboration on the above verses. The context of a pastoral community is made clear when Kṛṣṇa tells Balarāma that as the present wood is exhausted and no grass is left, they should move on to another wood, Vṛndāvana:

ārya nāsmin vane śakyam gopālaiḥ saha krīḍitum |8|
avagītam idaṃ sarvam āvābhyām bhuktakānanam[a] |
prakṣīṇatṛṇakāṣṭham ca gopair mathitapādapam |8|[58]

The account of the settlement of the cowherds in Vṛndāvana with details regarding their building of enclosures etc.,[59] reinforces this impression of historicity.

The description of Vṛndāvana in the words of Kṛṣṇa contains many elements already familiar from the verses discussed above, interspersed with conventional poetic imagery more or less applicable to any wood. Vṛndāvana is, for example, said to be covered with abundant grass:

śrūyate hi vanaṃ ramyaṃ paryāptatṛṇasaṃstaram |[60]

This is an image which fits in with the picture of Vṛndāvana as an ever-green pasture found in the verses discussed above. Vṛndāvana is also said to be the abode of all seasons:

snigdhaśītānilavanaṃ sarvartunilayaṃ śubham |[61]

Presumably this means that all the seasons exist at once, and this resembles the already mentioned concept of a hot summer season having the qualities of the rainy season.

Reference is made to Govardhana mountain, which is compared with the heavenly mountain, Mandara:

tatra govardhano nāma nātidūre girir mahān |
bhrājate dīrghaśikharo mandanasyeva mandaraḥ |[62]

The motif of Govardhana is apparently again related to the cow theme. The term itself appears to be derived from *go + vardhana,* or 'causing the cow to increase, strengthening the cow'[63] and in the *Hariv.* and *BhP.* account of the Govardhana story it is linked with Goloka.[64] The comparison here with Mandara can be seen primarily as a conventional poetic simile, but might also be intended as an echo of the celestial nature of the place.

The imagery of water and tree is pronounced in this passage. Vṛndāvana is said to have many Kadamba trees and to be situated on the bank of the Yamunā:

kadambapādapaprāyam yamunātīrasamśritaṃ |[65]

Further on, an immense Nyagrodha tree called Bhāṇḍīra is described as standing in the middle of Vṛndāvana:

> *madhye cāsya mahāśākho nyagrodho yojanocchritaḥ* |
> *bhāṇḍīro nāma śuśubhe nīlamegha ivāmbare* |26|[66]

Yamunā is mentioned yet again as dividing Vṛndāvana and is compared to the celestial Nalinī of Nandana, just as Govardhana was to the Mandara:

> *madhyena cāsya kālindī sīmantam iva kurvatī* |
> *prayātā nandanasyeva nalinī saritām varā* |27|[67]

In the final verse the tree, mountain and river are all brought together as the essential features of Vṛndāvana:

> *tatra govardhanam caiva bhāṇḍīram ca vanaspatim* |
> *kālindīṃ ca nadīṃ ramyāṃ drakṣyāvaś carataḥ* |28|[68]

(ii) The *Viṣṇu Purāṇa*: The *ViP.* contains a passage, V. 6.29-30, describing Vṛndāvana in remarkably similar terms to those used in II.9.32-33 of the *Hariv.*, though verse 34 is entirely omitted.

As in that passage the first verse connects Vṛndāvana with cow-imagery by saying that Kṛṣṇa chose Vṛndāvana so that he might nourish the cattle:

> *vṛndāvanam bhagavatā kṛṣṇenākliṣṭakarmaṇā* |
> *śubhena manasā dhyātam gavām vṛddhim abhīpsatā* |29|[69]

The similarity between this verse and that from the *Hariv.* can best be seen if the corresponding phrases are set side by side:

Hariv.	*ViP.*
kṛṣṇena	*kṛṣṇena*
gavām vai hitakāriṇā	*gavām vṛddhim abhīpsatā*
vanacāriṇā	*akliṣṭakarmaṇā*
śivena manasā dṛṣṭam	śubhena manasā dhyātam
tad vanam	*vṛndāvanam*
pūrvam eva	*bhagavatā*

The analysis shows that only the phrases *pūrvam eva* and *bhagavatā* are totally different in meaning.

The general trend of the differences in vocabulary is a more heavy emphasis on the divinity of Kṛṣṇa. This can be seen in the application of the adjective *bhagavatā*, which has no duplicate in the *Hariv.* verses. Similarly, though the terms *akliṣṭakarmaṇā* and *vanacāriṇā* have the same connotations of acting freely, the former is much more overtly divine in its connotations and does not fit in as well with the general imagery of cows and woods as the latter. This emphasis would seem to be, however, more on the divinity of Kṛṣṇa as an *avatāra* on earth than on the cosmological concept of Kṛṣṇa in a divine realm.

The similarity with the *Hariv.* continues in verse 30 where the same imagery of grass growing in the hottest driest season and the comparison with the rainy season is used:

tatas tatrātirūkṣe 'pi gharmakāle dvijottama |
prāvṛṭkāla ivodbhūtaṃ navaṃ śasyaṃ samantataḥ |[70]

This can be compared with the *Hariv.* verse:

Hariv.	*ViP.*
tato	*tatas*
rūkṣe	*atirūkṣe*
gharme māse	*gharmakāle*
varṣatīvāmṛtam deve	*prāvṛṭkāla iva*
vyavardhata	*udbhūtam*
tṛṇam	*sasyam*
nirāmaye	*dvijottama*

Here *nirāmaye* and *dvijottama* are the only phrases totally different in meaning.

Here, if anything, extraterrestrial overtones are less evident than in the *Hariv.* *Prāvṛṭkāla iva*, which takes the place of *varṣatīvāmṛtaṃ deve*, has no connotations beyond an unequivocally earthly rainy season. Thus while in the *ViP.* the divinity of Kṛṣṇa is stressed, the underlying cosmogonic nature of the whole scene is lost.

(iii) The *Bhāgavata Purāṇa*: The basic Vṛndāvana motifs discussed above do exist in the *Bhāgavata Purāṇa* as well, though not so immediately apparent.

The concept, for example, of an unpleasant, hot, summer season assuming the qualities of a pleasant season can be found at X.18.2, though here spring has taken the place of the rainy season:

vraje vikrīḍator evaṃ gopālacchadmamāyayā |
grīṣmo nāmartur abhavan nātipreyān śarīriṇām |2|
sa ca vṛndāvanaguṇair vasanta iva lakṣitaḥ |
yatrāste bhagavān sākṣād rāmeṇa saha keśavaḥ |3|[71]

That this quality of Vṛndāvana is connected with the presence of Kṛṣṇa is brought out by the last line *yatrāste bhagavān* . . . which can be compared with the *yatra tiṣṭhati* . . . *madhusūdanaḥ* in both concept and phraseology.

The elaboration of the metaphysical dimension may be seen in the use of the term *māyā*. That such a connotation is intended finds confirmation through the inclusion of the terms *lakṣitaḥ* and *guṇa*, both of which have philosophical overtones as well.

Such metaphysical tendencies are even more pronounced in a description of Vṛndāvana occurring in the context of Brahmā's carrying away of the calves and cowherd boys. This in itself is an incident not found in either the *Hariv.* or *ViP*.

This episode seems to aim at illustrating the identical nature of the manifest Kṛṣṇa and the unmanifest Viṣṇu and so to negate the concept of *avatāra*. That the activity of Kṛṣṇa is fundamentally on a divine level finds expression in the fact that the calves and cowherd boys are all described as being part of himself and his sports are therefore *ātmavihāra*:

svayamātmātmagovatsān prativāryātmavatsapaiḥ |
krīḍann ātmavihāraiś ca sarvātmā prāviśad vrajam |20|[72]

The concept of the cowherds as incarnations of gods — a reference, possibly, to the *Mbh.* account of the incarnation of the gods with Kṛṣṇa — is specifically denied. They are, instead said to be Kṛṣṇa himself appearing in different ways:

naite sureśā ṛṣayo na caite tvam eva bhāsīśa bhidāśraye 'pi |[73]

The description of Vṛndāvana thus occurs in this context of the identity of the manifest and the unmanifest, the terrestrial and the celestial. It may be noted that Brahmā is said to see Vṛndāvana after Kṛṣṇa spreads the curtain of Nature:

nīśe 'pi drasṭuṃ kim idam iti vā muhyati sati |
cachādājo jñātvā sapadi paramo 'jājavanikām |[74]

This curtain of Nature can be seen as related to the *gopālacchadmamāyayā* of the previous passage, X.18.2-3. Vṛndāvana is thus seen as part of the whole process of self-manifestation accomplished through the divine power.

Echoes of the imagery found in the *Hariv.* and *ViP.* do persist, especially in the first verse, though in a much modified form. The first verse describes Vṛndāvana as being filled with trees providing a livlihood for the people and as being pleasant throughout the year:

> *sapady evābhitaḥ paśyan diśo 'paśyat puraḥsthitam |*
> *vṛndāvanam janājīvyadrumākīrṇaṃ samāpriyam |59|*[75]

The term *janājīvyadrumākīrṇaṃ* 'filled with trees providing a livelihood for the people' can be seen as related to the abundant grass of the *Hariv.* and *ViP.*, though the pastoral image has been more or less lost — people have replaced cows. The second term, *samāpriyam*, 'pleasant throughout the year', echoes the concept of summer having the qualities of the rainy season found in the *ViP.*, and *Hariv.*, as well as that of summer having the qualities of spring found in previous passage from the *BhP.*

However, the imagery in the second verse — that of human beings and animals that have natural enmity towards each other living together as friends — is unique to this passage:

> *yatra naisargadurvairāḥ sahāsan nṛmṛgādayaḥ |*
> *mitrāṇīvājitāvāsadrutaruṭṭarṣakādikam |60|*[76]

This imagery is very paradisal in appearance; it is reminiscent of the concept of the lion lying down with the lamb found elsewhere in descriptions of Paradise or Eden.

The next line continues this imagery by describing how his paradisal state exists because anger, desire and so forth have fled the place where Viṣṇu dwells. This description of a condition resulting from the presence of the divine can be compared with both the other passage from the *BhP.* (*yatrāste bhagavān . . .*) andd that of the *Hariv.* (*yatra tiṣṭhati . . . madhusūdanaḥ*). The difference lies in the perception of the result of he divine presence being expressed here in terms of moral qualities — absence of anger and desire — whereas in the other passages it was expressed in terms of physical well-being — abundant grass, pleasant weather. Going back to the *bhava* concept of the *Hariv.* passage, we could say that in this case the salvation aspect of *bhava* is emphasized to the exclusion of the material aspect.

(e) The Gauḍīya Approach to Kṛṣṇa-Viṣṇu

(i) The nature of the divinity: The first point which may be remarked is that whereas in the texts discussed above Kṛṣṇa and Viṣṇu are portrayed as two equal aspects of one divine reality, in the Gauḍīya text to be examined here, the *Laghubhāgavatāmṛta*, Viṣṇu is unmistakably denoted to an inferior position. Kṛṣṇa is envisaged as the most complete expression of the divine, while Viṣṇu represents an aspect of Kṛṣṇa.

The relation between Kṛṣṇa and Viṣṇu forms a major topic in the first part of the main body of the text, which is preoccupied with the question of the relation of various aspects of the divine with each other and with the question of their relative positions. This part of the text begins with a verse establishing the supremacy of Kṛṣṇa among all objects of worship, as well as making it clear that all aspects of the divine subsequently discussed are, in fact, forms of Kṛṣṇa:

> *athopāsyeṣu mukhyatvaṃ vaktum utkarṣabhūmataḥ* |
> *kṛṣṇasya tatsvarūpāṇi nirūpyante kramād iha* |10|[77]

In this way, the text from the beginning postulates the Kṛṣṇa aspect as the primary divine source.

As a means of distinguishing between Kṛṣṇa himself and the other aspects of Kṛṣṇa, the divinity is described as manifesting itself in the extraterrestrial realm in three ways:

> *svayaṃrūpas tadekātmarūpa āveśanāmakaḥ* |
> *ity asau trividhaṃ bhāti prapañcātītadhāmasu* |11|[78]

Among these, the first, the 'one who has independent form', is defined as not being dependent upon any other; in other words, it exists in itself and is not derived from any other source, it is self-formed and spontaneous:

> *ananyāpekṣi yadrūpaṃ svayaṃrūpaḥ sa ucyate* |12|[79]

It is with this independent form that Kṛṣṇa is identified through a quotation from the *Bṛhadbrahmasaṃhitā*:

> *īśvaraḥ paramaḥ kṛṣṇaḥ saccidānandavigrahaḥ* |
> *anādir ādir govindaḥ sarvakāraṇakāraṇam* |13|[80]

It is thus clear that Rūpa sees Kṛṣṇa-Govinda and the original source as one and the same.

Both the other forms are apparently derivative. They have as their source the independent form, Kṛṣṇa, and are thus subordinate to the Kṛṣṇa aspect. Among these, Viṣṇu is assigned to the category termed 'having a form identical with that'. The definition given of this form is that though in configuration it appears different from the independent form, Kṛṣṇa, it is the same in essence:

> *yad rūpaṃ tadabhedena svarūpeṇa virājate* ।
> *ākṛtyādibhir anyādṛk as tadekātmarūpakaḥ* ।14।[81]

Thus it is not the original form itself, but one of the modes of expression through which that form reveals itself.

The 'identical form' is further divided into two aspects, basically corresponding to extraterrestrial manifestation and manifestation through incarnation. The first, to which Viṣṇu is said to belong, is called a sportive manifestation (*vilāsa*). Its main characteristic is that it is assumed for the sake of diversion and is for the most part equal in power to the original form, though it appears to have a different shape:

> *svarūpam anyākāraṃ yat tasya bhāti vilāsataḥ* ।
> *prāyeṇātmasamaṃ śaktyā sa vilāso nigadyate* ।[82]

The verse identifying Viṣṇu as a sportive manifestation says that Viṣṇu is a sportive manifestation of Kṛṣṇa and Vāsudeva is a sportive manifestation of Viṣṇu:

> *paramavyomanāthas tu govindasya yathā smṛtaḥ* ।
> *paramavyomanāthasya vāsudevaś ca yādṛśaḥ* ।15।[83]

If Vāsudeva is taken as an epithet of Kṛṣṇa, as is frequently the case, this statement would amount to waying that Kṛṣṇa and Viṣṇu were *vilāsas* of one another; in other words, that Kṛṣṇa equals Viṣṇu and Viṣṇu equals Kṛṣṇa — a viewpoint basically in accord with the statement of the *BhP*. However, in subsequent portions of the text, Vāsudeva, the *vilāsa* of Viṣṇu and first of the *vyūhas* is clearly differentiated from Kṛṣṇa, son of Devakī. This is made clear during the discussion of the possibility of Kṛṣṇa being an incarnation of Vāsudeva, showing an identification of Vāsudeva with Viṣṇu. The final conclusion reached is that Kṛṣṇa is superior even to the first of the *vyūhas:*

> *ādyavyūhād api śresṭhaḥ kathyate devakīsutaḥ* ।[84]

A gradation is thus made between Kṛṣṇa, his manifestation Viṣṇu and finally Vāsudeva, the manifestation of Viṣṇu. Evidently, therefore, the Viṣṇu aspect is seen as an expression of the independent Kṛṣṇa, for the sake of sport and diversity, almost but not quite equal in power to Kṛṣṇa himself and thus subordinate.

Divine power (*śakti*) plays an important role in this process of manifestation. This emerges from the fact that the main difference between the two divisions of 'identical form' is that whereas *vilāsa* is said to possess this *śakti* to a more or less equal extent as the independent form, the partial manifestation (*svāṃśa*) of the divinity displays progressively diminished power:

> *tādṛśo nyūnaśaktīṃ yo vyanakti svāṃśa īritaḥ*|[85]

It may be noted that later in the text as well, to the question of how a hierarchy can exist between different forms of the divine, the answer given is that there is not manifestation of all the powers in all of them. The difference between the state of being a part (*aṃśatva*) and that of being full (*pūrṇatva*) or the possessor of parts (*aṃśitā*)[86] is that in the first only a small proportion of the powers are manifest, whereas in the second all of the powers are present and can be made manifest according to the divine will:

> *aṃśatvaṃ nāma śaktīnāṃ sadālpāṃśaprakāśitā*|
> *pūrṇatvañ ca svecchayaiva nānāśaktiprakāśitā*|46|[87]

Apparently therefore the cause of gradation is expression or non-expression of *śakti*.

(ii) The nature of incarnation: The *Laghubhāgavatāmṛta* differs from the *Purāṇas* discussed above not only in that Viṣṇu is subordinated to Kṛṣṇa but also in the nature of the relationship portrayed — namely, the substitution of a concept of manifestation for that of incarnation. The relation between Kṛṣṇa and Viṣṇu is described in non-historical terms. There is no question of a sequence of events within time and space. This is made evident through the stress laid on the extraterrestrial nature of the basic manifestations. Almost at the very beginning of this section comes the statement that all three types of divine form dwell in abodes beyond the material universe (see above p. 28), a statement which is more or less repeated at the end of the section:

> *prapañcātītadāmatvam eṣāṃ śāstre pṛthagvidhe*|
> *pādmīyottarakhaṇḍādau vyaktam eva virājate*|20|[88]

A result of perceiving the process in these terms is that, unlike the Purāṇic conception of incarnation where Viṣṇu becomes Kṛṣṇa, here Kṛṣṇa and Viṣṇu are envisaged as co-existent, each is dwelling in his own divine abode at the same time.

Nevertheless it is clear from the next section of the text that the term incarnation is still applied to Kṛṣṇa, though the concepts associated with this term are somewhat different from those of the *Purāṇas.* As in the beginning of the previous section Kṛṣṇa was described as pre-eminent among objects of worship, so the first verse of this section states that Kṛṣṇa is perfect among incarnations:

> *athāvatārāḥ kathyante kṛṣṇo yeṣu ca puṣkalaḥ*|[89]

The *atha* used in the beginning of both these verses indicates the start of a new section, the one dealing with Kṛṣṇa as a *svarūpa* in the extraterrestrial realm, the other with Kṛṣṇa as an *avatāra* in the material universe.

The connection of incarnations with the physical universe is quite plain in the definition which follows:

> *pūrvoktā viśvakāryārtham apūrvā iva cet svayam*|
> *dvārāntareṇa vāvir syur avatārās tadā smṛtāḥ*|[90]

According to this verse the divine forms discussed above become manifest for the sake of effects in the world (like a transcendental causal link), either by themselves or through a medium: the importance of the material universe in this context is apparent from the phrase *viśvakāryārtham.* From the *śloka* it would follow that any activity on the part of the divine pertaining to the universe involves incarnation. Such activity would include creation as well as the entrance of the divine into the phenomenal world after creation.

It may be noted that the word *apūrva* is a technical term used in Mīmāṃsā to describe the unseen efficacy which brings results (*kārya*) not immediately connected with the cause (*kāraṇa*),[91] the intermediary between an act and its effect; for example the link between the performance of a sacrifice and the attainment of heaven. In this context it would indicate the way in which the incarnations constitute a link between the effects displayed in the world and the original divine cause.

Another point which may be made is that the verb used for their appearance *āvir bhū* may be seen as indicating a physical appearance as well as an event within time. This is in contrast with the verbs *bhā* and *virāj* used to describe the divine forms in the previous section, both of which appear to have connotations of a continuous state of being rather than an event, and also to convey a shining forth more than an appearance as opposed to disappearance.

That in this text, as in the *Purāṇas,* Viṣṇu, unlike Kṛṣṇa, is not envisaged as an incarnation but instead as a source of incarnations becomes clear in the following verse where mediums through which an incarnation can take place are discussed. According to this verse the means of incarnation can be divided into two types — one being *tadekātmarūpa* and the other *tadbhakta,* i.e., adherents of him, apparently more or less the same as the *āveśa* of the previous section:

> *tat tac ca dvāraṃ tadekātmarūpas tadbhakta eva ca* |
> *śeṣaśāyādiko yadvad vasudevādiko 'pi ca* |2|[92]

Viṣṇu, here identified as the one who sleeps on Śeṣa, is said to belong to the *tadekātmarūpa* category, which is consistent with the previous discussion of Viṣṇu, where he is called a *vilāsa,* i.e., one division of *tadekātmarūpa.* The reference to Viṣṇu as a means through which incarnation takes place may be seen as in accordance with statements from the *BhP.* quoted later in this text where Puruṣa, identified with Viṣṇu, is called the storehouse of incarnations[93] which is glossed in the text as being the place of origin of various incarnations:

> *etad rūpaṃ tu nānāvatārāṇām udayāspadam* |68|[94]

Thus the role of Viṣṇu in incarnation remains to a large extent similar in nature to that portrayed in the *Purāṇas;* it is through Viṣṇu that incarnation takes place and yet he is not himself an incarnation.

The Kṛṣṇa incarnation, however, is seen as unique and does not involve Viṣṇu as a medium. This becomes clear in a further verse which, referring back to the various forms of divine expression, categorizes incarnations as being for the most part either *svāṃśa* or *āveśa,* while only one incarnation is *svayaṃrūpa,* the identity of which is to be revealed later in the text:

> *prāyaḥ svāṃśas tathāveśā avatārā bhavanty amī* |
> *atra yaḥ syāt svayaṃrūpāḥ so 'gre vyaktībhaviṣyati* |3|[95]

The identity of this *svayaṃrūpa* incarnation as Kṛṣṇa becomes clear later in the text, where after rejecting various theories about the source of the Kṛṣṇa incarnation, the conclusion is reached that, in fact, it has no source. It is self-manifest and independent.

The verse indicating the nature of Kṛṣṇa as the independent incarnation states that from the term *svayam* used in the texts such as the *BhP.* it has been revealed that Kṛṣṇa is *svayaṃrūpa:*

ataḥ svayampadādibhyo bhagavān kṛṣṇa eva hi |
svayaṃrūpa iti vyaktaṃ śrīmadbhāgavatādiṣu |[96]

This is presumably a reference to *BhP.* I.3.28 (discussed above, p. 19). It may be noted that whereas in the *BhP.* the *svayam* is used to show the identity of Kṛṣṇa with Viṣṇu, Rūpa is trying to draw a distinction between Kṛṣṇa who is the Lord himself, and Puruṣa who is the source of incarnations. This is thus an example of the use of the words of the *BhP.* re-interpreted so as to express a meaning different from the original.

The verb *vyaktam* in the above verse is an indicator of the fact that it is intended as a direct sequel of the previous verse discussed above. While that verse said that the identity of the independent incarnation would be revealed subsequently — *agre vyaktībhaviṣyati* — here the same verb is used in the past tense — its identity has now been revealed; in other words Kṛṣṇa is the independent incarnation.

In a verse previous to this an apparently conscious use of vocabulary very nearly identical with that employed in the account of Kṛṣṇa as *svayaṃrūpa* (in the first section of this text) has the effect of forming a distinct link beween the two statements. The verse in question says that the account of Kṛṣṇa's superiority to all of his forms shows that he must be greater than Paramavyomanātha Viṣṇu, while through the use of the term 'himself' (*svayam*) his independence is proclaimed:

sarvebhyas tatsvarūpebhyaḥ kṛṣṇotkarṣanirūpaṇāt |
ādhikyaṃ paramavyomanāthād apy asya darśitam |
svayaṃpadena cāsyānyanairapekṣyam udīritam |121|[97]

The three terms of particular interest here are *svayam, utkarṣa* and *nairapekṣyam.* The term *svayam* needs little explanation since it evidently refers back to the term *svayaṃrūpa.* It may be remembered that v.10 of the first section spoke of Kṛṣṇa's superiority (*utkarṣa*) among objects of worship while here the same term is used to describe his superiority to all his other forms. Furthermore the definition of *svayaṃrūpa* was that it was dependent on no other (*ananyāpekṣin*) and similarly here the Kṛṣṇa incarnation is said to have independence (*nairapekṣyam*). This shows that just as Kṛṣṇa is considered *svayaṃrūpa* among the *svarūpas,* he is also *svayaṃrūpa* among the incarnations. Unlike other incarnations the Kṛṣṇa incarnation does not have its basis in any other entity.

Rūpa takes the different characteristics which in the *Purāṇas* all belong to one Viṣṇu entity and attributes them to separate entities who are seen as aspects of Viṣṇu. They are then placed in a hierarchy apparently based on their degree of involvement in creation. The relative gradation of the four main aspects is stated in a verse which says that Viṣṇu, the lowest, is said to be an incarnation of Puruṣa, indicating the superiority of Puruṣa; greater than Puruṣa is Vāsudeva and greatest of all is Mahāvaikuṇṭhanāyaka:

triṣu puṃso 'vatāreṣu rudrāt padmabhavāt tathā |
bhṛgvādikṛtanirddhārād viṣṇur eva mahattamaḥ |
kiṃ punaḥ puruṣas tatra vāsudevo 'tra kintarām |
tatrāpi kintamāṃ so 'yam mahāvaikuṇṭhanāyakaḥ |[98]

In this sequence Viṣṇu, here seen as the embodiment of *sattva guṇa,* is the effective cause of the material universe and so involved in the grossest level of creation. Puruṣa, on the other hand, is the primal cause of creation, and so though unmistakably a cosmic entity, on a higher plane. Vāsudeva, as the first *vyūha,* may be seen as involved in what is called in Pañcarātra terms pure creation.[99] He is thus on the transcendental level, but in the process of evolving towards the cosmic level. Finally, Mahāvaikuṇṭhanāyaka, the Lord of the celestial realm, is utterly transcendent and totally uninvolved in cosmic activity. Argument offering these aspects of Viṣṇu as sources for Kṛṣṇa are demolished one by one in the course of the text, starting on the lower end of the scale with Puruṣa and Viṣṇu.

Whereas the cosmic aspects, Viṣṇu and Puruṣa are treated as incarnations, the transcendent Vaikuṇṭhanāyaka and Vāsudeva are termed *vilāsas.* Two of the three types of incarnation are described as *puruṣa* and *guṇa,* the category to which Viṣṇu is assigned, the third type being the non-cosmic *līlā* incarnation of which Kṛṣṇa is one, again showing his non-cosmic nature:

puruṣākhyā guṇātmāno līlātmānaś ca te tridhā |[100]

With reference to the *BhP.*, Puruṣa is called the first incarnation:

ādyo 'vatāraḥ puruṣaḥ parasya |[101]

and as such is the source of all other incarnations — an aspect of the Viṣṇu entity discussed above. Paramavaikuṇṭhanātha and Vāsudeva, on the other hand, are consistently referred to as *vilāsas.* Some examples have already been seen above and others can be found. For example, at p. 149 Vāsudeva is termed a *vilāsa* of Mahāvaikuṇṭhanāyaka:

mahāvaikuṇṭhanāthasya vilāsatvena viśrutaḥ |[102]

A further reference to Mahāvaikuṇṭhanāyaka as a *vilāsa* of Kṛṣṇa can be found at p. 207:

tasmāt paramavaikuṇṭhanātho 'py asya vilāsakaḥ |133 |[103]

The difference between *vilāsa* and incarnation is indicated in a verse which is actually giving the viewpoint of the opponent in the argument (the *pūrvapakṣa*). Here it is said that though, because of his manifestation of *līlās* such as birth, Kṛṣṇa is an incarnation of Mahāvaikuṇṭhanāyaka, because of the abundance of his excellence he is called a *vilāsa*:

> *janmādilīlāprākaṭyād avatāratayāpy asau* |
> *prokto vilāsa eva syāt sarvotkarṣātibhūmataḥ* |[104]

Though the argument as applied to Kṛṣṇa is refuted in the text, the basic distinction between the two aspects appears to hold good. This means that the *vilāsa*, unlike the incarnation, does not get born; in other words, it does not become manifest within the phenomenal universe. Moreover, the *vilāsa* is apparently a more complete expression of the divine than the incarnation, a conclusion which agrees with the hierarchy discussed above.

It may be observed that the treatment of the formless Brahman appears more or less to correspond to that of Viṣṇu. In the *BhP.* the contrast between Kṛṣṇa and Brahman is made in the same way as the contrast between Kṛṣṇa and Viṣṇu, suggesting that the Brahman aspect and Viṣṇu aspect are deemed identical. If Kṛṣṇa is Viṣṇu with form, he is equally Brahman with form. Thus Viṣṇu-Brahman represent together the transcendent, formless, impersonal, cosmic aspect with Kṛṣṇa as the immanent personal aspect with form. In the *Laghubhāgavatāmṛta*, the formless Brahman is subordinated to Kṛṣṇa, just as is Viṣṇu. The relation of Brahman with Kṛṣṇa is compared to that of the sun and its rays:

> *brahma nirdharmakaṃ vastu nirviśeṣam amūrtikam* |
> *iti sūryopamasyāsya kathyate tatprabhopamam* |[105]

The two are essentially identical but the rays are dependent upon and so subordinate to the sun, which is the source.

It is clear from the above account that in many ways the basic characteristics of Viṣṇu and Kṛṣṇa have remained the same as in the *Purāṇas*. Viṣṇu here as well incorporates the transcendent and cosmic elements of the divine nature while Kṛṣṇa represents the personal, theistic aspect. The difference lies in the subordination of the Viṣṇu aspect to the Kṛṣṇa aspect which leads to a difference in the conception of the incarnation process. Viṣṇu does not become Kṛṣṇa, instead Kṛṣṇa himself takes incarnation. It is thus more a manifestation than an actual incarnation. There is no question of a transformation of one entity into another through the process of becoming incarnate. Here Kṛṣṇa appears as Kṛṣṇa within the phenomenal world.

(iii) Manifest and unmanifest *līlā* in the context of incarnation: The difference between Kṛṣṇa as an incarnation and Kṛṣṇa as a *svarūpa* is explained in terms of manifest (*prakaṭa*) and unmanifest (*aprakaṭa*) *līlā*. According to the text Kṛṣṇa eternally performs his *līlā* through innumerable appearances (*prakāśa*), and sometimes through one appearance he manifests his activities such as birth within the phenomenal world:

> *prakaṭāprakaṭā ceti līlā seyaṃ dvidhocyate* |
> *tathāhi* |
> *sadānantaiḥ prakāśaiḥ svair līlābhiś ca sa dīvyati* |
> *tatraikena prakāśena kadācij jagadantare* |
> *sahaiva svaparīvārair janmādi kurute hariḥ* |[106]

The term *prakāśa* is discussed earlier in the section on *svarūpa* where it is described as the manifestation of one form at the same time and in which there is no difference of any sort between the different forms:

> *anekatra prakaṭatā rūpasyaikasya yaikadā* |
> *sarvathā tatsvarūpaiva sa prakāśa itīryate* |[107]

This means that in the unmanifest *līlā*, each of the *līlās* is taking place simultaneously — Kṛṣṇa is being born at the same time as he is performing *rāsa* with the *gopīs*. There is thus no sequence of events, all of these *līlās* take place outside of time and place. During incarnation, however, the *līlās* are manifest within time and place and so appear to occur one after the other.

The difference between the manifest and the unmanifest is illustrated again when the text says that Kṛṣṇa eternally exists as the son of Yaśodā (that is in the unmanifest *līlā*) while in the manifest *līlā* she serves as a means through which he enters into the material universe:

> *so 'yaṃ nityasutatvena tasyā rājaty anāditaḥ* |
> *kṛṣṇaḥ prakaṭalīlāyāṃ taddvāreṇapy abhūt tathā* |163|[108]

The identification of Yaśodā as a medium through which the *avatāra* takes place may be compared with the earlier statement about the *tadbhakta* category of mediums such as Vasudeva. The text goes on to say that Kṛṣṇa having become manifest then goes on to manifest in sequence *līlās* such as those of childhood, which he also performs in thousands of unmanifest appearances:

atha prakaṭatāṃ labdhe vrajendravihite mahe |
tatra prakaṭayaty eṣa līlā bālyādikāḥ kramāt |
karoti yāḥ prakāśeṣu koṭiśo 'prakaṭeṣv api |[109]

The contrast here between the manifest historical sequence and the unmanifest eternally simultaneous existence is made clear.

The question of the historical nature of the incarnation is also raised in another verse where the opponent is made to argue that Kṛṣṇa, the offspring of the Yadus, became manifest at the end of the Dvāpara age, therefore Mahāvaikuṇṭhanāyaka, who is eternal, cannot be his sportive manifestation:

nanv eṣa dvāparasyānte prādurbhūto yadūdvahaḥ |
sa vaikuṇṭheśvaro 'nādis tadvilāsaḥ kathaṃ bhavet ||[110]

This statement clearly put forward the historicizing point of view — i.e., the concept that Kṛṣṇa is an event indicated by text such as the *ViP*. and the *Hariv*. This is refuted by the present text which maintains that the birth *līlā* of Kṛṣṇa who is without beginning is also beginningless:

maivam asyādiśunyasya janmalīlāpy anādikā |
svacchandato mukundena prākaṭyaṃ nīyate muhuḥ |[111]

This again affirms the fact that existence of Kṛṣṇa is a theological principle and not a historical event.

It may also be noticed that in the above verse the manifestation of Kṛṣṇa within the material universe is said to happen again and again. This is expressed in another place through comparing the incarnation with the manifestation on fire, which is latent in various places but only appears through the striking together of certain objects:

tatra tatra yathā vahnis tejorūpeṇa sanna api |
jāyate maṇikāṣṭhāder hetuṃ kañ cid avāpya saḥ |
anādim eva janmādilīlām eva tathādbhutām |
hetunā kena cit kṛṣṇaḥ prāduṣkuryyāt kadācana |140|[112]

In the same way Kṛṣṇa is said to manifest the *līlās* such as birth from time-to-time. Thus the incarnation itself is not an event which takes place once and for all and never again. Since it is going on eternally it can take place at any time, given the appropriate circumstances.

While a degree of continuity with Purāṇic representations of the character of Kṛṣṇa and Viṣṇu is thus maintained, the Gauḍīya perception of the relationship between the two shows considerable reinterpretation. The difference involves a rejection of the mythic approach and apparently an attempt to re-state the original nature of these two entities as symbolizing metaphysical concepts. Such a tendency is in line with the outlook of the Braj Bhāṣā texts to be examined in the following section.

Kṛṣṇa-Viṣṇu and the Concept of *avatāra* in Braj Bhāṣā Literature

Braj Bhāṣā texts can be divided into those which accept the mythological structure of the *Purāṇas* and those which do not. In the first, represented by the apparently non-sectarian *Sūrasāgara,* Kṛṣṇa and Viṣṇu have the same characteristics of being two essentially identical and equal aspects of one divine entity as was seen in the *BhP*. In the second, found with certain modifications in all the sectarian poetry discussed, the gradation between Viṣṇu and Kṛṣṇa, subordinating Viṣṇu, expressed in the Gauḍīya literature, is maintained.

(a) The Non-sectarian Approach — The *Sūrasāgara*

In the *Sūrasāgara* the contrast between a *'parama* Viṣṇu' and an *avama* Kṛṣṇa is frequently stressed, the first being transcendent, inaccessible and cosmic; the second immanent, accessible and theistic. At the same time the basic identity of these two modes of expression is equally emphasized.

It may be noted that the epithet 'Viṣṇu' is never in fact applied by the *Sūrasāgara* to the transcendent aspect, though references to such well-known attributes as being the husband of Ramā, lying on Śeṣa and taking the three steps are sufficient to warrant an identification with the Viṣṇu entity of the Purāṇic texts. That a distinct epithet 'Viṣṇu' is not in fact employed, while the epithet 'Hari' is used indiscriminately for both aspects indicates the emphasis on the identity of the two aspects.

The contrast and identity are exemplified in *pada* 621 which consists of a series of relative clauses which first describe the transcendent aspect and then proceed to simultaneously contrast and identify it with the immanent aspect, the two being connected by the pronouns *tāhi, soi, so,* i.e., 'he, that one'. The first three verses run:

> *ādi sanātana hari abināsī* | *sadā niramtara ghaṭa ghaṭa bāsī* |
> *pūrana brahma purāna bakhānaiṃ* | *caturānama siva aṃta na jānaiṃ* |
> *gunagana agama nigama nahiṃ pāvai* | *tāhi jasodā goda khilavai* |[113]

The first two and a half verses describe the first aspect which is given the epithet Hari and is identified with Brahman. Its transcendent and inaccessible nature is indicated by the statement that Brahmā and Śiva know not his limit, and that the scriptures cannot reach him. The final half verse, 'Him Jasodā has play in her lap', provides a total contrast, presenting as image of utter accessibility. At the same time an identification is made between the inaccessible Brahman and the child in the lap. In other words the child Kṛṣṇa aspect is at the same time the transcendent Viṣṇu.

The rest of the *pada* similarly consists of a series of contrasting statements. The characteristics of the first aspect are given as:

(a) Cosmic — he is called *viśvaṃbhara,* sustainer of the universe.[114] He is the creator of the universe and also its destroyer.[115]

(b) Transcendent — he has no sense organs or limbs:

> *locana srabana na rasanā nāsā |*
> *binu pada pāni karai paragāsā |*[116]

He is uninvolved in birth and death, and has no human relationships.[117]

(c) Identification with Viṣṇu attributes. He lies on the waters: *acyuta rahai sadā jalasāī |*[118]

His relations with Lakṣmī is also mentioned — she eternally rubs his feet: *carana kamala nita ramā palovai |*[119]

These attributes are contrasted with the activities of Kṛṣṇa, which are:

(a) Personal rather than cosmic; accessible instead of transcendent. They involve a personal relationship with the devotee, as, for example, when Kṛṣṇa is bound to the churning rod by his mother:

> *so ūkhala bāṃdhyau mahatārī |*[120]

(b) Instead of Lakṣmī he is associated with the *gopīs* and Rādhā, and whereas Lakṣmī is portrayed as serving him, he is under the control of Rādhā:

> *so rādhā basa kuṃja bihārī |*[121]

(c) The same connection with cows seen in the *Purāṇas* is observable here. He runs after the calves[122] and takes the cows to graze:

> *soi gopa kī gāi carāvai |*[123]

A frequent device used to convey the contrast between these two aspects in other *padas* is to compare Viṣṇu's triple *vikramaṇa* which encompasses the entire universe with the child-like act of Kṛṣṇa being unable to cross the threshold of the house. This can be seen in *pada* 731, for example, which describes how it has become difficult even to cross the threshold for the one who was not fatigued measuring the earth in three steps:

> *basudhā tripada karata nahiṃ ālasa tinahiṃ kaṭhina bhayau dehari ulaṃghanā* |[124]

The taking of three steps is, of course, one of the most characteristic activities of Viṣṇu as far back as the *Ṛg Veda*, where it can be seen as a creation myth — through measuring out the universe Viṣṇu in fact creates it. It is probable that the notion of creation is implicit in the use of this image in the *Sūrasāgara*; the most explicit connotation is, however, that of transcendence — the entire earth is not sufficient for his three steps. The image thus incorporates both the cosmic and the transcendent quality of Viṣṇu, while the inability to cross the thershold equally epitomizes the characteristics of the second aspect.

The myth of the churning of the ocean is made use of to a similar end, contrasted here with Kṛṣṇa churning the butter. *Pada* 761 describes how when Kṛṣṇa takes hold of the churning rod[125] all of the participants involved in the churning of the ocean react as if this episode were about to be repeated. Vāsuki, the serpent who was used as a rope, and the Asuras are afraid.[126] The sea, apprehensive of another churning, shrinks, while Śiva is anxious as to how he will be able to drink the poison which emerges.[127] Lakṣmī, on the other hand, is overwhelmed with love and joy at the thought of being married to Viṣṇu.[128] The churning of the ocean is a celestial and cosmic activity involving gods, demons, the birth of Lakṣmī, and so forth. The churning of milk, on the other hand is terrestrial. It is also purely play; it has no creative function. Despite this difference, the reactions portrayed to this Kṛṣṇa activity show that he is in fact identical with Viṣṇu who performed the cosmic act. Thus once again a Viṣṇu myth is contrasted with a Kṛṣṇa activity so as to bring out the difference and similarity simultaneously.

In the *Sūrasāgara* the relation between the two aspects is described in terms of incarnation. The transcendent Brahman is said to have taken incarnation as Kṛṣṇa:

> *brahma liyau avatāra duṣṭa ke dāvana re* |[129]

Other terms used for this process include *janama liyau,*[130] 'took birth'; as well as *deha dhari,*[131] 'assumed a body', and *rūpa dhari,*[132] 'assumed a form'; and finally *pragaṭe,*[133] 'manifested'.

All of these terms imply a degree of involvement in time and place, similar to that evinced in the *Purāṇas* discussed above. To that extent Kṛṣṇa is portrayed in a mythological rather than purely metaphysical context.

That the relation between the two — Kṛṣṇa and Viṣṇu — is basically a metaphysical one, though expressed in mythological terms, is indicated by a number of references to the Kṛṣṇa incarnation itself taking place again and again. Obviously, therefore, the incarnation is not an event which occurred once at a particular point in history and never again. *Pada* 1569 follows the expected statement that Kṛṣṇa took birth in Braj with the infomation that he always sports in Braj because he likes this *līlā*. The explanation as to how this is possible is that he takes body again and again:

braja janma liyau |
brajahī maiṃ nita karana bihārana | . . .
yaha līlā inakauṃ ati bhāvai |
deha dharata puni puni pragaṭāvai |[134]

This same idea emerges in *pada* 1115, which says that Kṛṣṇa takes incarnation from age-to-age in Braj, and he never leaves the *gopīs*, cowherd-boys, Vṛndāvana, Yamunā and all the other components of his *līlā* there:

juga juga braja avatāra leta prabhu | . . .
yei gopī yeī gvāla yahai sukha yaha līlā kahuṃ tajata na sātha |
yahai bihāra karata nisi bāsara yeī haiṃ jana ke pratipāla |[135]

The term *avatāra* as applied to Kṛṣṇa in the *Sūrasāgara,* in fact, appears to designate a state of having a form as opposed to being formless, being manifest as opposed to being unmanifest.

The problem of the relation between Kṛṣṇa and 'Viṣṇu' is further complicated by the fact that the only attestations of the epithet Nārāyaṇa represent this Nārāyaṇa as existing simultaneously with Kṛṣṇa. *Pada* 1682 describes how the sound of Kṛṣṇa's flute reached Vaikuṇṭha and hearing it, Nārāyaṇa and Lakṣmī were overjoyed:

muralī dhuni baikuṇṭha gaī |
nārāyaṇa kamalā suni daṃpati ati ruci hṛdaya bhaī |[136]

Nārāyaṇa further expresses his sense of inferiority by saying that the *rāsa* which Kṛṣṇa performs is far beyond him:

rāsa bilāsa karata nandanandana so hamataiṃ ati dūrī |[137]

This concept of a Nārāyaṇa who exists at the same time as Kṛṣṇa and who longs to participate in his sport but is unqualified to do so is found in the other Braj Bhāṣā texts, as will be seen below.

Despite, therefore, the *Sūrasāgara* being generally more or less in accord with the *BhP.* in its approach, it does succeed in incorporating features which are closer to the sectarian viewpoint. This leads to the impression that while the work is in the *BhP.* tradition, it has made an attempt to adapt that tradition to prevalent beliefs of the time.

(b) The Sectarian Approach

(i) Nandadāsa — Vallabha: Though Nandadāsa in his themes and style appears, like Sūradāsa and unlike poets such as Dhruvadāsa, to be close to the Purāṇic tradition, a closer examination shows more radical differences than might at first be expected. This emerges in his treatment of the relation between Kṛṣṇa and Viṣṇu, where he seems to adhere to the approach wherein Viṣṇu is envisaged as a less complete manifestation of Kṛṣṇa rather than the two being identical and equal.

Relevant to this discussion is the passage I.34-37 of the *Rāsapañcādhyāyī* in which verse 34 describes the relation between Kṛṣṇa with form and the formless Brahman. The all-pervasive Brahman is defined as being the light shining from the body of Kṛṣṇa:

mohana adbhuta rūpa kahi na āvati chabi tāki।
akhila-aṃḍa-vyāpī ju brahma ābhā hai jākī।34।[138]

The divergence of this approach from that of Sūradāsa is marked. Whereas in the *Sūrasāgara,* as in the *BhP.*, Brahman became Kṛṣṇa, here the unmanifest Brahman is reduced to being the radiance shining from the Kṛṣṇa-form. According to this point of view the divine in reality has only one aspect — the manifest Kṛṣṇa. That which is seen as unmanifest is due to an incomplete perception. This is very similar to the concept found above in the Gauḍīya texts.

The next two verses proceed to delineate the relation between Kṛṣṇa and Nārāyaṇa in such a way as to imply that Kṛṣṇa is the divinity in its entirely and perfection while Nārāyaṇa is a partial aspect. This is expressed through the use of the terms *dharmī* and *dharma* in the sense of 'possessor of qualities' and 'qualities'. The youthful (*kiśora*) Kṛṣṇa is described as the *dharmī* whereas it is through these qualities (*dharama kari*) that he is Nārāyaṇa:

paramātama parabrahma sabana ke aṃtarajāmī।
nārāyaṇa bhagavāna dharama kari saba ke svāmī।35।
bāla kumāra pugaṇḍa dharama āsakta ju lalita tana।
dharmī nitya kisora kānha mohata saba ko mana।36।[139]

The use of terms *dharmī* and *dharma* in this way can be compared with the use in Braj Bhāṣā of *avatārī* as the origin of the incarnation and *avatāra* as the incarnation itself; similarly *aṃśī* as the possessor of parts or the whole, and *aṃśa* as the part.[140] In this way Nārāyaṇa is depicted as an expression of certain attributes of Kṛṣṇa and so as less complete.

The relation between Kṛṣṇa and Viṣṇu is discussed in similar terms in the *Siddhāntapañcādhyāyī*:

> *ṣaṭaguna aru avatāra dharana nārāyaṇa joī* |
> *sabakauṃ āśraya avadhibhūta naṃdanaṃdana soī* |7|[141]

In this verse Kṛṣṇa and Nārāyaṇa are on the one hand identified with each other — he who is Nārāyaṇa is Kṛṣṇa. At the same time, in the description of the characteristics of each, a gradation between the two seems intended. To Kṛṣṇa are ascribed the qualities of being the support of all, of encompassing all. Nārāyaṇa, on the other hand, is the one who takes incarnation, a more limited function.

The fact of Kṛṣṇa being Viṣṇu and at the same time more than Viṣṇu is reflected in a number of passages where Lakṣmī and the *gopīs* are compared. The *Rāsapañcādhyāyī* says that though Lakṣmī always serves his (Viṣṇu-Kṛṣṇa's) lotus feet, she cannot obtain this *rasa*, i.e., of the dust of Vṛndāvana:

> *jadapi padakamala kamalā amalā sevata nisidina* |
> *yaha rasa apanai sapanai kabahūṃ nahiṃ pāyau tina* |33|
> *binu adhikārī bhae nahina bṛṃdāvana sūjhai* |
> *renu kahāṃ teṃ sūjhai jaba lauṃ bastu na būjhai* |34|[142]

Here Kṛṣṇa and Nārāyaṇa are identified through the connection of Lakṣmī with Nārāyaṇa's feet. At the same time the supremacy of the Kṛṣṇa aspect is demonstrated by the fact of the dust of Vṛndāvana, the Kṛṣṇadhāman, being unobtainable to Lakṣmī. A similar image is used in the *Siddhāntapañcādhyāyī* according to which Lakṣmī cannot get the same *rasa* as the women of Braj, though she disports herself on his (again Kṛṣṇa-Viṣṇu's) bosom:

> *jadapi bachasthala ramati ramā ramani vara kāmini* |
> *tadapi na yaha rasa pāyo pāyo jo braja bhāmini* |118|[143]

In verse 7 from the *Siddhāntapañcādhyāyī* discussed above, not only is Viṣṇu made subordinate to Kṛṣṇa, in addition Kṛṣṇa is dissociated to some extent from the incarnation process. This appears to be inevitable if Kṛṣṇa is to be regarded, not as one of two aspects of the divine, but as the supreme divine form. Any question of the divinity taking form, i.e., Viṣṇu becoming Kṛṣṇa, is then irrelevant. Accordingly, the need to present the appearance of Kṛṣṇa as an event is also lost. Kṛṣṇa eternally as Kṛṣṇa.

Some indication of the rejection of the theory of incarnation as applied to Kṛṣṇa can be found in the *Bhramaragīta* where Uddhava uses this theory as one of his arguments against the *gopīs*. According to Uddhava, Kṛṣṇa has assumed a body by becoming incarnate for the sake of sport, but only through *yoga* can the abode of the supreme Brahman be obtained:

līlā ko avatāra lai dhari āe tana syāma |
joga juguta hī pāiyai pārabrahma-pada-dhāma ||[144]

In other words, the Kṛṣṇa form is only a temporary manifestation of the divine which in its supreme state is formless and unmanifest.

The *gopīs* and through them Nandadāsa reject this proposition and insist on the supreme nature of the Kṛṣṇa form as of the activities associated with Kṛṣṇa. They, in fact, propound a relation between Kṛṣṇa with form and the formless Brahman in terms corresponding to those found in I.34 from the *Rāsapañcādhyāyī* discussed above. The *gopīs* compare Kṛṣṇa to the form of the sun which is hidden in its own light; both can be seen only by those whith the gift of divine sight:

tarani akāsa prakāsa jāhi meṃ rahyau durāī |
divya dṛṣṭi binu kahau kauna pe dekhyau jāī |[145]

A similar image is used in another verse of the same text which says that people know not the real form; they reject the manifest sun to grasp at reflected rays:

nāstika hai je loga kahā jānaiṃ nija rūpai |
pragaṭa bhāru koṃ chāṃḍi gahata parachāīṃ dhūpai |[146]

Here again Brahman is regarded as no more than the brilliance emitted from the divine form.

As in the Gauḍīya texts, though the theory of Kṛṣṇa being no more than an incarnation is refuted, the process of incarnation is still recognized as an aspect of Kṛṣṇa. According to the *Siddhāntapañcādhyāyī*, the *gopīs*, through their re-enactment of the Kṛṣṇa *līlās*, illustrated to devotees the essential unity of Kṛṣṇa as infant, child and youth, and showed now he incorporated within himself the *avatārī*, the *avatāras* and all the manifestations (*vibhūtis*):

aru je āhiṃ upāsaka tinahiṃ abheda batāyau |
sisu kumāra paugaṃḍa kānha ekai dikharāyo |78|
avatārī avatāra dharana aru jitaka bibhūtī |
iha saba āśraya ke adhāra jaga jihi kī ūtī |79|[147]

This reflects a position close to that of the Gauḍīya portrayal of Kṛṣṇa as both the one who takes incarnation and the incarnation itself — i.e., Kṛṣṇa manifested himself in the world as Kṛṣṇa.

It is presumably this approach which enables Nandadāsa to include in the *Rāsapañcādhyāyī* verses based closely on the *BhP.* which speak of the manifestation of Kṛṣṇa as an event. The *gopīs* are quoted as saying that since Kṛṣṇa manifested in Braj, it has been adorned by Lakṣmi:

kahana lagīṃ aho kuṃara kānha braja pragaṭe jaba te |
avadhibhūta iṃdirā alaṃkṛta hvai rahī taba teṃ |[148]

This can be compared with a verse from the *BhP.* where the *gopīs* similarly describe how the *vraja* prospers more because of the birth of Kṛṣṇa, since Lakṣmī resides there permanently:

jayati te 'dhikaṃ janmanā vrajaḥ śrayata indirā śaśvad atra hi |[149]

This can equally be seen as the explanation for the acceptance of the term *avatāra* as applied to Kṛṣṇa in the *Bhāṣā daśama skandha* of Nandadāsa, which purports to be no more than a translation of the *BhP.* and so could be expected to adhere most closely to the *BhP.* terminology. The typical *avatāra* theory is, for example, put in the words of Kaṃsa who says that Viṣṇu will take incarnation through Devakī in order to kill him:

devakī viṣai viṣṇu avatarihaiṃ |
mere vadha kau uddima karihaiṃ |[150]

Nevertheless, even in this text, changes are made which, though apparently slight, alter the total import considerably and once again raise Kṛṣṇa above Viṣṇu. For example, the *BhP.* has a passage where Garga tells Nanda that Kṛṣṇa has all of the qualities of Nārāyaṇa:

tasmān nandakumāro 'yaṃ nārāyaṇasamoguṇaiḥ |
śriyā kīrtyā 'nubhāvena tatkarmasu na vismayaḥ |22|[151]

Nandadāsa repeats this statement but adds that Kṛṣṇa has these qualities to an even greater extent than Nārāyaṇa:

nārāina madhi guna haiṃ jite |
tere suta meṃ jhalakata tite |
śrī kīrti saṃpati rasamaī |
nārāina hū teṃ adhikaī |[152]

In this way the meaning of the passage is of changed utterly; instead of being equal to Viṣṇu, Kṛṣṇa is a more complete expression of the divine.

If Sūradāsa can be said to introduce sectarian elements while retaining the fundamental concepts of the *BhP.*, Nandadāsa retains the structure of the *BhP.* but changes the basic perception of the relation between Kṛṣṇa and Viṣṇu. Essentially he expresses a viewpoint similar to that of the Gauḍīya texts and performs a similar function, i.e., that of giving credibility to sectarian concepts through affiliating them with a text of traditional authority.

(ii) Dhruvadāsa — Rādhāvallabha: The poetry of Dhruvadāsa is far more unequivocal than that of Nandadāsa in its repudiation of any attempt to depict Kṛṣṇa in a mythological context. Kṛṣṇa is throughout depicted as an eternal principle uninvolved in either creation or incarnation.

The term *avatāra* itself is used in the sense of a minor deity, rather than as the action performed by a deity. It is nowhere applied to Kṛṣṇa himself, and the *avatāras* are depicted as co-existent with him. In a verse from the *Vṛndāvana sata* the partial incarnations (*aṃśa* and *kalāvatāras*):

vṛndāvana rasa sabana teṃ rākhyo dūri durāi |42|
aṃśa kalā autāra je te sevata haiṃ tāhi |
aise bṛṃdā vipina kauṃ mana baca kai avagāhi |43|[153]

Kṛṣṇa and Rādhā are the source of the *rasa*, so the distinction between Kṛṣṇa and the *avatāras*, as well as their co-existence, is evident.

In the poetry of Dhruvadāsa, Viṣṇu retains his cosmic attributes found in all the texts examined so far. As in the Gauḍīya texts, Kṛṣṇa is, on the other hand, eternally involved in the divine sport (*vihāra*) which is outside of creation.

The function of Viṣṇu as creater is described in the *Bṛhadbāvana Purāṇa*. The eternal *sakhī* is said to appear before the Vedas, who wishs to know about the nature of the eternal *rasa* of the divine sport, and tells them that she must first carry out the command of the Lord:

> *prabhu ājñā ika bhaī hai so pahile kari laiṃhu* |
> *tā pāchai jo pūchi hau tākau uttara daiṃhu* |6|[154]

She thinks of Śrīpati, i.e., Viṣṇu, who appears and is ordered to create the universe:

> *sakhī kiyo jaba ciṃtavana śrīpati pragaṭe āi* |
> *prabhu ājñā tinasoṃ bhaī sṛṣṭi racāvahu jāi* |62|[155]

After she has communicated the commands of the Lord, the *sakhī* explains to the Vedas that Kṛṣṇa is eternally engrossed in the divine sport which is unaffected by creation and destruction. The Vedas realize that the bewildering process of creation is nothing but a manifestation of a portion of the divine, represented by Nārāyaṇa and the *avatāras*, whereas Kṛṣṇa as he appears engaged in the eternal sport is complete:

> *vedahu jāne aṃśa saba miṭyau bharama tehi kāla* |
> *samujhe pūrana sabani para nitya bihārī lāla* |[156]

Creation is then initiated when Viṣṇu directs his thoughts towards Puruṣa and Prakṛti and arouses in them the desire for sport:

> *śrīpati citayau hai jabahiṃ puruṣa prakṛti kī koda* |
> *tihi china upajīhīya meṃ kījai kachuka binoda* |71|[157]

In this way the involvement of Viṣṇu in creation is clearly stated, as well as his inferior position with respect to Kṛṣṇa, all of which is fully in accord with the Gauḍīya outlook.

Where Dhruvadāsa differs most radically from the Gauḍīya approach is with regard to the question of Kṛṣṇa becoming manifest. Dhruvadāsa draws a distinction between Kṛṣṇa in Vṛndāvana and Kṛṣṇa in Braj, and it is only in the context of Braj that manifestation is regarded as a possibility. A work called *Brajalīlā* describes how the divine couple, Kṛṣṇa and Rādhā, manifest themselves for the sake of the devotees:

> *nandalāla vṛṣabhāna kiśorī rasikani hita pragaṭī yaha jōrī* |3|[158]

The use here of the epithets 'Son of Nanda' and 'Daughter of Vṛṣabhāna' may be noted. Neither is commonly used by Dhruvadāsa, and through their reference to the parents of Rādhā and Kṛṣṇa, they evoke connotations of birth. The connection of the manifestation with Braj is made clear in two verses where it is described as having taken place in Braj, in both cases for the sake of devotees (*rasikas*). The first says that Rādhā and Kṛṣṇa made manifest in Braj the *līlā* which is a treasure of *rasa* and gives happiness to the devotees:

rasa nidhi līlā braja pragaṭāī rasika janani kau ati sukhadāī |5|[159]

The second similarly describes how the youthful couple became manifest in Braj for the sake of devotees:

rasikani hita vivi kuṃvara bara bhaye pragaṭa braja āṃni |[160]

Even in the above verses terms such as taking birth or becoming incarnate are avoided. It is a manifestation, as in the Gauḍīya texts, not an incarnation. It is a revelation of the divine sport of devotees. It is not, however, on the same level as the *nitya vihāra* in Vṛndāvana in which only the *sakhīs* can participate, and in this respect Dhruvadāsa differs from the Gauḍīya approach.

The distinction between Kṛṣṇa in Braj, where he performs *rāsa* with the *gopīs*, and Kṛṣṇa in Vṛndāvana, where the eternal sport of Rādhā and Kṛṣṇa occurs, is also indicated in the *Bṛhadbāvana Purāṇa*. Kṛṣṇa tells the Vedas, who want to sport with him, to become manifest in Braj, where he will also manifest himself:

tina prati taba vānī bhaī yaha prabhu tinhīṃ māni |
pragaṭa hohu braja jāya tuma hamahūṃ pragaṭaiṃ āni |57|[161]

Once again the concept of manifestation is used with regard to Kṛṣṇa in Braj alone and this is differentiated from the *nitya vihāra* in Vṛndāvana.

In this way Dhruvadāsa rejects the mythological structure of the *BhP.* much more totally than either Nandadāsa or the Gauḍīya texts. The divine sport as an ever-present symbolic expression of the essential nature of the divinity as alone stressed.

(iii) Bihārinadāsa — Haridāsī: With regard to the relation of Kṛṣṇa and Viṣṇu, Bihārinadāsa differs very little from Dhruvadāsa. Once again the Viṣṇu aspect is distinctly subordinated and there is no question of Kṛṣṇa being an incarnation of Viṣṇu.

The distinction between Vṛndāvana Kṛṣṇa and Braj Kṛṣṇa is even more marked in the poetry of Bihārinadāsa than in that of Dhruvadāsa. Here Braj Kṛṣṇa is relegated to roughly the same category as Viṣṇu. This gradation is made very explicit in a verse which says that neither Lakṣmīpati (Viṣṇu) nor Rāmakṛṣṇa (Kṛṣṇa and Balarāma) are unable to participate in the *bihāra* — the sport of Rādhā and Vṛndāvana Kṛṣṇa:

śrībihāridāsa bihāra kauṃ lachamīpati lalacāi |
e deva pitara līneṃ phirai hyāṃ rāmakṛṣṇa na samāi |[162]

The same sentiment is echoed in another verse which says that the *rasa* is unobtainable even to the women of Braj; Nārāyaṇa longs for it and the jewel of Braj, i.e., Braj Kṛṣṇa, falls at the feet of the *sakhīs* overcome by desire for this *rasa*:

kyoṃ pāyeṃ rasarīti prīti bina durlabha niju brajajāyana |
yā rasa koṃ lalacāta lajāte lachimīpati nārāyana ||
ihi rasa vivasa bhayau vrajabhūṣana laṭaki lagyau paripāṃyana |[163]

The fact that Bihārinadāsa makes a distinction between Braj Kṛṣṇa and Vṛndāvana Kṛṣṇa is pertinent to the problem of incarnation, for like Dhruvadāsa, he associated the process of *avatāra* exclusively with Braj Kṛṣṇa-Vṛndāvana Kṛṣṇa is totally detached from it. This can be seen in a verse which describes Lakṣmīpati and Brajapati as both being the supreme source of all incarnations, who assume bodies for the sake of *līlā* according to their wish. The eternal youth, Vṛndāvana Kṛṣṇa, who eternally sports is inaccessible even to these than whom no-one could be more qualified to experience him:

ichyā vigraha dhari līlā vapu saba avatārani para avatārī |
lachamīpati brajapati kauṃ dullabha inataiṃ kauna baḍau adhikārī |
nitya kisora niraṃtara biharata sevata srīharidāsa dulārī |[164]

Whereas in the poetry of Nandadāsa, Kṛṣṇa was said to be both *avatārī* and *avatāra,* here in his essential form he is neither; he is dissociated from the entire process, which is all on a lower plane than the eternal *vihāra.*

Elsewhere in the poetry of Bihārinadāsa the contrast between Braj Kṛṣṇa and Vṛndāvana Kṛṣṇa is described in terms of the distinction between the eternal (*nitya*) and that which has a particular purpose (*nimitta*). Vṛndāvana Kṛṣṇa represents the *nitya,* while Braj Kṛṣṇa expresses the *nimitta,* an event which has a purpose and so a beginning and an end. In *pada* 150 Bihārinadāsa emphasizes the inappropriateness of the concept of time in the context of the eternal *vihāra*:

sarvopari nityavihāra su nyārau |
barasa māsa aru pakṣa pahara pala kāhe koṃ gani dina dhārau |[165]

This would appear to be a direct reference to the mythological depiction of Kṛṣṇa in the *Purāṇas* where the *līlā* is expressed in terms of time. That this is what he has in mind is born out by the next line where he distinguishes the participants in this eternal *vihāra* from Kṛṣṇa as son of Nanda and Rādhā as daughter of Vṛṣabhānu who experience birth and action:

janama karama vṛṣabhānusuta naṃdanaṃdana siṣṭācārau |[166]

He finally expresses this difference as that between the *nitya* and the *nimitta,* which must be understood in order have a true comprehension of the nature of the *vihāra*:

nitta nimitta saṃdhi samajhe binu sodina svāda bigārau |[167]

There is thus very little difference between the approaches of Bihārinadāsa and Dhruvadāsa, both in their apprehension of the relative position of Kṛṣṇa and Viṣṇu and in their presentation of Vṛndāvana Kṛṣṇa as being totally uninvolved in the process of incarnation. If anything, Bihārinadāsa is more explicit in the distinction he draws between Vṛndāvana Kṛṣṇa and Braj Kṛṣṇa.

(iv) Harivyāsadeva — Nimbārkīya: Harivyāsadeva expresses essentially the same concepts as those found in the poetry of Dhruvadāsa and Bihārinadāsa. It is only in his much more extensive use of philosophical terminology that he differs from them and resembles more closely a poet such as Nandadāsa.

That the resemblance to Nandadāsa is more than purely accidental is suggested by the fact that one of the *padas* which discusses the relation between Kṛṣṇa and Viṣṇu is close in its wording to the passage from Nandadāsa (I. 34-37, discussed above, p. 42). It begins with a description of the formless Brahman which is almost a word for word repetition of the Nandadāsa verse, apart from the fact that Brahman is said to be the glow from the toe-nail of Kṛṣṇa rather than of his body:

akhila brahmāṇḍa brahma vyāpaka hai joī |
tihāre carana nakha ābhā hai soī |[168]

This means that Brahman's position relative to Kṛṣṇa is even further reduced. The next line states that Paramātmā, whose body is the universe, and who is Nārāyaṇa-Viṣṇu, is the attribute (*dharma*) of Kṛṣṇa, who is the possessor of these attributes (*dharmī*):

> *paramātama viśvakāya nārāyaṇa viṣṇu* |
> *dharma haiṃ tihāre tuma dharmī jaga jiṣṇu* |[169]

The implication of the statement by Nandadāsa are here made explicit and unequivocal. Whereas Nandadāsa was attempting to bridge the difference between the *BhP.* and sectarian concepts; Harivyāsadeva is expressing the sectarian viewpoint in philosophical terms. This greater sectarian emphasis suggests that the verse of Nandadāsa is the earlier upon which Harivyāsadeva has based his statement.

The cosmic role of Viṣṇu is found described in the poetry of Harivyāsadeva as well. In a number of places Paramātmā, who in the above verse is synonymous with Viṣṇu, is called a portion (*aṃśa*) of Kṛṣṇa, and is depicted as being involved in creative activity. *Pada* 16 says that Paramātmā, who is Lord of Prakṛti and Puruṣa (cf. Dhruvadāsa describes how Śrīpati directs his thoughts towards Prakṛti and Puruṣa in the beginning of creation) and lord of the world, is a portion of Kṛṣṇa:

> *jāko aṃsa paramātamā prakṛti puruṣa ko īsa* |
> *para icchā ādhīna hvai jagamagāta jagadīsa* |2|[170]

The dependence of Paramātmā upon *icchā* described in this verse is significant in view of the identification of *icchā* with the *sakhī* in a further verse:

> *priyā śakti ahalādinī piya ānanda svarūpa* |
> *tana vṛndāvana jagamagaiṃ icchā sakhī anūpa* |9|[171]

In this verse not only is *icchā* identified with the *sakhī*, by Rādhā with *hlādinī-śakti* and Kṛṣṇa with the *svarūpa* of bliss, very much long Gauḍīya lines. Referring back to the dependence of Paramātmā upon *icchā*, it would seem that this could be compared with the role of the *sakhī* in the *Bṛhadbāvana Purāṇa* where it is she who conveys the order of the Lord of Viṣṇu (see above p. 47).

The cosmic role of Viṣṇu Paramātmā is also described in a further *pada* according to which Paramātmā was created by Kṛṣṇa for the sake of creating the universe:

> *paramātma parabrahma kari visatārana jaga jāla* |
> *jana pālana jaya jaga mahā rāsabihārīlāla* ||[172]

It goes on to say that through this one part, the *avatāra* Paramātmā, which is dependent upon *icchā*, Kṛṣṇa has created the entire expanse of the universe:

> *jāke eka hī aṃsa kari paramātama avatāra* |
> *para icchā ādhīna hvai kīnoṃ saba vistāra* |[173]

In the above passages it may be noted that Viṣṇu is described as the incarnation of Kṛṣṇa and not *vice versa,* thus reversing the Purāṇic position. The role of Viṣṇu as the source of all other incarnation nevertheless remains unchanged. Both of these ideas are expressed in a verse which says that the one Paramātmā, taking incarnation, becomes many in the endless universe:

> *aise viśva ananta meṃ eka hī ye bahu aṃsa* |
> *paramātama avatāra hvai nirvikāra nirasaṃsa* |5|[174]

This can be compared with the Gauḍīya description of Viṣṇu as the *guṇa avatāra* who is at the same time the source of other incarnation.

In the use of terms such as *paramātmā, icchā-śakti,* and *hlādinī-śakti,* Harivyāsadeva comes closer to theological discussion in the manner of the Gauḍīya Gosvāmīs, than do other Braj Bhāṣā poets such as Dhruvadāsa and Bihārinadāsa. He is, however, as uncompromising as they are in his rejection of any mythic interpretation of Kṛṣṇa. He does not indeed even refer to the possibility of Kṛṣṇa taking incarnation.

The above discussion illustrates how even in the Braj Bhāṣā texts the basic characteristics of Viṣṇu and Kṛṣṇa, as traced in the Sanskrit texts, from the *RV.* to the Gauḍīya Gosvāmīs, remains fundamentally unchanged. This continuity can be found even in poets such as Dhruvadāsa who diverge most radically from the Purāṇic outlook. Viṣṇu is still the creator of the universe, while Kṛṣṇa is totally uninvolved in cosmic activity. Kṛṣṇa is still the manifest while Viṣṇu is the unmanifest.

The differences lie mainly in the approach to the relation between Kṛṣṇa and Viṣṇu and so to the concept of incarnation. Attitudes vary in this respect, ranging from acceptance of the mythological Purāṇic structure by Sūradāsa, to its total rejection by Dhruvadāsa. To attempt an analysis of these differences on sectarian grounds would appear to be mistaken since certainly texts belonging to the Rādhāvallabha, Haridāsī and Nimbārkīya sects are almost identical in their views, while even those from the Gauḍīya and Vallabha are very similar in many respects. A division into sectarian and non-sectarian would seem to be more fruitful.

References

1. The formation of the word Vṛndāvana is unclear. A plant name as first member could be expected, but there is no attested support for the modern explanation *vṛndā=tulasī*. Equally, Vṛndā used as a name for Rādhā, a *sakhī* or a goddess (*Brahmavivarta Purāṇa*, *Nārada Pañcarātra*, etc.) lacks independent confirmation. It seems not improbable that the word is pre-classical: lengthening of *vṛnda-* in Vṛndāvana would be comparable with Vedic vowel-lengthening in compound junctive (e.g. *RV. gárta-ruh=gártāruh*). One might suppose equally a connection with *vṛndāraka* 'chief', *vṛndiṣṭha* 'best', which seem to be related to the common formations *vṛndavṛndaiḥ*, etc. 'in groups'. In that case, the popular etymology, envisaging *vṛndā*, would be of no importance, and the word would be derived from *vṛnda* 'multitude, assembly'. Given the attestation of *yativṛnda* 'assembly of ascetics' (P. Olivelle, *Vāsudevāśrama: Yatidharmaprakāśa*, Vienna, 1976, I, 37), Vṛndāvana may be a synonym of *tapovana.*

   Vaikuṇṭha is attested in Vedic material as Indra Vaikuṇṭha, the traditional *Anukramaṇikā* author of *RV.* 10.48-50. This name is, on the face of it then likely to be a patronymic; implausibly, the *Anukr.* sees Vaikuṇṭha as a metronymic from Asurī Vikuṇṭhā. Its use as a place-name is therefore secondary (following Vṛndāvana). Such a conclusion is supported by its use even in the *Mbh.* for Viṣṇu rather than for Viṣṇudhāman. Such evidence as there is suggests something in the context of Vāmana, i.e., related to a physical defect. Vaikuṇṭha is probably derived from *vikuṇṭha* meaning 'blunt, dull' which is also connected with *kuṇtha* 'crippled, lame' and *kuṇṭhati* 'maims'.

2. *Ṛg Veda, Die Hymnen des Ṛigveda*, ed. Th. Aufrecht Berlin, 1861, i.154.5-6.
3. J. Gonda, *Die Religionen Indiens,* Vol. I, Stuttgart, 1960. pp. 238-39.
4. *Ibid.*, p. 242.
5. *Ibid.*, p. 243.
6. *RV.* op. *cit.*, i.26.2; i.44.6.
7. *Ibid.*, v. 11.1.

   jánasya gopā ajaniṣṭa jāgṛvir agníḥ sudákṣaḥ suvitāya návyase |

   'Born recently for easy access as the watchful protector of the people, Agni, the capable one.'
8. *Ibid.*, i.1.9.

   sá naḥ pitéva sūnáve ágne sūpāyanó bhava |
   sácasvā naḥ svastáye |

   'Like a father to his son, Agni, become accessible lto us. Associate with us for our well-being.'
9. *Ibid.*, x.95.10. For a discussion of this hymn see J.C. Wright, 'Purūravas and Urvaśī' *BSOAS* XXX (1967), pp. 526-47.
10. *Ibid.*, x.95.11.
11. *Ibid.*, x.95.7.
12. *Ibid.*, x.95.6.
13. *Ibid.*, x.95.8.
14. *Kapiṣṭhala-kaṭha-saṃhitā*, ed. Raghu Vira, Delhi, 1968, 7.6.
15. *Śatapatha-brāhmaṇa*, Ajmere, 1902, XI.5.1.
16. *Ahirbudhnya-saṃhitā*, ed. M.D. Rāmānujācārya, Adyar, 1916, Vol. I. I.7.38-41.
17. *Viṣṇu-Purāṇa*, ed. Jīvānanda Vidyāsāgara, Calcutta, 1882, I.3.1924.

18. *Aitareya-brāhmaṇa*, ed. Kāśīnātha Śāstrī Āgāśe, Ānanda Āśrama, 1896, Vol. I, I.1. 'Agni is the lowest of the gods, Viṣṇu is the highest; between them are all the other gods.'

19. *Mahābhārata*, ed. V.S. Sukthankar, Poona, 1936, I.17.18-19
evaṃ sutumule yuddhe vartamāne bhayāvahe |
naranārāyaṇau devau samājagmatur āhavam |18|
tatra divyaṃ dhanur dṛṣṭvā narasya bhagavañ api |
cintayāmāsa vai cakraṃ viṣṇur dānavasūdanam |19|
'Thus, when the clamorous, terrible battle was raging, Nara and Nārāyaṇa, the two divinities, entered the fray. There seeing the divine bow of Nara, Lord Viṣṇu also thought of his discus, the destroyer of demons.'

20. *Bhagavadgītā*, ed. W.D.P. Hill, London, 1928, 18.78. 'Where Kṛṣṇa, lord of Yoga, and Pārtha, the bow-man, remain, there prosperity, victory, right conduct and well-being are firm; this is my opinion.'

21. *Ibid.*, I. 189.31. 'And Hari plucked out two hairs, one white the other black. Those two hairs would enter two women in the family of Yadus—Rohiṇī and Devakī. Of them one became Baladeva, the second dark one became Keśava.'

22. *Mbh.*, *op. cit.*, I. 58.26. 'Then the demons who had been defeated often by the gods in battle and who had lost their supremacy, arose here on earth.'

23. *Ibid.*, I. 58.46.
asyā bhūmer nirasituṃ bhāraṃ bhāgaiḥ pṛthakpṛthak |
asyām eva prasūyadhvaṃ virodhāyeti cābravīt |
'He said, "In order to remove the burden of this earth, let each one separately, in part, be born there, for the sake of opposing (the demons)." '

24. *Ibid.*, I.58.51. 'For the sake of purifying the earth, Indra said to Puruṣottama, "Descend in part" and Hari agreed.'

25. *Ibid.*, I.61.90. 'He who is called Nārāyaṇa, eternal god of gods, his part among men was the powerful Vāsudeva.'

26. *RV.*, *op. cit.*, x.90.

27. *Viṣṇu Purāṇa*, *op. cit.*, V.1.59-60.
ujjahārātmanaḥ keśau sītakṛṣṇau mahāmune |59|
uvāca ca surān etau matkeśau vasudhātale |
avatīrya bhuvo bhārakleśahāniṃ kariṣyataḥ |60|
'(Viṣṇu) took out two of his hairs, one black and one white, and said to the gods, "These two hairs of mine will descend to the earth and will remove the distress (caused by) the burden (which has encumbered) the earth." '

28. *Ibid.*, V.1.2.
aṃśāvatāro brahmarṣe yo 'yam yadukulodbhavaḥ |
viṣṇos taṃ vistareṇāhaṃ śrotum icchāmy aśeṣataḥ |2|
'I wish to hear of the partial incarnation of Viṣṇu who was born in the Yadu family, completely and at length.'

29. *Ibid.*, V.1.3.
cakāra yāni karmāṇi bhagavān puruṣottamaḥ |
aṃśāṃśenāvatīryorvyāṃ tatra tāni mune vada |3|
'Those deeds which Lord Puruṣottama performed when he descended to earth through various

parts, relate, O sage.'

30. *Ibid.*, V.i.4. 'Maitreya, listen to that about which you have asked—Viṣṇu's performance of birth by various parts for the welfare of the world.'
31. *Harivaṃśa*, ed. P.L. Vaidya, Poona, 1969, 1.5.
    tatra janma kurūnāṃ vai tvayoktaṃ lomaharṣaṇe |
    na tu vṛṣṇyandhakānāṃ vai tad bhavān prabravītu me |
    'There you have related the origin of the Kurus, O Lomaharṣaṇa, but not that of the Vṛṣṇis and Andhakas. Please relate that to me.'
32. *Ibid.*, 43. 62.
    aṃśāvataraṇaṃ sarve surāḥ kuruta mā ciram |
    'Let all you gods become incarnate in part without delay.'
33. *Ibid.*, 43.76-77. 'Hear further how Viṣṇu descended to the earth for the sake of the people, the Lord, Master of life. Then Lord Nārāyaṇa, desirous of fame, was born in the renowned family of wise Vasudeva, born of the lineage of Yayāti.'
34. *Ibid.*, 45.38. 'Having caused yourself to descend to earth by means of yourself, gladden the wombs of Devakī and Rohiṇī.'
35. *Bhāgavata Purāṇa*, Tenth Canto, Bombay, 1867, X.1.2 'Describe to us the heroic deeds of Viṣṇu when he became incarnate in part.'
36. *BhP.*, Bombay, 1905, I.3.1. 'In the beginning the Lord assumed the form of Puruṣa, which arises from those principles commencing with Intellect, and which has sixteen parts, out of desire to create the world.'
37. *Ibid.*, I.3.5.
    etan nānāvatārāṇāṃ nidhānaṃ bījam avyayam |
    yasyāṃśāṃśena sṛjyante devatiryaṅnarādayaḥ |
    'This is the storehouse of various incarnations, the indestructible seed, by its various part are created gods, animals, men and so forth.'
38. *Ibid.*, I.3.28. 'These are all parts of fractions of the Puṃs, but Kṛṣṇa is the Lord himself.'
39. The epic form of this myth can be found in *Mbh.*, *op. cit.*, I.60.22-23 and IX.43.10-11. Especially interesting is the fact that the seed bearing Kārttikeya is first thrown in a river and that the child himself is found in a thicket of reeds.
40. *ŚBr.*, *op. cit.*, 11.5.1.4.
41. *BhP.*, *Tenth Canto*, *op. cit.*, X.11.35. 'Seeing Vṛndāvana, Govardhana and the banks of the Yamunā, Rāma and Mādhava had the highest joy, O king.'
42. For a discussion of this concept of cosmic water in the myths of other cultures, cf. M. Eliade, *Patterns in comparative religions*, London, 1958, pp. 188-93.
43. Cf. M. Eliade, *Ibid.*, pp. 193-94.
44. *Ibid.*, pp. 273-378.
45. *Ibid.*, pp. 287-93.
46. *Ibid.*, pp. 282-83.
47. *Kauṣītaki-upaniṣad*, in *Aṣṭādaśa-Upaniṣadaḥ*, ed. V.P. Limaye and R.D. Vādekara, Vol. I, Poona, 1958, 1.3. *vijarā nadī* | *ilyo vṛkṣaḥ* | 'The river Vijarā, the tree Ilya'.
48. M. Monier-Williams, *A Sanskrit English dictionary*, Oxford, 1899, p. 950, col. 2.

49. *Kauṣītaki-upaniṣad, op. cit.*, 1.3.
 vijarāṃ vā ayaṃ nadīṃ prāpat |
 na vā ayaṃ jarayiṣyatīti |
50. *The Principle Upanisads*, ed. S. Radhakrishnan, London, 1953, p. 756.
51. *KKS., op. cit.*, 7.6.
52. *ŚBr. op. cit.*, 11.5.1.13.
53. *Harivaṃśa*, this reading is from the R. Kiṃjavaḍekara, Poona, 1936 edition, II.9.32. 'First Kṛṣṇa looked favourably upon that grove as he was wandering through various groves tending the cows.'
 Poona, 1969 edition (53.32) variant reading:
 a. *satkārakāriṇā*
54. M. Monier-Williams, *op. cit.*, p. 1298, col. 2.
55. *Hariv., op. cit.*, II. 9.33 'Then in the last dry hot month (called) "healthy" grass sprang up there, as in the rains.' variant reading (53.33): a. *tataḥ pakṣe gharmamāsi.* The term *nirāmaya* means literally 'free from disease' which in this context does not seem particularly appropriate. However it is used in the *Mbh.* as well in conjunction with *gharmamāsa* (*Mbh.*, I. 3545, cf. O. Böhtlingk, *Sanskrit Wörterbuch*, p. 179, col. 2). This might indicate that it was, in fact, the name of a particular month in the hot season.
56. *Ibid.*, II.9.34. 'Where Madhusūdana remains for the salvation of the worlds, there calves, cattle and other people do not perish.'
57. M. Monier-Williams, *op. cit.*, p. 748, col. 3; p. 749, col. 1.
58. *Hariv., op. cit.*, II.8.8-9. 'O noble one, it is not possible to disport in this wood with the cowherd boys. This entire wood has been enjoyed by us and is worn out. Its grass and timber has been exhausted and the plants agitated by the cowherd boys.' variant reading (52.8-9) a. *bhuktabhojanam.*
59. Ibid., II.9.27-30.
60. *Ibid.*, II.8.22. 'It is said that there is a beautiful wood covered with abundant grass.'
61. *Ibid.*, II.8.24. 'A wood having a moist cool breeze, the abode of all the seasons, auspicious.'
62. *Ibid.*, II.8.25 'There, not very far away, the great mountain named Govardhana shines, having a high peak, like the Mandara of Nandana.'
63. M. Monier-Williams, *op. cit.*, p. 926. col. 1.
64. *Hariv.*, II.19.30.
65. *Hariv., op. cit.*, II.8.23. ' . . . which has many Kadamba trees and is situated on the bank of the Yamunā.'
66. *Ibid.*, II.8.26. 'And in the middle of this a Nyagrodha tree, having great branches, a *yojana* high, named Bhāṇḍīra, looks beautiful like a dark cloud in the sky.'
67. *Ibid.*, II.8.27. 'And through it, Kālindī has wended its way as if making a parting, like the Nalinī of Nandana, the best of rivers.'
68. *Ibid.*, II.8.28. 'And there we two will see Govardhana and the the Bhāṇḍīra, and the beautiful river Kālindī, pleasant for the traveller.'
69. *ViP., op. cit.*, V.6.29. 'The Lord Kṛṣṇa, whose actions cannot be frustrated fixed his mind favourably on Vṛndāvana, so that he might nourish the cattle.'

The term *akliṣṭakarman* can have two meanings: (1) He who brings about his aims easily, who can do anything; (2) He who is tireless in performing Vedic rites (cf. M. Monier-Williams, *op. cit.*, p.3, col. 1). In the context of Kṛṣṇa the first interpretation would seem to be more appropriate.

70. *Ibid.*, V.6.30. 'And so there even in that most arid hot season, O best of the twice-born, new grass grows as in the rainy season.'

71. *BhāP.*, *op.cit.*, X.18.2-3. 'While the two of them played thus in the *vraja* in the guise of cowherd boys through their pretence, the summer season started which is not dear to embodied beings, but through the qualities of Vṛndāvana, where Lord Keśava remained in person with Rāma, it appeared like spring.'

72. *Ibid.*, X.13.20. 'He who is independent, restraining the calves who were himself by means of the cowherd boys who were himself, and disporting through self-sports, the universal soul entered the *vraja*.'

73. *Ibid.*, X.13.39. 'These are neither gods nor sages; you alone, Lord, shine through separate receptacles.'

74. *Ibid.*, X.13.57. 'Knowing (Brahmā) to be unable to see and bewildered, wondering what all this was, the Supreme Unborn immediately spread the curtain of Nature.' *cf. Śvetāśvataropaniṣat*, I.9. in *Aṣṭādaśa-Upaniṣadaḥ*, *op. cit.*, for *ajā* in the sense of Prakṛti or Nature.

75. *Ibid.*, X.13.59. 'Suddenly looking on all sides, he saw before him Vṛndāvana filled with trees providing a livelihood for the people, pleasant throughout the year.'

76. *Ibid.*, X.13.60. ' . . . where human beings and animals that have natural enmity towards each other were living together as friends, anger, desire and so forth having fled the place where Ajita dwells.'

77. Rūpa Gosvāmī, *Laghubhāgavatāmṛta*, ed. Jvālāprasāda Miśra, Bombay, 1902, p. 8, v. 10. 'Now in order to declare the superiority of Kṛṣṇa because of (his) abundance of excellence, his forms will be examined in succession here.'

78. *Ibid.*, p. 9, v. 11. 'As one who has independent form, as one indentical with that, and as the possessed one, thus he appears triply in the abodes beyond the phenomenal universe.'

79. *Ibid.*, p. 9, v. 12. 'That form which depends on no other is called "the one having independent form".'

80. *Ibid.*, p. 10, v. 13. 'The supreme Lord, Kṛṣṇa, having a form of existence, consciousness and bliss, without beginning, the very beginning, Govinda, the cause of all causes.'

81. *Ibid.*, p. 11, v. 14. 'That form which is as if in its own form not different from that and owing to factors such as shape appears different, belongs to (the category) of "form identical with that".'

82. *Ibid.*, p. 11, v. 15. 'That form of him which, out of short, appears to have a different shape, for the most part equal to himself in power, is to be termed "diversion form".'

83. *Ibid.*, p. 11, v. 15. 'As the Lord of the supreme heaven is declared (to be) of Govinda, and as Vāsudeva is of the Lord of the supreme heaven.'

84. *Ibid.*, p. 153, v. 87. 'The son of Devakī is said to be superior to even the first of the *vyūhas*.'

85. *Ibid.*, p. 12, v. 16. 'In the same way that which displays progressively diminished power is termed "a partial manifestation of himself".'

86. The term *aṃśatva* and *aṃśitā* are contrasted in a later verse; *Ibid.*, p. 124, v. 50:

ekatvam ca pṛthakatvam ca tathāṃśatvam utāṃśitā |
'Oneness and manifoldness, and being a part and being possessor of parts.'

87. *Ibid.*, p. 122, v. 46. 'The state of being a portion is that in which always a portion of the powers are manifest; completeness is when many powers are manifest in accordance with his will.'

88. *Ibid.*, p. 15. v. 20. 'Of these the state of having an abode beyond the material universe is clearly apparent in a separate Śāstra such as the last canto of the *Pādmīya.*'

89. *Ibid.*, p. 16, v. 1. 'Now the incarnations are described amongst whom Kṛṣṇa is perfect.'

90. *Ibid.*, p. 16, v.1. 'If the aforesaid appear for the sake of effects in the world, like a causal link, either by themselves or through some means, then they are declared by *Smṛtis* to be incarnations.'

91. M. Monier-Williams, *op. cit.*, p. 56, col. 2.

92. *Laghubhāgavatāmṛta*, op. cit., p.17, v.20. 'And each intermediary form is either the one who is identical with him or a follower of him; as for example (the Viṣṇu) who lies on Śeṣa and Vasudeva.'

93. *Ibid.*, p. 136, v. 67. (*BhP.*, *op. cit.*, 3.1.5). 'This one is the storehouse of various incarnations, the indestructible seed.'

94. *Ibid.*, p. 138, v. 68. 'This form is the seat of the appearance of various incarnations.'

95. *Ibid.*, p. 17. v. 3. 'These incarnations are for the most part "partial manifestations of himself" and "possessed", and the one who is "independent" will be revealed subsequently.'

96. *Ibid.*, p. 207, v. 132. 'Therefore through terms such as "himself", it has been revealed in texts such as the *BhP.* that Lord Kṛṣṇa is indeed the independent form.'

97. *Ibid.*, p. 190, v. 121. 'Through the description of Kṛṣṇa's superiority to all of his forms, the fact that he is greater than Paramavyomanātha is shown, and through the term "himself" his independence is described.'

98. *Ibid.*, p. 188, v. 118. 'Among the three incarnation of Puṃs, Viṣṇu is the greatest, (greater) than Brahmā and Rudra, as has been established by Bhṛgu, etc. What to speak then of Puruṣa himself, and how much more is Vāsudeva, while greatest of all is Mahāvaikuṇṭhanāyaka.'

99. Cf. discussion of *śuddhasṛṣti* in F.O. Schrader, *Introduction to the Pāñcarātra*, Adyar 1916, pp. 31-38.

100. *Laghubhāgavatāmṛta* , *op. cit.*, p. 17, v.3. 'They (the *avatāras*) are threefold as: that called Puruṣa, those that have the nature of *guṇas*, and those embodied for *līlā*.

101. *Ibid.*, p. 18, v. 4. (*BhP.*, *op. cit.*, II. 6.40) 'Puruṣa is the first incarnation of the Supreme.'

102. *Ibid.*, p. 149, v. 79. 'He is famed through being a *vilāsa* of Mahāvaikuṇṭhanātha.'

103. *Ibid.*, p. 207, v. 133. 'Therefore Paramavaikuṇṭhanātha also has the nature of being his *vilāsa.*'

104. *Ibid.*, p. 169, v. 103.'Though through the manifestations of *līlās* such as birth, he is known as an incarnation, through the abundance of all his excellence he is a *vilāsa.*'

105. *Ibid.*, p. 164, v. 99. 'Brahman, which is a thing without qualities, without distinctions, without form, can be compared to the light of Kṛṣṇa is compared to the sun.'

106. *Ibid.*, p. 230, v. 156. 'The *līlā* is said to be twofold as manifest and unmanifest. Moreover he always sports through his endless appearances and *līlās* and sometimes through one appearance in the world he takes birth etc., together with his attendants.'

107. *Ibid.*, p. 16, v. 18. 'That manifestation of one form at the same time, altogether having the same

nature as that (independent form), is called "appearance".'

108. *Ibid.*, p. 235, v. 163. 'Kṛṣṇa remains without beginning as her eternal son and in manifest *līlā* he comes through means of her.'

109. *Ibid.*, p. 236, v. 164. 'Then having become manifest in the festival arranged by the lord of Vraj, there he manifests the *līlās* such as those of childhood in sequence, which he performs in thousands of unmanifest appearances also.'

110. *Ibid.*, p. 208, v. 135. 'Surely this offspring of the Yadus appeared at the end of Dvāpara. How then can the Lord of Vaikuṇṭha who is without beginning be his manifestation.'

111. *Ibid.*, p. 208, v. 135. 'Not so, the *līlā* of this one who is without beginning is also beginningless. Out of his own free will it is manifest by Mukunda from time-to-time.'

112. *Ibid.*, p. 214, v. 140. 'Just as though fire exists in various places in the form of heat, it is produced through flint, wood, etc., having got a cause; in the same way, Kṛṣṇa sometimes for some reason manifests his beginningless, marvellous *līlā* of birth etc.'

113. Sūradāsa, *Sūrasāgara*, ed. Nandadulāre Vājapeyī, Vol. 1, Kāśī, 1953, *pada* 621. 'Hari, who is primeval, eternal and indestructible, who dwells ever in each body, whom the *Purāṇas* describe as the fullest Brahman, whose limits Śiva and Brahmā know not, whose virtues are unapproachable even to the scriptures; that one Jaśodā has play in her lap.'

114. *Ibid.*, v. 7. *viśvambhara nija nāma kahāvai* | 'He is called the sustainer of the universe.'

115. *Ibid.*, v. 16. *loka racai rākhai aru mārai* | 'He creates, sustains and destroys the world.'

116. *Ibid.*, v. 6, 'He has neither eyes, nor ears, nor tongue nor nose; without hands and feet he manifests himself.

117. *Ibid.*, v. 10. 'He is devoid of old age and death, without illusion; (he has) no father or mother, no son or relative, no wife.'

118. *Ibid.*, v. 15. 'He is Acyuta, ever reclining upon the waters.'

119. *Ibid.*, v. 22. ' Ramā always rubs his lotus feet.'

120. *Ibid.*, v. 17. 'That one is bound by his mother to the churning-rod.'

121. *Ibid.*, v. 23. 'That one sports in the bower under the control of Rādhā.'

122. *Ibid.*, v. 11. *so bacharani ke pāchaiṃ ḍolai* | 'He runs after the calves.'

123. *Ibid.*, v. 14. 'He takes the cows of the cow-herd boys to graze.'

124. *Ibid.*, *pada* 762. 'He who was not fatigued measuring the earth in three steps, finds it difficult to cross the threshold.'

125. *Ibid.*, *pada* 761. *japa dadhiripu hari hātha liyau* | 'When Hari took in his hand the churning rod.'

126. *Ibid.*, *khagapati-ari ḍara asurani saṃkā bāsarapati ānamda kiyau* | 'The enemy of Garuḍa was afraid, the demons were alarmed, the sun was happy.'

127. *Ibid.*, *bibukhi siṃdhu sakucata siva socata garalādika kimi jāta piyau* | 'The sea shrunk back in pain; Śiva pondered how he would drink the poison.'

128. *Ibid.*, *ati anurāga saṃga kamalā tana praphulita aṃga na samāta hiyau* | 'Kamalā was overjoyed and could not contain her love.'

129. *Ibid.*, pada 646. 'Brahman has taken incarnation as destroyer of the wicked.'

130. *Ibid.*, *pada* 886. *gokula janama liyau sukhakārana* | 'The source of happiness has taken birth in

Gokula.'

131. *Ibid., pada* 1012. *bhakti ke basa syāma suṃdara deha dhare āvaiṃ* I 'Through the force of devotion, Śyāma has come, assuming a beautiful body.'

132. *Ibid., pada* 1004. *nirguna saguna rūpa dhari āe* I 'The attributeless one has assumed a form with attributes.'

133. *Ibid., pada* 2220. *dhani gokula pragaṭe banavārī* I 'Blessed in Gokula where Banavārī has manifested.'

134. *Ibid., pada* 1569. 'He was taken birth in Braj. In Braj he always disports himself. This *līlā* he likes exceedingly; he assumes a body again and again and so manifests himself.'

135. *Ibid., pada* 1115. 'From age-to-age the Lord takes incarnation in Braj. These *gopīs,* these cowherd-boys, this happiness, this *līlā,* he never abandons. Night and day he performs this sport; he is the protector of the people.'

136. *Ibid., pada,* 1682. 'The sound of the flute reached Vaikuṇṭha. On hearing it, the couple, Nārāyaṇa and Kamalā felt pleasure in their hearts.

137. *Ibid.*, 'That *rāsa* sport which Kṛṣṇa performs is far from us.'

138. Nandadāsa, *Rāsapañcādhyāyī,* in *Nandadāsagraṃthāvalī,* Kāśī, 1949, I.34. 'The beauty of Mohana's marvellous form cannot be described; its glow is Brahman who pervades the entire universe.'

139. *Ibid.*, I.35-36. 'The supreme soul, supreme Brahman, inner conscience of all, through his attributes is Lord Nārāyaṇa, master of all. That charming body is endowed with the attributes of infancy, childhood and boyhood; the possessor of these attributes is the eternal youth Kānha, who amazes the heart of all.'

140. This does not seem to be entirely in accord with classical Sanskrit usage. Cf. M. Monier-Williams, *op. cit.*, where *avatārin* is the one who has taken incarnation (p. 90, col.1) and *aṃśin* is the one who has a part or share (p. 1, col. 1.).

141. Nandadāsa, *Siddhāntapañcādhyāyī* in *Nandadāsagraṃthāvalī, op. cit.* v. 7 'He who is Nārāyaṇa for the sake of taking incarnation and (possessing) the six (divine) qualities is Nandanandana, the resort and limit of all.'

142. Nandadāsa, *Rāsap., op. cit.*, v. 33. 'Though the pure Kamalā serves his lotus feet night and day, she cannot even dream of experiencing that *rasa.* Unless one is qualified no-one can perceive Vṛndāvana. How can you see the dust as long as you have not understood the matter.'

143. Nandadāsa, *Siddhāntap., op. cit.*, v. 118. 'Though the beautiful Ramā, best of women, sports upon his breast, still she cannot obtain that *rasa,* which the women of Braj obtained.'

144. Nandadāsa, *Bhramaragīta* in *Nandadāsagraṃthāvalī,* op. cit., v. 11. 'Śyāma has taken incarnation and assumed a body for the sake of sport; only through the way of *yoga* can the abode of the supreme Brahman be obtained.'

145. Ibid., v. 24. 'The sun in the sky is hidden in its light, without divine sight who can see it.'

146. *Ibid.*, v. 28. 'How can those who are atheists know his real form. Leaving aside the manifest sun, they grasp at reflected rays.'

147. Nandadāsa, *Siddhāntap., op. cit.*, vv. 78-79. 'And to the worshippers they showed the unity; they displayed the oneness of Kānha as infant, child and boy. The one who takes incarnation, the taking of incarnation, and all the manifestations, he is the basis of all these, the sustenance of the world.'

148. Nandadāsa, *Rāsap., op. cit.*, III. 1. 'And they said, "Since the youthful Kṛṣṇa manifested in Braj, Indirā, the limit of all has adorned the place.'

149. *BhP., op. cit.*, X. 31.1. 'Victory to you through whose birth the *vraja* prospers more, (since) Indirā is permanently here.'

150. Nandadāsa, *Bhāṣā daśama skandha*, in *Nandadāsagraṃthāvalī, op. cit.*, I., p. 223. 'Viṣṇu will become incarnate through Devakī; he will be intent upon my death.'

151. *BhP., op. cit.*, X.8.19. 'Therefore, because Nandakumāra has the same qualities as Nārāyaṇa — in fortune, fame and experience — there should be no astonishment at his deeds.'

152. Nandadāsa, *Bhāṣā daśama skandha, op. cit.*, VIII, p. 244. 'All the qualities which are in Nārāyaṇa shine in your son. Fortune, fame, riches and *rasa* (are in him) even greater in quantity than in Nārāyaṇa.'

153. Dhruvadāsa, *Vṛndāvana sata līlā*, in *Bayālīsa līlā, op. cit.*, vv. 42-43. 'The *rasa* of Vṛndāvana is far from all. The incarnations, both portions and parts, serve it. Let your mind and speech be immersed in such a Vṛndā forest.'

154. Dhruvadāsa, *Bṛhadbāvana Purāṇa bhāṣā līlā*, in *Bayālīsa līlā, op. cit.*, v. 6. 'There is a command of the Lord which I will first carry out. After that I will give the reply to the question you have asked.'

155. *Ibid.*, v. 62. 'When the *sakhī* contemplated, the Lord of Śrī appeared manifest. The Lord's command to him was, "Let the world be created".'

156. *Ibid.*, v. 69. 'Then the Vedas recognised all as parts and their confusion was removed. They understood Bihārlāla to be complete, above all the eternal.'

157. *Ibid.*, v. 71. 'When the Lord of Śrī thought in the direction of Puruṣa and Prakṛti at that moment arose in their heart the desire for sport.'

158. Dhruvadāsa, *Braja līlā*, in *Bayālīsa līlā, op. cit.*, v. 3. 'The son of Nanda and the daughter of Vṛṣabhāna, for the sake of devotees this couple manifest itself.'

159. *Ibid.*, v. 5. 'They made manifest in Braja the *līlā* which is treasure of *rasa*, and gives happiness to the devotees.'

160. *Ibid.*, v. 9. 'For the sake of devotees the youthful couple became manifest in Braj.'

161. *Ibid.*, v. 57. 'Then they heard a voice which said that the Lord had agreed to this — "You become manifest in Braj; I will also become manifest".'

162. Bihārinadāsa, in *Sarvopari-nityavihāriṇī-rasa sāgara*, Vṛndāvana, 1969. 'Bihārinadāsa says that even Lakṣmīpati longs for this sport; let alone gods and forefathers, even Rāma and Kṛṣṇa cannot enter it.'

163. *Ibid.*, p. 449, *pada* 148. 'How can this way of *rasa* be achieved without love? It is impossible even for the women of Braj to obtain. Longing for this *rasa*, even Nārāyaṇa, the Lord of Lakṣmī, feels ashamed (of his own lowliness). Overcome by this *rasa*, the jewel of Braj, falls at the feet (of the *sakhīs*).'

164. *Ibid.*, p. 290, v. 28. 'To them who assume a form at will, a body for the sake of *līlā*, the supreme source of all the incarnations, even to that Lakṣmīpati and Brajapati than whom no-one has greater authority, it is unobtainable. The eternal youth sports forever and Haridāsa serves him with affection.'

165. *Ibid.*, p. 452, *pada* 150. 'That eternal sport is above all and distinct; why pass your days counting the years, months and hours, moments and minutes.'

166. *Ibid.*, p. 452, *pada* 150. 'The daughter of Vṛṣabhānu and the son of Nanda have birth and action; they behave in accordance with human codes of conduct.'

167. *Ibid.*, p. 452, *pada* 150. 'Without understanding the nature of the relation between the eternal and that which has a purpose, the taster spoils the taste'.

168. Harivyāsadeva, *Mahāvāṇi*, ed. Kuñjabihāriśaraṇa, Vṛndāvana, 1976, *Siddhānta sukha*, 33.1, p. 130. 'That Brahman who pervades the entire universe is the brilliance shining from your toe-nail.'

169. *Ibid.*, 33.2, p. 130. 'Paramātma, whose body is the universe, who is Nārāyaṇa-Viṣṇu, is your attribute and you are the possessor of attributes, O Lord of the world.'

170. *Ibid.*, 16.2, p. 100. 'He (Kṛṣṇa) whose portion is Paramātmā, Lord of Puruṣa and Prakṛti, who is dependent upon the Supreme Will, and who shines forth as Lord of the world.'

171. *Ibid.*, p. 101, v. 16.9. 'Rādhā is power causing bliss, Kṛṣṇa the form of bliss itself. Vṛndāvana is their form shining forth, and divine Will is the unique *sakhī*.'

172. *Ibid.*, p. 104, v. 17.1. 'To that one who created Paramātmā Parabrahma in order to spread out the net of the universe and for the protection of the people, victory to that performer of the *rāsa* who is supreme is the world.'

173. *Ibid.*, p. 104, v. 17.2. 'He who through his one portion, the incarnation Paramātmā, who is dependent on the Supreme Will, created all this expanse.'

174. *Ibid.*, p. 101, v. 16.5. 'Thus in the endless universes he is one with many parts, this Paramātmā having taken incarnation, without modification, without doubt.'

3

Vṛndāvana and its Role in *Līlā*

VṚNDĀVANA is the *līlādhāman* of Kṛṣna. In other words, it is the symbolic representation of that aspect of the divinity which forms the 'space' for the performance of divine self-manifestation. As *līlā* is an activity, it must have an area in which to manifest itself — an area which is, however, not limited by the physical notions of time and space. The image of Vṛndāvana puts this concept into concrete terms of a mentally conceivable place. In order to understand the nature of Vṛndāvana it is therefore necessary to examine the concept of *līlā*.

The Nature of *Līlā*

The term *līlā* means play or action performed not for a purpose, but as a form of divine self-expression.[1] As a manifestation of divine nature this concept of play is frequently connected with creative processes. This is illustrated by a passage from the *Bṛhadāraṇyaka-upaniṣad* which says that in the beginning there was only one, and the divinity could not sport alone:

> *sa vai naiva reme*[2]

The verb *ram* used here indicates the same sense of expression and exprience of internal delight as *līlā*. The passage implies that the expression of delight is inherent in the divine and is manifested through play. Thus creation takes place through the play of the divinity which takes the form firstly of division into two[3] and through these two evolves the whole of creation.[4] Creation, in this context, is an expression of the essential nature of the divine. It differs therefore from the cyclic notion of creation as a function basically external to the divine nature.

Though all of the texts to be examined regard *līlā* as the manifestation of the divine, certain texts draw a distinct line between creation and the essential nature of the divine. When this happens *līlā* becomes either totally disconnected from creation or the creative aspect is regarded as secondary.

(A) *Līlā* in the *Purāṇas*

In the *BhP.* *līlā* is envisaged as incorporating both the manifestation of creation and self-manifestation in the form of incarnation. The text itself begins with the sages asking the reciter of the *Purāṇa* to describe to them the noble actions of that one who becomes divisible in sport (*līlayā*):

tasya karmāṇy udārāṇi parigītāni sūribhiḥ |
brūhi naḥ śraddadhānāṃ līlayā dadhataḥ kalāḥ | [5]

In effect, this informs the reader that the *BhP.* is about the manifest aspect of the divinity, and as can be seen from the contents of the text, these activities include both creation and incarnation. The phrase *līlayā dadhataḥ kalāḥ* indicates how the manifestation takes place through *līlā*. *Kalā* denotes a part of a whole and is commonly used for the digits of the moon which are said to be sixteen in number.[6] Therefore 'assuming parts' would appear to imply becoming divisible in contrast to the unmanifest, indivisible Brahman.

The connection between having *kalās* and being manifest is substantiated in another passage according to which the divine took the form of *puruṣa* which has sixteen *kalās* through desire to create the world:

jagṛhe pauruṣaṃ rūpaṃ bhagavān mahadādibhiḥ |
saṃbhūtaṃ ṣoḍaśakalām ādau lokasisṛkṣayā || [7]

The *puruṣa* form of the divine is here evidently the active, manifest from involved in creation. It is this form which is described as having sixteen *kalās*, again connecting the possession of parts with activity and manifestation.

While in the first passage it was through *līlā* that the process of manifestation took place, in the second passage it is through the innate desire for creation (*lokasisṛkṣayā*). That the two terms are used in very similar contexts, suggests again that *līlā* and the desire for creation are seen as synonymous.

That the cosmic process in inseparable from *līlā* is further indicated by a verse which says that it is through self-sport (*ātmalīlā*) that the creation, protection and destruction of the world takes place:

ya eka īśo jagad ātmalīlayā sṛjaty avaty atti na tatra sajjate | [8]

The whole process is thus a form of self-expression of the divinity.

Not only creation but also the entrance of the divine into creation, i.e., incarnation, is a part of *līlā*. In one verse the sages ask to hear the stories of the incarnation (*avatārakathāḥ*) of Hari who performs *līlā* through his own incomprehensible power (*ātmamāyā*):

> *athākhyāhi harer dhīman avatārakathāḥ śubhāḥ|*
> *līlā vidadhataḥ svairam īśvarasyātmamāyayā|*[9]

Thus the events of the incarnation are effected when the divine is performing *līlā*.

The use of the term *ātmamāyā* in the above passage is significant since in another passage it is said to be through *ātmamāyā* that creation takes place :

> *sa evedaṃ sasarjāgre bhagavān ātmamāyayā|*
> *sadasadrūpayā cāsau guṇamayyāguṇo vidhuḥ||*[10]

It is therefore through the same *ātmamāyā* that both incarnation and creation occur, showing how they are both essentially the same process. In other words there is no real difference between creation and the entrance of the divine into creation. Both are expressions of the divine self-manifestation.

In conformity with their nature as epic texts, neither the *Hariv.* nor the *ViP.* give much overt prominence to the *līlā* concept. The few references there are suggest a standpoint not differing essentially from that of the *BhP.*

The *ViP.* prefaces its account of creation with a statement to the effect that the activities of Viṣṇu are like those of a child playing:

> *vyaktaṃ viṣṇus tathāvyaktaṃ puruṣaḥ kāla eva ca|*
> *krīḍato bālakasyeva ceṣṭhāṃ tasya niśāmaya||*[11]

This distinctly suggest that creation is of the nature of *līlā*.

The connection between *līlā* and incarnation appears in a passage where Balarāma is said to ask Kṛṣṇa why he is acting like a human to the extent of allowing Kālīya to overpower him. Balarāma tells Kṛṣṇa that he has descended among mortals for the sake of the world, because of his desire to remove the burden of evil which was weighing it down.[12] This incarnation is called human *līlā* (*mānuṣyalīlā*) and is said to be imitated by the gods who remain with Kṛṣṇa:

> *mānuṣyalīlāṃ bhagavan bhajatā bhavatā surāḥ|*
> *viḍambayantas tvallīlāṃ sarva eva sahāsate||*[13]

So far the impression is that this form of *līlā* is primarily for a purpose, i.e., the protection of the earth, but the next line belies this and shows how it is basically for the expression of the divine nature. According to this verse the goddesses were first made to descend to the *Gokula* and afterwards Kṛṣṇa descended with play as his aim:

avatārya bhavān pūrvaṃ gokule tu surāṅganāḥ |
krīḍārtham ātmanaḥ paścāt avatīrṇo 'si śāśvata ||[14]

Pure sport is thus the only real motivation for the incarnation.

Though references to *līlā* are even rarer in the *Hariv.* than in the *ViP.*, there are still sufficient allusions to suggest that the basic concept is inherent in the account. One passage, for example, describes how Kṛṣṇa sported with the other cowherd boys as he had previously sported in heaven:

sa tatra vayasā tulyair vatsapālaiḥ sahānagha |
reme vai vāsaraṃ kṛṣṇaḥ purā svargagato yathā ||[15]

Here an identification is made between terrestrial and celestial sport and such sport is seen as innate to the nature of Kṛṣṇa.

(B) *Līlā* in the Sectarian Philosophical Texts

In contrast to the Purāṇic position discussed above, whereby creation is an aspect of *līlā* not basically different from incarnation, the philosophical texts of both the Vallabha and Gauḍīya sects draw a distinction between *līlā* as an expression of the essential nature of the divine and the creative process.

(i) The Vallabha texts : The distinction between creation and inner *līlā* can be seen in the *Tattvārthadīpanibandha* ascribed to Vallabhācārya, which says that at times the divinity delights within itself and at other times it disports itself in the phenomenal universe :

kadācid ramate svasmin prapañce 'pi kvacit sukham ||[16]

In another verse from the same text the sport which takes place within the divine itself (*svasmin*) is called *ātmarati*.[17] According to this verse, liberation does not entail the disapperance of the material universe (*prapañca*) but only of the illusion which makes the soul unable to perceive the world as an expression of the divine. At the time of Kṛṣṇa's *ātmarati*, however, even the material universe itself is absorbed into him. The manifestation of the universe is, therefore, envisaged as an expression of divine sport. At the same time, there is an even higher and more complete expression of *līlā* within the being of the divinity.

The inner sport (*ātmarati*) is described in the *Subodhinī* in terms of the *rāsa* with the *gopīs*. Vallabha discusses the problem of how Kṛṣṇa can be sporting within himself alone at the same time as he is sporting with the *gopīs*. The solution found for this problem is that even when sporting with the *gopīs*, he has placed himself in the *gopī* and so in reality the sport is within himself:

> *asyām api daśāyām ātmarata eva rasādhāratvāya tasyām ātmānaṃ sthāpitavān*।[18]

The *rāsa* is thus a manifestation of his own essential being; it is the play of the divine within itself for the sake of self-expression.

A similar situation is postulated with regard to the entrance of human souls into the divine *līlā*. The *Anubhāṣya* describes how souls transcend the material body formed of qualities and obtain a body which is beyond the qualities and is suitable for *līlā*.

> *prākṛtaguṇamayaṃ prapañcam atikramya guṇātītaṃ*
> *prapañcaṃ sākṣāllīlopayoginaṃ prāpnotīty avagamyate*।[19]

It goes on to say that the divine which is formed of bliss enters the soul which then experiences the *rasa*, first of the pain of separation (as the *gopīs* did before the *rāsa*) and then of the manifested divine from itself:

> *jīve tv ānandamayaḥ puruṣottamaḥ praviśatīti rasātmakatvād ānandātmakam eva virahabhāvarasābdhim anubhūya paścāt prādurbhūtaprabhusvarūpaṃ prāpya na bibheti*।[20]

The concept here of the divine entering into the soul for the sake of *līlā* is similar to that of Kṛṣṇa entering into the *gopīs* for the sake of *ātmarati* as described in the *Subodhinī*. This *līlā* is evidently not the same as the process whereby souls are involved in the material condition, i.e., creation.

In the philosophy of Vallabha, creation of the material universe is in fact conceived as a process of concealment of the divine nature rather than manifestation. The most perfect expression of the divinity lies in total manifestation of the qualities of existence (*sat*), consciousness (*cit*) and bliss (*ānanda*). In addition to these three qualities the supreme expression of the divinity has six unique qualities (enumerated as *aiśvarya, vīrya, yaśas, śrī, jñāna* and *vairāgya*) which are concealed in all other forms, even when the quality of bliss is partially manifested. In the material universe the bliss aspect is concealed, while in the unmanifest aspect of the divinity, idenitfied as *akṣara brahman,* bliss is obscured so as to become finite and the six divine qualities are concealed. In the *Aṇubhāṣya* it is said that the unmanifest *akṣara brahman* cannot be the supreme goal because in it *ānanda* is limited:

> *athavā akṣarabrahmaṇy ānandātmake saty api tasya*
> *paricchinnatvān na paramaphalatvam* |[21]

It is thus full manifestation rather than the absence of qualities or activities which constitutes the essential nature of the divine, and accordingly *līlā* is regarded as the highest expression of the divine.

The idea of different levels of *līlā* can be related to the Vallabha concept of reality as three levels of manifestaion: (i) the divine (*ādhidaivika*) in which all three qualities of existence, consciousness and bliss are fully manifested. (ii) The spiritual (*ādhyātmika*) in which the bliss is partially concealed. (iii) The material (*ādhibhautika*) in which both consciousness and bliss are concealed. These three terms are found in an explanation in the *Subodhinī* of the epithet *sākṣānmanmathamanmatha* used for Kṛṣṇa by the *BhP*. Vallabha says that the material Kāma has the form of the god; the spiritual Kāma is in the hearts of all beings; and the divine Kāma is Kṛṣṇa because Kṛṣṇa is the essence of everything:

> *ādhibhautiko manmathaḥ devatārūpaḥ* |
> *tata ādhyātmika sarvahṛdayeṣu sākṣānmanmathaḥ* |
> *tasyāpy ayaṃ maṇḍalathaḥ ādhidaivikaḥ* |
> *sarvasyāpi sarvatvāt* ||[22]

In the *Siddāntamuktāvalī* there is a verse in a similar vein which compares Gaṅgā with the divinity, each of which is said to have three forms. The material universe is compared to the water of the river; the *bṛhat* (i.e., *akṣara brahman*) is compared to the invisible power of Gaṅgā which rewards those who live on its banks; finally, the actual goddess, Gaṅgā, is compared with Kṛṣṇa himself:

> *yathā jalaṃ tathā sarvaṃ yathā śaktā tathā bṛhat* |
> *yathā devī tathā kṛṣṇas tatrāpy etad ihocyate* ||[23]

Though the terms *ādhibhautika*, *ādhidaivika* and *ādhyātmika* are not actually used in this verse, the commentator on the text uses these terms in his interpretation.[24]

It seems possible to see in the concept of *līlā* a parallel to the above idea of three levels of reality. The *ādhidaivikī līlā* would be equivalent to *ātmarati* — the highest expression of the divinity wherein it manifests all of its divine qualities. *Ādhyātmikī līlā* involves the expression of the divine as the unmanifest, formless *akṣara brahman*. Here there is concealment of the six divine qualities and a limitation of the bliss aspect. Finally in *ādhibhautikī līlā* the creation is manifested through a further process of concealment.

(ii) The Gauḍīya texts : Creation is relegated to an even more subsidiary position as an expression of the divine in Gauḍīya texts than in those of the Vallabha texts. An even greater distinction is drawn between the eternal divine *līlā* and *līlā* as a cosmic process.

The Gauḍīya understanding of the role of creation in divine self-expression is closely connected with their concept of the relation between the divinity and its powers (*śaktis*). This *śaktis* are described by Jīva Gosvāmī in his *Bhagavat-saṃdarbha* as being three in number.[25] The first is called *antaraṅga-* or *svarūpa-śakti;* the term *antaraṅga* indicates that it is intrinsic to the divinity and, in fact, constitutes its essential being. Through this power the divinity expresses its own divine nature and realizes itself in its bliss. This relationship can be seen as corresponding to the *ātmarati* of the Vallabha texts discussed above.

Creation is, on the other hand, the function of the *bahiraṅga-* or *māyā-śakti*[26] which is external to the divinity and cannot affect its essential nature. Creation is, therefore, a form of manifestation of divine power, and to this extent can be regarded as an aspect of *līlā*. However, the Gauḍīya texts differ from those of the Vallabha texts in showing no direct involvement of the divinity in creation.

The situation of the soul is expressed in terms of the third *taṭastha-* or *jīva-śakti.* As long as the *taṭastha-śakti* which forms the soul is under the influence of *māyā-śakti,* obscuring its pure consciousness, it is bound. When the soul is released from this bondage, it becomes a part of the *svarūpa-śakti* and takes part in the eternal, divine *līlā*.[27] This can be compared with the account of the soul transcending its material body and entering into the *līlā* seen above in the Vallabha texts.

The intrinsic *līlā,* the display of the *svarūpa-śakti,* is described by the Gauḍīya texts in terms of the activities which in the *BhP.*, for example, were associated with incarnation; that is to say, the activities of Kṛṣṇa and not of Viṣṇu. The separation of the cosmic aspect of divine manifestation from the divine *līlā,* coincides therefore with the emphasis on the eternal nature of Kṛṣṇa *līlā*. It is the Kṛṣṇa *līlā* alone which is the intrinsic expression of the divine being.

Within Kṛṣṇa *līlā* itself, the sport of Kṛṣṇa with the *gopīs* is regarded as the innermost essence of the divine. It may be remembered that in the Vallabha texts, as well, the *ātmarati* was identified with the *rāsa*. In his *Śrīkṛṣṇa-saṃdarbha,* Jīva states that in the *gopīs* the essence (*sāra*) of the experience of love (*premarasa*) is displayed; this experience of love is itself the essence of that power by which bliss is experienced and caused (*hlādinīsāra*).[28] He goes on to say that because of the abundant display of this power in the *gopīs*, the supreme bliss of the divinity is manifest in them and hence the desire for sport arises:

> *tatprācuryaprakāśena śrībhagavato 'pi tāsu paramollāsaprakāśo bhavati tena tābhī ramaṇecchā jāyate* |[29]

Where the Gauḍīya texts differ from those of Vallabha is in their further singling out of Rādhā among the *gopīs* as expressing the highest degree of the supreme love (*premotkarṣaparākāṣṭhā*) and, in fact, as being identical with the *hlādinī-śakti*. Jīva states that Kṛṣṇa with Rādhā is the most wonderful of the manifestations of the divine:

> *rādhayā yugalitas tu kṛṣṇaḥ paramādbhutaprakāśaḥ* |[30]

Such an emphasis on the *līlā* of Rādhā and Kṛṣṇa is significant in view of the fact that this *līlā* alone is regarded as the eternal, divine sport by Braj Bhāṣā texts of the Rādhāvallabha and Haridāsī sects.

(C) The Braj Bhāṣā Treatment of Divine Sport

Braj Bhāṣā texts divide into those which speak of *līlā* as the supreme expression of the divine and those which postulate *nitya vihāra*, expressed through the sport of Rādhā and Kṛṣṇa only, as being an even higher expression than *līlā*. The poets which concentrate on *nitya vihāra* are more or less the same as those which rejected the validity of incarnation in the context of Kṛṣṇa.

(i) Texts which describe *Līlā*

(a) Sūradāsa : In the *Sūrasāgara*, *līlā* involves a manifold expression of the divine for the sake of devotees. This comes across clearly in a *pada* where Sūradāsa describes how Kṛṣṇa who cannot be reached by Śiva and other gods, laughs when he is rocked by Yaśodā, and concludes by saying that Kṛṣṇa takes many guises for the sake of his devotees:

> *sūra syāma bhaktani hita kārana nānā bheṣa banāvaiṃ* |[31]

In this sense, the performance of *līlā* is an assumed condition, not the one and only expression of the divine.

The above understanding of *līlā* fits in with the concept of the divine as having two aspects — Kṛṣṇa and Viṣṇu. When the divinity performs *līlā* he is Kṛṣṇa. The paradox of the two aspects — the inaccessible as the utterly accessible — creates the wonder of *līlā*. Thus Sūradāsa concludes a description of the two aspects — Viṣṇu who measures the earth in three steps and Kṛṣṇa who cannot even cross the threshold — by wondering at the greatness of this *līlā* which cannot be described even by Śeṣa:

> *sūradāsa prabhu kī yaha līlā parati na mahimā seṣa bakhānī* |[32]

The *Sūrasāgara* differs from the *BhP.* insofar as *līlā* is distinguished from creation. This can be seen for example in a verse which says that the Supreme Being who creates, preserves and destroys the universe, assumes līlā in the company of the cowherd boys:

> *loka racai rādhai aru mārai* |
> *so gvālani saṃga līlā dhārai* ||[33]

Here *līlā* is equated with Kṛṣṇa sporting in Braj with cowherd boys, not with any engagement in cosmic porcesses.

(b) Nandadāsa : A number of verses in the poetry of Nandadāsa reflect markedly the influence of the Vallabha definition of *ātmarati* discussed above. In his *Siddhāntapañcādhyāyī,* for example, Nandadāsa says that in order to manifest the *līlā* which finds expression in *rāsa,* Kṛṣṇa made the *gopīs* equal to or like himself:

> *ramyo cahata rasa rāsa inahīṃ apanī samasari kari* |[34]

This is almost identical with the image of Kṛṣṇa placing himself in the *gopīs* found in the *Subodhinī.*

In another place in the same work, Nandadāsa states that the divine Lord draws all within himself in order to disport himself, and this sport is spontaneous (*sahaja*) — a natural manifestation of his own nature:

> *je jaga maiṃ jagadīsa kahai ati rahe garva bhari* |
> *saba kara kiyau nirodha nija sahaja khela kari* ||[35]

This can be compared with Vallabha's description of the dissolution of the material universe during the divine self-sport (discussed above p. 66).

This description of divine sport is close to the concept of *nitya vihāra* which will be seen in the poetry of Dhruvadāsa and Bihārinadāsa, but is not identical with it. Its similarity lies in the fact that the divine sport is envisaged as taking place within the divine itself and not really as being a form of manifestaion. However, there is not the same emphasis on its unceasing nature. In the first example cited above, the use of the verb *kari* 'having made' gives the sense of an action being initiated, rather than that of a continuous state. The second example similarly gives the impression of the *sahaja khela* as being a condition entered into from time-to-time.

There is, moreover, an emphasis on *līlā* as a response to devotion, similar to that of Sūradāsa, which is not found in the concept of *nitya vihāra*. The love of the *gopīs* is described as the reason why Kṛṣna initiates the sport :

jadapi ātmarāma ramana bhae navala neha basa |[36]

Devotion is thus the moving force behind *līlā*.

This aspect of *līlā* is further emphasized in the Braj Bhāṣā adaptation of the *BhP*. by Nandadāsa, where he states that when the divinity had the desire to perform *līlā*, he first caused his devotees to take incarnation on earth for the sake of *līlā*:

jaba hari līlā icchā karaiṃ |
jagata maiṃ prathama bhakta avataraiṃ ||
tina kai prabhu kau parikara jitau |
pragaṭa ho'a līlā hita titau ||[37]

Thereupon Kṛṣṇa himself descends to fulfil the desires of the devotees:

taba śrī kṛṣṇa avatarahiṃ āi |
siddha karaiṃ bhagatana ke bhāi ||[38]

In this passage Hari first has the inherent desire to perform *līlā*, thus showing that the desire to disport himself is an essential part of his nature. At the same time the *līlā* becomes manifest for the sake of the devotees.

The emphasis on the role of devotion in *līlā* is much greater here than in the *BhP*. There it is not the devotees who become incarnate along with the divinity but the gods. The concept of devotees being involved in the incarnation would appear to reflect a sectarian slant, since it is also echoed in the *Vidvanmaṇḍana* of Viṭṭhalanātha. This text says that when the divine descends for the sake of play, some suitable souls are also caused to descend:

svāvatārasamaye krīḍārthaṃ sākṣād yogyās ta eva
bhavantīti tān apy avatārayīti punar nirgamayogyatvam |[39]

Thus once again, the *BhP.* is seen to be modified by Nandadāsa in line with Vallabha sectarian considerations.

Whereas the *līlā* of Sūradāsa includes the childhood sport of Kṛṣṇa as much as the *rāsa* performed with the *gopīs,* the *nitya vihāra* is confined to the expression of love between Rādhā and Kṛṣṇa. In this respect again, Nandadāsa takes the line of compromise, similar to that taken by the Gauḍīyas. In the *Rāsapañcādyāyī,* for example, describes the childhood and adolescent aspects of the *līlā* as conditions of the divine, while Kṛṣṇa as a youth is its essential form:

bāla kumāra pugaṃḍa dharama āsakta ju lalita tana |
dharmī nitya kisora kānha mohata saba ko mana ||[40]

This indicates that it is the activities of the youth aspect which display the essence of *līlā.*

(ii) Texts which describe *Nitya Vihāra*

(a) Dhruvadāsa : The distinction between *līlā* and *nitya vihāra* is connected with the way in which the texts distinguish between Braj Kṛṣṇa and Vṛndāvana Kṛṣṇa. According to Dhruvadāsa the *līlā* which was manifested by Kṛṣṇa in Braj for the sake of devotees was only the first stage of love:

pahilī pairī prema kī kīnhī vraja bistāra |
bhaktani hita līlā karī karunānidhi sukumāra ||[41]

The term *bistāra* which comes from the Sanskrit root *vistṛ,* meaning 'to spread out, expand, diffuse', in this context appears to give the sense of expansion and manifestation as opposed to the inner essence. Thus *līlā* is seen to be a form of expansion of the reality performed through the divine power but not the innermost essence of that divine reality. Moreover, this manifold expression is not regarded as the acme of divine sport because it has a purpose — it is performed for the sake of devotees. Here a difference from the poetry of both Sūradāsa and Nandadāsa may be noted, where the greatness of *līlā* lay in the very fact of its being an expression of love for devotees.

The contrast between the inner essence — *vihāra* — and the manifold expression — *līlā* — comes across clearly in a further verse of Dhruvadāsa where he says that *vihāra* is the essence of all manifold *līlā* which took place in Braj:

braj meṃ jo līlā carita bhayau jo bahuta prakāra |
sabako sāra bihāra hai rasikani kiyau nirdhāra ||[42]

Similarly, in his *Sata bhajana*, Dhruvadāsa states that one who has in his heart the beauty of Kṛṣṇa as he appears in the *vihāra*, i.e., as a youth, will not like the *līlās* of adolescence, childhood and so forth:

> *nautana vaisa kiśora chabi basata hai jihi ura nitta* I
> *paugaṃḍa bāla līlādihūṃ bhāvata nahiṃ tehi citta* II[43]

This verse can be compared with that of Nandadāsa discussed above (see p. 73). The difference lies in the fact that though Nandadāsa regarded the youthful aspect as the essence, he still accepts the other activities as valid expressions of the divine, while Dhruvadāsa regards them as inessential distractions from the essential reality.

(b) Bihārinadāsa : Bihārinadāsa expresses views similar to those discussed above when he describes the different stages of approach to the divine reality. He first describes *bhakti*, i.e., devotion in the form of ritual service of the deity, as a swamp which must be crossed in order to reach the Braj *līlā*:

> *bhakti daladalai kyauṃ tarai braja lauṃ sakai na jai* I[44]

This Braj is in turn described as being very large; its threshold is high, so that one may climb high and then slip and fall:

> *so braja parama visāla hai tākī baḍī su pauri* I
> *ūṃce caḍhe khisale pare nīcaiṃ āvata bhauṃri* I[45]

In other words, one may get lost in and bewildered by the manifold manifestation of the divine as expressed in Braj *līlā*. This Braj *līlā* is said to have three main aspects personified by the *gopīs*, cows and *gopas* — all participants in the *līlā* as described, for example, by Sūradāsa:

> *tā braja ke āvarana suni gopī gāi guvāla* I[46]

According to Bihārinadāsa, however, the essential expression of the divine reality, that is Kṛṣṇa performing *vihāra*, is far from all of these:

> *tina hūṃ te biharata duraiṃ rasikana ke pratipāla* II[47]

The intrinsic nature of this *vihāra* is expressed in another verse where Bihārinadāsa praises the founder of the sect, Haridāsa, saying that he alone could filter the *madhura rasa* eliminating ritual practice, knowledge, devotion and even the splendour of Braj; he alone could describe the *vihāra*:

> *śrī haridāsa rasika ananya binu ko pai parata bihāra bakhāṃyauṃ*।
> *karma gyāna dūra bhakti braja vibho vākasa chāṃdi madhura rasa chāmyau*॥[48]

The nature of *vihāra* as an eternal fact, basic to the nature of the divine and different from the manifold expression displayed in *līlā* is thus described by both Dhruvadāsa and Bihārinadāsa. It could, in fact, be claimed that the *vihāra* is the divine itself and Rādhā and Kṛṣṇa are instruments through which it is expressed, such is the importance attached to it.

The Role of Vṛndāvana in *Līlā* — An Aspect of the Divine —

(A) In the *Purāṇas*

The fact that creation and incarnation are both essentially seen as the same process in the *BhP.* implies that the 'space' in which both occur is also the same. There is in fact only one divine space in which the divine displays its nature and which is essentially of the nature of the divine. There can, therefore, be no distinction between a heavenly Vṛndāvana and an earthly Vṛndāvana.

Because the nature of the activities of Kṛṣṇa as *līlā* is less overtly expressed in the *Hariv.* and *ViP.*, consequently the nature of Vṛndāvana as a *līlādhāman* is also less apparent than in the *BhP.* It is represented more as a place on earth where certain events occurred within time and space. The ambiguous nature of the imagery used to describe Vṛndāvana has, however, been examined, which indicates that in actuality the *līlādhāman* aspect of Vṛndāvana is implicitly recognized.

(B) In the Sectarian Philosophical Texts

(i) Vallabha : The representation of an aspect of the divinity as the divine abode can be seen in the *Aṇubhāṣya* of Vallabha where he explains that the reason for the description of *akṣara brahman* as the 'tail' shows that it is subsidiary to the Supreme Being, forming his substratum or abode:

> *tasmād hīnatvaṃ ceti pṛṣṭhabhāgād api dūrasthita-*
> *puccharūpatvaṃ brahmaṇa ucyate*।
> *puruṣottamādhiṣṭhānatvāt pratiṣṭhārūpatvaṃ ca*।[49]

A statement along similar lines can be found in a later Vallabha work, the

Prameya-ratnārṇava, where it is said that to devotees *akṣara brahman* appears as the abode of the Lord of Vyāpivaikuṇṭha:

> *tatra bhaktānāṃ puruṣottamadhāmavyāpivaikuṇṭhādyātmakatvādidharmavat pratīyate*|[50]

Vallabha similarly identifies Vyāpivaikuṇṭa with *akṣara*:

> *guhāyāṃ hṛdayākāśe yad āvirbhūtaṃ paramaṃ vyomākṣarātmakaṃ vyāpivaikuṇṭhaṃ tasya puruṣottamagṛharūpatvāt tatra nihitaṃ sthāpitam iva vartamānaṃ yo veda sa bhakto brahmaṇā nityāvikṛtarūpeṇa vipaścitā*|[51]

Akṣara brahman is an aspect of the divine reality possessing all the same qualities, though the *ānanda* aspect is limited. These statements, therefore, in identifying the *dhāman* with *akṣara brahman* represent it as an aspect of the divine reality. *Akṣara brahman* is that expression of the divine nature through which the *līlā* takes place, or to put it in a different way, it is the 'abode' in which the divine resides when performing the *līlā* of creation.

A question which arises is whether the *ātmarati* takes place in the same *dhāman.* There does appear to exist in the Vallabha texts a concept of a divine Vṛndāvana associated with the activities of the intrinsic divine *līlā.* The *Aṇubhāṣya* describes how the manifestation of the divine which causes first the pain of separation and then supreme bliss is not to be found in the world or even in Vaikuṇṭha:

> *loke kvacid api na dṛṣṭaṃ śrutaṃ va vaikuṇṭhe 'pīti*|[52]

These things are said to be found only in Gokula which is even more excellent than Vaikuṇṭha, and which is beyond nature and time, etc.:

> *uktāni vastūni pare prakṛtikālādyatīte vaikuṇṭhād api śrīgokula eva santīti śeṣaḥ*|[53]

In other words, Gokula is beyond both the material and the spiritual realms and is the divine realm of *ātmarati.*

(ii) Gauḍīya : Vṛndāvana is clearly depicted as an aspect of the divinity itself in the Gauḍīya texts. According to Jīva Gosvāmī in his *Bhagavat-saṃdarbha,* the *dhāman* of the

Lord is also an expression of the power expressing his intrinsic nature (*svarūpa-śakti*). It is eternal and beyond *prakṛti*, which is an effect of the *māyā-śakti* itself, so that the soul can never reach it as long as he is subject to that *śakti*. This realm consists of the three attributes of existence, consciousness and bliss, as does the divinity itself.[54] In *Śrīkṛṣṇa-saṃdarbha*, Jīva describes the *dhāman* as the place where there is an excess of intrinsic divine bliss — *svarūpānandasukhotkarṣa*; the *dhāman* is thus an expression of the highest *hlādinī-śakti* itself.[55]

These philosophical concepts find poetic expression in the *Vṛndāvanamahimāmṛta* of Prabodhānanda. Vṛndāvana is described, for example, as being situated on an island of sweetness, which is in the ocean of the divine light of inner bliss and which is beyond the three *guṇas*:

> *traiguṇyātītapūrṇojjvalavimalamahākāmabījātmadivyajyotiḥ-*
> *svānandasindhau kim api sumadhuraṃ dvīpam āścaryam asti* |
> *tasmin vṛndābanaṃ* . . .||[56]

This verse illustrates the way in which Vṛndāvana is regarded as the essence of the essence. The island is the essence of the ocean of bliss and Vṛndāvana is within this island. This resembles the Gauḍīya concept where *premarasa* is the essence of the *hlādinī* which is the essence of *svarūpa*.

Secondly, the non-material nature of Vṛndāvana is stressed. Vṛndāvana is beyond the three material qualities and so is untouched by *māyā*. This means that is part of the *svarūpa-śakti*. This can also be seen in the fact that said to be in the sea of *svānanda*. The *ānanda* expresses the essential nature of the divine and so is equivalent to the *hlādini-śakti*; this would correspond to Jīva's description of the *dhāman* as *svarūpānandasukhotakarṣa*.

(C) Vṛndāvana in the Braj Bhāṣā texts

In the previous discussion of divine activity, Braj Bhāṣā texts have been shown to be divided into two groups:

(a) The *līlā* approach illustrated by Sūradāsa and Nandadāsa.

(b) The *nitya vihāra* approach found in the poetry of Dhruvadāsa and Bihārinadāsa. This division can be seen reflected in the portrayal of Vṛndāvana.

In both approaches Vṛndāvana is regarded as an aspect of the divine itself, indispensable to the expression of divine activity. However, in the *lılā* approach, divine activity is a manifold manifestation of the divine in contrast to its still aspect, and thus can be revealed or concealed according to the wish of the divine. Corresponding to the revelation and concealment, Vṛndāvana assumes and casts off its role as a place.

In the *nitya vihāra* concept, on the other hand, a continuous flow of activity is seen as expressing the essential nature of the divine. Vṛndāvana is the means for this essential manifestation and accordingly the role of Vṛndāvana as divine space is eternal and unchanging.

(i) Vṛndāvana in *Līlā*

(a) Sūradāsa : In the *Sūrasāgara,* Vṛndāvana has an important role in the manifestation of *līlā,* though its nature as an aspect of the divine is not made so explicit. It is in Braj-Vṛndāvana alone that the Suprme Being displays its manifold *līlā* and becomes utterly accessible; it is here that the divinity experiences its own bliss to the fullest extent. According to Sūradāsa, the joy which Kṛṣṇa experiences in Vṛndāvana makes him forget the heavenly joys. One *pada* has Kṛṣṇa telling the cowherd boys that he likes Vṛndāvana exceedingly, and that tending cows here cause him to forget all the joys of Vaikuṇṭha — the wish-yielding cow, the divine tree and all his happiness with Lakṣmī:

> *bṛṃdāvana maukauṃ ati bhāvata* |
> *sunahu sakhā tuma subala srīdāmā braja taiṃ bana gaucarana āvata* |
> *kāmadhenu surataru sukha jitane ramā sahita baikuṃṭha bhulāvata* |[57]

A contrast is made here between Vaikuṇṭha and Vṛndāvana; between the divine wish-yielding cows and the cows of Vṛndāvana; between Lakṣmī and Kṛṣṇa's playmates in Vṛndāvana. The contrast is equivalent to that made between the transcendent Viṣṇu and the immanent Kṛṣṇa. That Vṛndāvana is equal or even superior to Vaikuṇṭha is shown by the fact that the charms of Vṛndāvana cause Kṛṣṇa to forget his celestial abode. Nevertheless, Vṛndāvana is not portrayed as the one and only eternal abode. Kṛṣṇa is shown to have two abodes in accordance with his two conditions of being.

(b) Nandadāsa : The nature of Vṛndāvana as an aspect of the divine is very apparent in the poetry of Nandadāsa, much more so than in the *Sūrasāgara.* In a verse from the *Rāsapañcādhyāyī* he describes Vṛndāvana as pure consciousness which has assumed an inert state for the sake of the playful sport of Kṛṣṇa:

> *śrī vṛndābana cidghana kachu chabi barani na jāi* |
> *kṛṣṇa lalita līlā ke kāja dhari rahyau jaḍatāi* ||[58]

The first point which may be noted about this verse is the use of the term *cidghana* as an adjective referring to Vṛndāvana, since (as seen above in the discussion of Vallabha philosophy) *cit* or consciousness is one of the three attributes used to describe the nature of the divine, the other two being existence (*sat*) and bliss (*ānanda*). So through the description of Vṛndāvana as *cidghana,* the verse indicates the nature of Vṛndāvana as an aspect of the divine which assumes the attributes of a place.

Secondly, the inseparable connection between *līlā* and Vṛndāvana is expressed in this verse. The existence of Vṛndāvana as a place is purely for the sake of *līlā* — *līlā ke kāja*. Though its essential nature as a part of the divine is pure consciousness, for the sake of the manifestation of divine activity it assumes a condition of unconsciousness — *jaḍatāi*.

The verse following this one in the same text is also relevant to this discussion, since it describes how in Vṛndāvana all of the mountains, birds, deer, bowers, etc. are lovely with a splendour which is not derived from material qualities or time:

> *jahaṃ naga khaga mṛga kuṃja latā bīrudha tṛna jete*।
> *nahina kāla guna prabhā sadā sobhita rahe tete*।18।[59]

This illustrates once more the non-material nature of Vṛndāvana, since only that which is divine can be unconnected with time and material qualities. A place unrelated to either time or matter cannot be a place in the physical sense of the term. At the same time the verse visualizes Vṛndāvana in physical terms — mountains, animals, plants, etc. It is therefore symbolic space.

The way in which Vṛndāvana partakes of the nature of the divine similarly emerges from a verse in the *Siddhāntapañcādhyāyī* which says that just as the son of Nanda is solidified existence, consciousness and bliss, so Vṛndāvana, which devotees obtain in the world when they become imbued with *rasa*, and which scriptures praise as the eternal abode of Kṛṣṇa, is solidified consciousness:

> *saghana saccidānanda naṃdanaṃdana īśvara jasa*।
> *taiseī tinake bhagata jagata meṃ bhaye bhare rasa*।
> *śrī vṛndābana cidghana ghana ghana ghana chabi pāveṃ*।
> *naṃda sūnu ko nitya sadana śruti gana jihi gāveṃ*।।[60]

Thus both Kṛṣṇa and Vṛndāvana are essentially the same substance. Moreover, they are inseparable — Kṛṣṇa cannot exist except in Vṛndāvana.

In both of the above descriptions there is, nevertheless, a sense of contrast between the divine in its condition as pure existence, knowledge and bliss, when Vṛndāvana is also undifferentiated consciousness, and its condition when involved in *līlā* — when Vṛndāvana assumes the character of a place. This is reminiscent of the contrast found in the *Sūrasāgara* between Vṛndāvana and Vaikuṇṭha. Though the contrast in this case is less marked, there is still the sense, indicated, for example, by the phrase *dhari rahyau* 'assumed', that the *līlā* is a condition which is taken on, and accordingly that Vṛndāvana does not exist eternally and continuously as a *līlādhāman*.

(ii) Vṛndāvana in *Nitya Vihāra*

(a) Dhruvadāsa : The divine nature of Vṛndāvana as well as its indispensable role in the *nitya vihāra* is stressed by Dhruvadāsa. Vṛndāvana is, in fact, almost on a par with Rādhā, Kṛṣṇa and the *sakhīs* as one of the four eternal elements of the *nitya vihāra*. Dhruvadāsa describes how Rādhā and Kṛṣṇa eternally participate in an eternal pastime; Vṛndāvana is eternally co-existent; Lalitā and the rest are their eternal playmates; eternally they disport themselves in one single passion:

> *nita hī nitya vihāra karaiṃ yāme kachu na saṃdehu* |
> *nitya sahaja bṛndā bipina nitya sakhī lalitādi* |
> *nita hī bilasata eka rasa yugala kiśora anādi* ||[61]

The adjective *nityasahaja* applied to Vṛndāvana in this passage is capable of a number of interpretations. *Sahaja* in its original meaning denotes 'born with'.[62] Taken in this sense *nityasahaja* would imply 'eternally born with' or 'co-existent' with the *nitya vihāra* to which reference was made in the previous line. This would reflect the inseparable relation spoken of earlier between the divine activity and the divine place. Another possible interpretation is that Vṛndāvana is *nityasahaja* with the youthful couple (Rādhā and Kṛṣṇa) mentioned in the following line. This would illustrate the relationship between the divinity and the divine place, implying a certain similarity of nature between the divine couple and Vṛndāvana. In either case, it is evident that for the *nitya vihāra* all four elements are essential.

The divine nature of Vṛndāvana and its apartness from the material world is made explicit in a verse from the *Vṛndāvana sata*, where Dhruvadāsa says that the wind of creation which is derived from *māyā* and the three *guṇas* does not touch that forest which has no beginning or end and which gives eternal happiness:

> *ādi anta jākau nahiṃ nitya sukhada bana āhi* |
> *māyā triguna prapañca kī pavana na parasata tāhi* | 25 |[63]

The statement that Vṛndāvana is untouched by creation formed from the three *guṇas* is similar in concept to the verse previously quoted from the *Rāsapañcādyāyī* (see above p. 79). Here again the point is emphasized that Vṛndāvana is not part of material creation, and so has no beginning or end, either in the sense of time or of space. It is 'space' in a purely symbolic sense.

In these verses of Dhruvadāsa there is a decided emphasis on the eternal nature of the divine activity — the constant reiteration of the term *nitya*, 'eternal' conveys this sense. Such an emphasis corresponds to the concept of total manifestation and activity as the fullest expression of the divine and the unmanifest as incomplete reality. Since the activity is eternal, all of the elements involved in the activity are also eternal, and Vṛndāvana in its role as divine space must also be eternal.

(b) Bihārinadāsa : Though Bihārinadāsa does not discuss at length the nature of Vṛndāvana to the same extent as Dhruvadāsa, it is apparent that his views are basically similar. The *vihāra*, as we have seen above, is the essential expression of the divine, and this *vihāra* occurs only in Vṛndāvana. This can be seen, for example, in a verse where Bihārinadāsa says that Mathurā is greater than all pilgrimage centres, worlds and even than Vaikuṇṭha. Greater even than Mathurā is the glory of Braj which was described by Brahmā and the Vedas. Bihārinadāsa, however, serves only the groves in which the Lord of Rādhā disports himself — Vṛndāvana, the manifest temple of the Lord, the mine of *rasa*:

tīratha sakala loka baikuṃṭha taiṃ madhupurī adhika saṃdeha nasāṃnauṃ |
śrī bihārinidāsa nikuṃjani sevata jāmaiṃ rādhāravana ravāṃnauṃ |
vidyamāna hari mandira rājatu śrīvṛndāvana rasa khāna khadaṃnauṃ ||[64]

The non-material nature of Vṛndāvana comes across in a verse which contrasts the destructible dust of the material world with the indestructible dust of Vṛndāvana:

nasvara raja lagi jūjhaī nasvara pūta kahāi |
śrī bṛndāvana seye rahaiṃ so raja māṃhi samāi ||[65]

Thus in the poetry of both Bihārinadāsa and Dhruvadāsa just as *vihāra* is not a physical action, which must have a beginning and an end, so Vṛndāvana is not a 'place' which must also have a beginning and an end. At the same time, *vihāra* is expressed in terms of action which can, therefore, be termed symbolic action while the space in which it manifests itself is symbolic space. Vṛndāvana is, therefore, not merely a receptacle for the divine, but an aspect of the divine reality without which this reality cannot express itself.

References

1. For a discussion of the etymology of the word, see M. Mayrhofer, *A concise etymological Sanksrit dictionary*, Heidelberg, 1963. pt. 17, p. 104.
2. *Bṛhadāraṇyaka-upaniṣad*, in *Aṣṭādaśa-Upaniṣadaḥ*, *op. cit.*, I.4.3. 'Thus he did not delight.'
3. *Ibid.*, I.4.3.
   sa dvitīyam aicchat |
   sa haitāvan āsa yathā strīpumāṃsau saṃpariṣvaktau |
   sa imam evātmānaṃ dvedhāpātayat |
   tataḥ patiś ca patnī cābhavatām |

He wanted a second. He was as large as a woman and a man closely embracing. He divided this, himself, into two. He became a husband and a wife.'

4. *Ibid.*, I. 4.3.

   tāṃ samabhavat |

   tato manuṣyā ajāyanta |

   'He approached her and from that men were born.' The text goes on to describe how the various species of animals were born from the meeting of these two in the form of the male and female of each species.
5. *BhP.*, *op. cit.*, I.1.17. 'Describe to us who have faith, the noble deeds proclaimed by the sages, of him who in sport assumes parts.'
6. M. Monier-Williams, *op. cit.*, p 211, col. 3.
7. *BhP.*, *op. cit.*, I.3.1. 'The Lord, in the beginning, took the form of *puruṣa* which arose through principles beginning with *mahat* and which has sixteen parts, through his desire to create the world.'
8. *Ibid.*, I.10.24. 'That one Lord who through his self-sport, creates, preserves and devours this universe, but is not attached to it.'
9. *Ibid.*, I.1.18. 'Now relate, O intelligent one, the auspicious stories of the incarnation of Lord Hari, who sports according to his own will through his own power of *māyā*.'
10. *Ibid.*, I.2.30. 'That divine Lord who is without qualities, through his own *māyā* created all this which has the form of existence and non-existence and which is formed of qualities.'
11. *ViP.*, *op. cit.*, I.2.18. 'Viṣṇu is manifest and unmanifest, he is *puruṣa* and time. Hear the activity of that one who is like a child playing.'
12. *Ibid.*, V. 7. 38

    jagatyarthaṃ jagannātha bhārāvataraṇaecchayā |

    avatīrṇo 'si martyeṣu tavāṃśaś cāham agrajaḥ ||

    'O Lord of the world, you and also I, your portion and younger brother, have descended among men for the sake of the earth, because of your desire to take away its burden.'
13. *Ibid.*, V.7.39. 'O Lord, with you, who are engaged in human *līlā*, remain all the gods imitating your *līlā*.'
14. *Ibid.*, V.7.40. 'You caused the goddesses to descend first to the *gokula*; afterwards you yourself took incarnation for the sake of paly, O eternal one.'

15 *Hariv.*, *op. cit.*, II.11.24. 'Kṛṣṇa played there for a day with cowherd boys of his own age, O sinless one, as he had done previously when in heaven.'

16. Vallabhācārya, *Tattvārthadīpanibandha*, ed. Kedaranātha Miśra, Benares, 1971, v. 68. 'At times he sports within himself and at times in the phenomenal universe, happily.'
17. *Ibid.*, v. 24.

    saṃsārasya layo muktau na prapañcasya karhicit |

    kṛṣṇasyātmaratau tu 'sya layaḥ sarvasukhāvahaḥ ||

    'In salvation there is dissolution of *saṃsāra*, never of the material universe. In the *ātmarati* of Kṛṣṇa, however, there is dissolution of this (material universe), which brings all happiness.'
18. Vallabhācārya, *Rāsapañcādhyāyī-śrīsubodhinī*, ed. J. Caturvedī, Varanasi, 1971, X.27.34. 'Even in this condition he was sporting within himself; in order to have a foundation for the *rasa*, he had placed himself in her.'

19. Vallabhācārya, *Śrīmad aṇubhāṣyam*, ed. S.T. Pāṭhaka, Poona, 1921, I.1.11. 'It is known that (the soul) having transcended the material body, formed of qualities, obtains a body which is beyond qualities and is suitable for the *līlā* itself.

20. *Ibid.*, I.1.11. 'Puruṣottama, the divine, formed of bliss, enters the soul. (That soul) having experienced the *rasa*-ocean of the pain of separation, which because it is *rasa* is of the nature of bliss, afterwards having attained the manifest form of the Lord, does not fear.'

21. *Ibid.*, I.1.11 (p. 24, lines 24-25) 'Or though *akṣara brahman* has the nature of bliss, because of its being limited it does not have the nature of being the supreme goal.'

22. *Subodhinī, op. cit.*, X.29.2. 'Material Manmatha has the form of a god. Then the spiritual Manmatha himself is in the heart of all beings. This one (Kṛṣṇa) remaining in the circle, is the spiritual (form) of that; because he is the sum total of everything.'

23. Vallabhācārya, *Siddhāntamuktāvalī*, Bombay, 1918, v. 9. 'As is the water so is all this. As is the power so is the *bṛhat*. As is the goddess so is *Kṛṣṇa*. More about this is said here.'

24. *Ibid.*, commentary by Dīkṣitalāla Bhaṭṭa.

    brahmaṇo rūpatrayam |
    tatrādhidaivikaṃ param brahma kṛṣṇākhyaṃ prathamam |
    ādhyātmikam akṣarātmakaṃ dvitīyam |
    ādhibhautikaṃ prapañcātmakaṃ tṛtīyam |

    'Brahman has three forms. Here the first is the divine, the supreme Brahman called Kṛṣṇa. The second is the spiritual identified with *akṣara*. The third is the material, having the nature of the material world.'

25. Discussed in S.K. De, *Early history of the Vaiṣṇava faith and movement in Bengal*, Calcutta, 1942, pp. 210-11.

26. *Ibid.*, p. 211.

27. *Ibid.*, pp. 211-12.

28. *Ibid.*, p. 267.

29. *Ibid.*, p. 267. 'Because of the excess of the expression of that (*hlādinī-śakti*) there is an expression of the supreme joy of divine in them; because of that is born the desire to sport with them.'

30. *Ibid.*, p. 268.

31. Sūradāsa, *op. cit.*, pada 663. 'Śyāma of Sūra takes many guises for the sake of his devotees.'

32. *Ibid., pada* 762. 'The greatness of this *līlā* of the Lord of Sūradāsa even Śeṣa cannot describe.'

33. *Ibid., pada* 621. 'He who creates, preserves and destroys the world, he assumes *līlā* in the company of the cowherd boys.'

34 Nandadāsa, *Siddhāntap., op. cit.*, v. 66. '(Kṛṣṇa) wanted to enjoy the *rasa* of *rāsa*, having made those (*gopīs*) equal to himself.'

35. *Ibid.*, v. 9. 'That Lord of the world who is pre-eminent in the world, withdrew all (within himself), performing his own spontaneous sport.'

36. *Ibid.*, v. 62. 'Though experiencing bliss within himself, he began to sport (with them), overcome by the power of their fresh love.'

37. Nandadāsa, *Bhāṣā daśama skandha, op. cit.*, I.115-16 (p. 220). 'When Hari had a desire for *līlā*, first the devotees descended to earth. All of the attendants of the Lord manifested for the sake of *līlā*.'

38. *Ibid.*, I.117. 'Then Kṛṣṇa descended to fulfil the desires of his devotees.'

39. Viṭṭhalanātha, *Vidvanmaṇḍanam*, Ratnagopāla Bhaṭṭa ed., Benares, 1908, p. 97, lines 15-16. 'At the time of his own incarnation, he causes those souls which are suitable also to descend for the sake of play; (this is the meaning of) suitability for coming out again.'

40. Nandadāsa, *Rāsap.*, *op. cit.*, I.36. 'That beautiful body which is furnished with the qualities of childhood, boyhood and adolescence — the possessor of these qualities is eternally a youth, Kānha, who charms the hearts of all.'

41. Dhruvadāsa, *Bṛhadbāvana Purāṇa*, *op. cit.*, v. 24. 'As the first step of love he made the expanse of Braj; the youthful (Kṛṣṇa), a mine of compassion, sported for the sake of his devotees.'

42. *Ibid.*, v. 42. 'The many and varied episodes of *līlā* in Braj — the essence of all these is the *bihāra*. This is the certainty which the *rasikas* have established.'

43. Dhruvadāsa, *Sata bhajana*, in *Bayālīsa līlā*, *op. cit.*, v. 59. 'In whose heart eternally remains the beauty of that youth of fresh appearance, his mind does not like even the *līlā* of childhood and boyhood.'

44. Bihārinadāsa, *op. cit.*, v. 662, p. 244. 'One cannot cross the marsh of devotion: one cannot even reach Braj.'

45. *Ibid.*, v. 663. 'That Braj is very large, its threshold is high. You climb high, slip and fall, because when you look down you feel giddy.'

46. *Ibid.*, v. 664. 'Hear the coverings of the Braj — the *gopīs*, the cows and the cowherd boys.'

47. *Ibid.*, v. 664. 'Far from even these sports the protector of the *rasikas*.'

48. *Ibid.*, v. 22, p. 284. 'Apart from the *rasika*, Haridāsa who else could describe the *vihāra*. He filtered the *rasa* of love, leaving the remains of ritual acts, knowledge, devotion and even the splendour of Braj.'

49. Vallabha, *Aṇubhāṣya*, *op. cit.*, I.1.11. (p.33, lines 18-20). 'Therefore it has a subordinate position; because of its being at the back, Brahman is said to have the form of a tail which is situated far; and because of its being the resting-place of the Lord, it has the form of a foundation.'

50. Bālakṛṣṇa Bhaṭṭa, *Prameyaratnārṇava*, Varanasi, 1971, ch. III, p.55. 'That is recognized by devotees as having conditions such as having the nature of the abode of the divine or Vyāpivaikuṇṭha.'

51. Vallabha, *Aṇubhāṣya*, *op. cit.*, I.1.11. (p.25, lines 22-23). 'In the secret place, i.e., the space in the heart, that supreme Vyāpivaikuṇṭha, of the nature of *vyomākṣara*, which appears, because of its having the form of the abode of the divine, to be placed there, i.e., established, present there. He who knows this, that devotee is with Brahman who is wise, i.e., has an eternally unchanged form.'

52. *Ibid.*, IV.2.15, (p. 326, line 13). '. . . these are not seen or heard of anywhere in the world or in Vaikuṇṭha.'

53. *Ibid.*, line 14. 'These things exist only in the supreme Gokula which is more excellent than Vaikuṇṭha and which is beyond nature, time etc.; so it was left to be supplied.'

54. S.K. De., *op. cit.*, pp. 221-22.

54. *Ibid.*, p.254.

56. Prabodhānanda Sarasvatī, *Vṛndāvanamahimāmṛtam*, Vṛndāvana, 1967, III. 11. 'In the ocean of the divine light of intrinsic bliss, having the nature of the great *kāmabīja* (*mantra*), pure, fully brilliant and beyond the three material qualities, there is an astonishing sweet island; in that

is Vṛndāvana. . .

57. Sūradāsa, *op. cit., pada* 1067. 'I like Vṛndāvana exceedingly. Listen you friends, Subala and Srīdāmā, when I come to the wood from Braj to tend the cows, it makes me forget the wish-yielding cows, the divine trees and all the happiness with Ramā in Vaikuṇṭha.'

58. Nandadāsa, *Rāsap., op. cit.*, I.17. ' The beauty of Vṛndāvana, which is pure consciousness, cannot be described. For the sake of the playful sport of Kṛṣṇa it assumes an inert state.'

59. *Ibid.*, I.18. 'Where all of the mountains, birds, deer, bowers, creepers and plants are always lovely with a splendour which is not derived from time or material qualities.'

60. Nandadāsa, *Siddhāntap., op. cit.*, vv. 19-20. 'Just as the Lord, son of Nanda, is solidified existence, consciousness and bliss, so Vṛndāvana which devotees obtain in the world, having become imbued with *rasa,* is solid consciousness and solid beauty, the eternal abode of the son of Nanda, of which the scriptures sing.'

61. Dhruvadāsa, *Bṛhadbāvana Purāṇa, op. cit.*, vv. 66-67. 'No doubt but that eternally they (Rādhā and Kṛṣṇa) participate in an eternal pastime; Vṛndāvana is eternally co-existent; Lalitā and the rest are (their) eternal playmates; eternally they disport themselves in one single passion, the youthful couple without beginning.'

62. M. Monier-Williams, *op. cit.*, p. 1193, column 3.

63. Dhruvadāsa, *Vṛndāvana sata, op. cit.*, v. 25. 'That forest which has no beginning or end and gives eternal happiness, the wind of creation based on *māyā* and the three material qualities does not touch it.'

64. Bihārinadāsa, *op. cit.*, v. 60, p. 307. 'Madhupurī is greater than all pilgrimage centres, worlds and Vaikuṇṭha; all doubt about this matter has been destroyed. Greater than that is the glory of Braj which Brahmā and the Vedas have described. Bihārinadāsa serves the groves in which the Lord of Rādhā sports — Vṛndāvana, the manifest temple of the Lord, the mine of *rasa.*'

65. *Ibid.*, p. 165, v. 332. 'People die fighting for destructible dust, calling the destructible pure: reside in Vṛndāvana, become merged in that dust.'

4

Geography and Symbolism in the Representation of Vṛndāvana

IN any given text the portrayal of Vṛndāvana as a place clearly reflects the attitude of the writer to the concepts involved in Vṛndāvana as a mythic and symbolic place. Three distinct pictures emerge — the mythological, the symbolic and the geographical — though these may overlap in one single text.

The mythological depiction expresses the concept of sacred space in mythic terms. It is thus a reflection of the same process whereby the metaphysical contrast between the immanent and the transcendent becomes a mythological event through its expression as incarnation. It is therefore not surprising that the mythological picture of Vṛndāvana is found in texts where the theory of incarnation is incorporated. A basic characteristic of this picture is the 'linear' layout of Vṛndāvana in relation to Braj-Gokula and Mathurā. To this extent it is compatible with geographical considerations.

In contrast to this linear layout, the symbolic picture is circular in shape. That is to say,Vṛndāvana is portrayed as a cirtular area within the Mathurā region. In this plan there is a gradation of the three areas — Vṛndāvana, as the centre, being supreme. The images used in this case are frequently those of the *yantra*, suggesting a similarity of purpose, i.e., a symbolic representation of the transcendental realm. This *yāntric* Vṛndāvana invariably forms the scene, not for the incarnation of Kṛṣṇa, but for the eternal, unceasing union of Rādhā and Kṛṣṇa — the *nitya vihāra*. The texts using this form of representation can be further divided into two categories; the first being ritualistic and apparently intended for the practice of worship and meditation, the second concerned exclusively with the experience of *rasa*.

In the geographical picture Vṛndāvana appears as one of twelve forests surrounding Mathurā. In contrast to the above representations it is thus much more Mathurā-centred, which would apear to be related to the fact that these texts are concerned with pilgrimage. In this respect, they can be designated the most geographical in nature, since they are describing a place which can be visited in pilgrimage.

The Mythological Representation

The mythological representation predominates in the Purāṇic texts, and continues to play an important part in the poetry of Sūradāsa and Nandadāsa. All of these texts correspond in their division of the scene for the youthful activities of Kṛṣṇa into three localities, i.e., Mathurā, Vṛndāvana and Braj-Gokula. These three places are linked by the movements to and fro of Kṛṣṇa.

In considering the relation of Vṛndāvana with Braj-Gokula in this mythological picture of Vṛndāvana, it is necessary to look at the definition of Braj-Gokula itself, since these range from that of a general term for a cowherd encampment, to the present-day usage of Braj for the entire area and Gokula for a particular town. There can be no doubt that originally these two terms were used for the cattle station as well as for the actual herd of cows. The term *vraja* is attested in this sense as early as the *RV.*[1] while *gokula* first appears in the *Mbh.*[2] with similar connotations.

There is considerable evidence that the *Purāṇas* continue to use *vraja* and *gokula* as general terms rather than as proper nouns. Particularly relevant are the passages which describe the move to Vṛndāvana, since in all three *Purāṇas* it is clear that this does not involve a move from a place called Braj-Gokula as is later understood. In fact, the entire *vraja-gokula* is moved to Vṛndāvana, illustrating its nature as a movable encampment.

In the *Hariv.*, for example, the inhabitants decide that the entire *vraja* should be moved in order to avoid a massacre by the wolves who threaten them:

> *yāvad vṛkair vadhaṃ ghoraṃ na naḥ sarvo vrajo vrajet* |3|[3]

The aim of the move to Vṛndāvana is described as not only the welfare of the cows but also the establishment of the *vraja*:

> *teṣāṃ matam athājñāya gantuṃ vṛndāvanaṃ prati* |
> *vrajasya ca niveśanāya gavāṃ caiva sukhāya ca* ||[4]

Finally the beauty of the newly established *vraja* surrounded by the woods of Vṛndāvana is depicted:

> *tad vrajasthānam adhikaṃ cakāśe kānanāvṛtam* |[5]

All the above examples correspond with a conception of the *vraja* as a nomadic settlement rather than as the name of a particular place.

The pattern is identical in the *ViP*. The elders decide that they should depart from their present location to Vṛndāvana before a catastrophe befalls the *vraja*:

> *vṛndāvanam itaḥ sthānāt tasmād gacchāma mā ciram* |
> *yāvad bhaumamahotpātadoṣo nābhibhaved vrajam* |124|[6]

Here again the establishment of the *vraja* in Vṛndāvana is described:

> *sa samāvāsitaḥ sarvo vrajo vṛndāvane tataḥ* |[7]

No change in this respect can be detected in the *BhP*. Both the protection of the *vraja* as the motive for the move and the eventual re-establishment of the *vraja* in Vṛndāvana are in evidence here as well. The elders assemble to discuss the affairs of the *vraja*, the term evidently denoting the community as a whole and not the place:

> *gopavṛddhā mahotpātān anubhūya bṛhadvane* |
> *nandādayaḥ samāgamya vrajakāryam amantrayam* |20|[8]

Using *gokula* synonymously with *vraja*, the elders decide that out of concern for the welfare of the *gokula*, they should leave the place:

> *utthātavyam ito 'smābhir gokulasya hitaiṣibhiḥ* |[9]

Finally comes the description of the *vraja* settlement formed in Vṛndāvana with a semi-circle of carts:

> *tatra cakrur vrajāvāsaṃ śakaṭair ardhacandravat* |[10]

Other indications that *vraja* and *gokula* are employed as general terms can be found in their use in the plural as well as with the possessive qualification 'of Nanda' suggesting the possibility of other *vrajas* and *gokulas*. Such a use in the plural can be seen in a passage from the *Hariv.* which says that rich *vrajas* should move on to forests having fresh grass and that neither those who live behind closed doors nor those possessing house and fields are as praiseworthy as the *vrajas* which wander from place to place:

> *icchanty anupabhuktāni bhoktuṃ gāvas tṛṇāni ca* |
> *tasmād vanaṃ navatṛṇaṃ gacchantu dhanino vrajāḥ* |17|
> *na dvārabandhāvaraṇā na gṛhakṣetriṇas tathā* |
> *praśastā vai vrajā loke yathā vai cakracāriṇaḥ* |18|[11]

In this passage the nature of the *vraja* as a nomadic community is evident in the contrast with the settled possession of home and property. The *BhP.* elsewhere describes how during the move to Vṛndāvana the cowherds each prepared their own *vraja* for the journey, suggesting that the *vraja* as a whole consisted of a group of smaller *vrajas*:

vrajān svān svān samāyujya yayū rūḍhaparicchadāḥ |[12]

The nature of *vraja* as a term for a particular type of settlement emerges from another passage from the *BhP.* which describes how Pūtanā wandered, killing children in towns, villages and *vrajas*:

śiśūṃś cacāra nighnantī puragrāmavrajādiṣu |2|[13]

Again *vraja* is used in the plural, while its use with 'town' and 'village' place it in a similar category of meaning.

A few examples from the three *Purāṇas* will suffice to show the identification of the *vraja-gokula* where Kṛṣṇa resided as belonging to Nanda. The *Hariv.* speaks of Kṛṣṇa and Balarāma being herdsmen in the *govraja* of Nanda:

govraje nandagopasya ballavatvaṃ prakurvataḥ |1|[14]

The *ViP.* describes how for seven days it rained on the *gokula* of Nanda:

saptarātraṃ mahāmeghā vavarṣur nandagokule |[15]

The *BhP.* states that because it was the dwelling-place of Hari, Lakṣmī disported herself in the *vraja* of Nanda, endowing it with all wealth:

tata ārabhya nandasya vrajaḥ sarvasamṛddhimān |
harer nivāsātmaguṇair ramākrīḍam abhūn nṛpa |18|[16]

All of these uses imply the existence of *vraja-gokulas* belonging to others than Nanda, and so contradict the notion of Braj-Gokula as the name of a particular place.

Vaudeville sees a distinction between *vraja* as the pasture-land and *gokula* as the encampment of the cowherd tribe.[17] Such a distinction is not, however, substantiated by the Purāṇic texts. The pasture-land is the *vana*, in particular Vṛndāvana, which is contrasted with the *vraja* and *gokula* which are both used for the inhabited area, though *vana* and the *gokula-vraja* together comprise the rural scene as opposed to the city of Mathurā.

Contrast between *vana* and *vraja*, wherein the *vraja* is the habitation of the cowherds and *gopīs*, while *vana* is the wild area where the cattle are taken to graze, can be frequently observed in the *Hariv*. One example may be seen in the incident where Kṛṣṇa is struggling with Kāliya in a pool of the Yamunā specified as being in Vṛndāvana by an earlier verse.[18] At that time the cowherd boys are said to return to the *vraja* to inform the others such as Nanda of the misfortune, thus indicating the nature of the *vraja* as an inhabited area:

> *etasminn antare bhītā gopālāḥ sarva eva te* |
> *krandamānā vrajaṃ jagmur vāṣpasaṃdigdhayā girā* |14|[19]

The term *gokula* is used much less frequently by the *Hariv*. and if any difference of meaning can be detected, it is that *gokula* can be understood as the actual herds of cattle rather than the encampment. For example, in the context of the lifting of Govardhana it is said that the *gokula* was kept dry:

> *nirjalaṃ gokulaṃ kṛtvā dhṛto govardhano giriḥ* |[20]

Here there is no clear indication, as there was with *vraja* above, that *gokula* is meant to be understood as an encampment.

No such ambiguity remains in the *ViP*. and *BhP*. where *gokula* and *vraja* are used with equal frequency and clearly synonymously. The *ViP*., for example, speaks of Kṛṣṇa as living in *gokula* when Pūtanā arrives:

> *vasatāṃ gokule teṣām pūtanā bālaghātinī* |[21]

The contrast between the *vraja-gokula* is as evident in the *ViP*. as it is in the *Hariv*. A passage describes, for example, how Kṛṣṇa and Balarāma return to the *vraja* in the evening with cows and cowherd boys after wandering in the wood during the day:

> *krīḍantau tau vane tasmiṃś ceratus tuṣṭamānasau* |49|
> *vikāle ca samaṃ gobhir gopavṛndasamanvitau* |
> *vihṛtyātha yathāyogaṃ vrajam etya mahābalau* |50|[22]

The *vana* versus *vraja* contrast is similarly evident in the *BhP*. Kṛṣṇa tells the *gopīs* who have come to the *vana* attracted by the music of his flute, to return to the *vraja*:

pratiyāta vrajaṃ neha stheyaṃ strībhiḥ sumadhyamāḥ |[23]

He says that they have seen the beauties of the *vana*, which he describes as blossoming, lit by moonbeams, and adorned with trees rustling in the breeze from the Yamunā river:

dṛṣṭaṃ vanaṃ kusumitaṃ rākeśakararañjitam |
yamunānilalīlaijattarupallavaśobhitam ||[24]

All of these images evoke the atmosphere of the wood, romantic and uninhabited, which is in total contrast to the *vraja*, the *goṣṭha*, where the relatives of the *gopīs* are lying asleep, and to which Kṛṣṇa urges them to return and serve their husbands:

tad yātaṃ mā ciraṃ goṣṭhaṃ śuśrūṣadhvaṃ patīn satīḥ ||[25]

A contrast is thus maintained in all three *Purāṇas* between the *vraja-gokula*, the inhabited area, where the child Kṛṣṇa is brought up, and Vṛndāvana, the uncultivated, wooded pasture-land, where the boy Kṛṣṇa takes the cattle to graze, plays with the cowherd boys, and sports with the *gopīs*.

An almost identical pattern is to be found in the *padas* of the *Sūrasāgara*. The same contrast between Braj-Gokula and Vṛndāvana may be observed, for example, in numerous *padas* dealing with the theme of Kṛṣṇa taking the cows to graze in Vṛndāvana. In one *pada*, Kṛṣṇa expresses concern about the fact that night may fall while they are still in the forest and says that they should return to Braj:

brajahiṃ calau āī aba sāṃjha |
surabhī sabai lehu āgaiṃ kari hoi jani banahīṃ māṃjha |[26]

Other *padas* describe the beauty of Kṛṣṇa as he returns from the forest to Braj in the evening. He is described as being surrounded by the cows and cowherd boys who have been wandering in the forest all day:

saṃdhya samaya gopa godhana saṃga bana taiṃ bani braja āvata |[27]

Sūradāsa, thus, maintains the same contrast between the inhabited Braj-Gokula and the uninhabited *vana* as the three *Purāṇas* discussed above.

Like the *Purāṇas,* Sūradāsa sees Braj-Gokula as the location for the majority of the babyhoold *līlās,* as well as incidents connected with the birth of Kṛṣṇa. This can be seen in a *pada* describing the celebration of this birth:

> *ānaṃda atisai bhayau ghara ghara nṛtya thāvaṃhiṃ thāṃva* |
> *naṃda dvāraiṃ bheṃṭa lai lai umahyau gokula gāṃva* |[28]

Vṛndāvana, on the other hand, besides being the place where the cattle are taken to graze, also forms the background for the *rāsa.* Sūradāsa describes how the *gopīs* go running to the wood when they hear the sound of the flute.[29] As in the *BhP.*, Kṛṣṇa asks the *gopīs* why they have come to the wood at night:

> *nisi kāhaiṃ banakauṃ uṭhi dhāīṃ* |[30]

The contrast between Vṛndāvana and the inhabited community of Braj emerges when Kṛṣṇa laughingly suggests that they have lost their way to Braj as they were returning from selling curds in Mathurā:

> *haṃsi haṃsi syāma kahata haiṃ suṃdari kī tuma braja māragahiṃ bhulāīṃ* |
> *gaī rahīṃ dadhi becana mathurā tahāṃ āju avasera lagāī* |[31]

In the *Sūrasāgara,* the *vana* is also the scene of the meeting of Rādhā and Kṛṣṇa — an aspect of Vṛndāvana absent from the Purāṇic portrayal. Kṛṣṇa is quoted as asking Rādhā to go with him to Vṛndāvana:

> *bātani laī rādhā lāi* |
> *calahu jaiva bipina brṃdā kahata syāma bujhāi* |[32]

Further *padas* describe how the youthful Rādhā and Kṛṣṇa, imbued with the essence of love, disport themselves in Vṛndāvana:

> *navala gupāla navelī rādhā naye prema rasa pāge* |
> *aṃtara bana bihāra dou krīḍata āpu āpu anurāge* |[33]

In fact, the concept of Rādhā and Kṛṣṇa together as a couple is generally in the context of Vṛndāvana, not Braj. Sūradāsa does describe a few episodes where Rādhā meets Kṛṣṇa in Braj, as for example, when Kṛṣṇa calls her to milk the cows and all the *sakhīs* question why she who is from Vṛṣabhānupurā has come to milk in Braj.[34] However, even in situations such as these Rādhā and Kṛṣṇa are not actually united, so it can be argued that the *vana* alone is the scene for their true union.

Though the essential contrast between Braj-Gokula and Vṛndāvana is basically the same in the *Sūrasāgara* as in the *BhP.*, there does appear to be a basic difference in the definition of Braj-Gokula, i.e., its use suggests the connotation of a proper name rather than that of a general term. Sūradāsa never uses Braj or Gokula in the plural, nor does he ever qualify them with the possessive adjective 'of Nanda'. The one and only *pada* which mentions the move to Vṛndāvana is inconclusive. It merely says that Yaśodā and Nanda decide that since disasters befall them daily in Gokula, they should go and settle in Vṛndāvana:

> *mahara mahari kaiṃ mana yaha āī* |
> *gokula hota upadrava dina prati basie bṛṃdāvana maiṃ jāī* |[35]

This does not make it clear whether Gokula is a place or a movable enacampment. Apart from this single verse which could well be a later interpolation attempting to put the *Sūrasāgara* in line with the *BhP.* there is every indication that Braj-Gokula is a settled place near Vṛndāvana, and that no move is involved; especially since Braj-Gokula continues to be the term given to the inhabited area in verses which in the time sequence of the events of Kṛṣṇa's life should follow the above verse.

The frequent juxtaposition of both Braj and Gokula with qualifying terms including 'village' (*gāṃva*) and 'town' (*śahara*) supports the supposition that Braj-Gokula has in the *Sūrasāgara* the connotation of a particular place. These suggest the sense of a proper name, i.e., 'the village called Gokula'. Sūradāsa says, for example, that at the birth of Kṛṣṇa all of the people of the city of Gokula were overjoyed:

> *ānaṃdaṃagana nara gokula sahara ke* |[36]

Braj is used in a similar sense in a verse which describes Kṛṣṇa as he returns to the city of Braj from grazing the cattle in the woods:

> *pahuṃce āi syāma brajapura maiṃ gharahiṃ cale mohana bala āche* |[37]

The difference of such statements from those of the *BhP.* where the *vraja* is specifically differentiated from both town and village (see above p. 90) is obvious.

The above discussion shows how the three *Purāṇas* and the *Sūrasāgara* share certain basic elements in the portrayal of Vṛndāvana, among which the contrast between the inhabited Braj-Gokula and forest Vṛndāvana is of primary significance. In this context the similar contrast in the Vedic myth of Purūravas and Urvaśī between the village (*grāma)* and the forest (*āraṇya*). The presence of this parallel suggests that such a contrast forms a basic mythological motif, possibly having reference to two stages in the evolution of creation — the *vana* representing Eden, while the *grāma* is the evolved material world of time and space.

It may be noted, however, that none of the above texts suggest any gradation between Vṛndāvana and Braj-Gokula in their respective importance — both are protrayed as being on the same plane. The interrelation between the two is reflected in the constant movement of Kṛṣṇa back and forth between Braj-Gokula and Vṛndāvana.

All of the four texts discussed above accept in one way or another the concept of the divinity as comprising two aspects — Viṣṇu as transcendent and Kṛṣṇa the immanent incarnation. In the *Hariv.* and *ViP.* the process of incarnation is presented as a series of events within time and space while the *BhP.* and the *Sūrasāgara* emphasize the metaphysical dimensions of the concept; nevertheless, all four texts accept the same basic mythological structure. It is not surprising, therefore, that all four use the same mythological pattern in their portrayal of Vṛndāvana.

The Symbolic Representation

The overlapping of the mythological and the symbolic pictures of Vṛndāvana can be seen in the *Laghubhāgavatāmṛta* of Rūpa and the works of Nandadāsa — which while not rejecting outright the concept of incarnation reinterpret it insofar as Kṛṣṇa is regarded, not as an incarnation of Viṣṇu, but of himself. This involves the existence of Vṛndāvana on two levels, i.e., in Gauḍīya terminology, the manifest (mythological) and the unmanifest (symbolic). In this way the two distinct approaches are reconciled, enabling the incorporation of the Purāṇic pattern to a certain extent.

The first significant difference observable in the portrayal of Vṛndāvana as found in the *Laghubhāgavatāmṛta* is the lack of importance attached to the contrast between Vṛndāvana and Braj-Gokula. This emerges from a verse describing the abodes of Kṛṣṇa, which first divides them into two, i.e., Māthura and into Gokula and the city (*pura*):

> *dhāmāsya dvividhaṃ proktaṃ māthuraṃ dvārvatī tathā* |
> *māthuraś ca dvidhā prāhur gokulaṃ puram eva ca* |[38]

There is thus a degree of identification of Mathurā and Gokula as being the two parts — urban and rural — of a single area, but there is no further division of Gokula, which must then be inclusive of Vṛndāvana.

The inclusive nature of the term Gokula as used by Rūpa, as well as his reinterpretation of the Purāṇic structure, is also implicit in a further statement, according to which Kṛṣṇa goes to and fro between Gokula, Mathurā and Dvāravatī in the manifest *līlā* alone:

tatra prakaṭalīlāyām eva syātām gamāgamau|
gokule mathurāyāṃ ca dvāravatyāṃ ca śārṅgiṇaḥ|[39]

Here again Gokula must stand for the entire Gokula-Vṛndāvana area. The movement from one to another of these three abodes is said to occur only in the manifest *līlā*, i.e., in the mythological context. This concept of manifest *līlā* is used to explain the separation of Kṛṣṇa from the *gopīs* in another passage:

vraje prakaṭalīlāyāṃ trīn māsān viraho 'munā|[40]

This is in contrast to the unmanifest *līlā* where Kṛṣṇa disports himself in Vṛndāvana continuously and always with the inhabitants of Gokula:

preṣṭhebhyo 'pi priyatamair janair gokulavāsibhiḥ|
vṛndāraṇye sadaivāsau vihāraṃ kurute hariḥ|[41]

Thus the manifest *līlā* retains the Purāṇic pattern of the contrast and relation between Braj and Mathurā, but this is absent in the unmanifest *līlā* where the sport in Braj-Vṛndāvana is an unbroken process.

A further respect in which Rūpa differs from the Purāṇic texts is in the obvious gradation which may be seen in the presentation of the various abodes. This emerges even from the verse discussed above from the order in which the *dhāmans* are enumerated. That is to say Māthura comes before Dvāravatī, indicating the precedence of Māthura; then, in the further division of Māthura, Gokula precedes the *pura*, showing the supremacy of Gokula above all the other abodes. The pre-eminence of Gokula becomes even more explicit in a further passage according to which though Kṛṣṇa disports himself in all three abodes eternally (i.e., in the unmanifest *līlā*) in Gokula his sweetness is greatest; that is to say, he finds his most complete expression:

iti dhāmatraye kṛṣṇo viharaty eva sarvadā|
tatrāpi gokule tasya mādhurī sarvato 'dhikā||[42]

This particular sweetness which is said to exist in Braj-Gokula alone (*vraja eva*) is fourfold, consisting of majesty, sport, flute and beauty of form:

caturdhā mādhurī tasya vraja eva virājate |
aiśvaryakrīḍayor veṇos tathā śrīvigrahasya ca ||[43]

All of these statements point to an intentional and overt elevation in the status of Gokula-Vṛndāvana above that of Dvāravatī and Mathurā, an elevation possibly inherent in the *BhP.* but never emphasized in this way.

Nandadāsa resembles Rūpa insofar as he retains the *BhP.* mythological structure of Vṛndāvana-Braj-Mathurā, but gives importance only to the contrast between Mathurā and Vṛndāvana-Braj, not to that between Vṛndāvana and Braj. This can be seen in the *Bhramaragīta* where both Vṛndāvana and Braj are contrasted with Mathurā. The use of Braj in this context can be seen in a verse where the *gopīs* tell Uddhava that in leaving Mathurā and coming to Gokula to teach Yoga, he has made a mistake since only people with love live here:

madhubana sudhihiṃ bisārikai āye gokula māhiṃ |
ita saba premi basata haiṃ tumarau gāṃhaka nāhiṃ |[44]

Vṛndāvana is used in a similar way when Uddhava entreats Kṛṣṇa, who is in Mathurā to return to Vṛndāvana and the company of the *gopīs*:

puni puni kahai he syāma jāya bṛṃdābana rahiyai |
parama prema ko puṃja jahām gopī saṃga lahiyai ||[45]

Something of the Gauḍīya concept of manifest and unmanifest *līlā* would also appear to be reflected in the *Virahamañjarī* of Nandadāsa which, though the whole poem is based on the theme of Kṛṣṇa's absence from Braj-Vṛndāvana, says in the introduction that Kṛṣṇa always resides in Vṛndāvana:

sadā basau bṛṃdāvana dhāmā |[46]

The reference must be to the unmanifest *līlā*. A similar allusion is also detectable in the last verse of the *Bhramaragīta* which says that Kṛṣṇa showed himself to be one with the *gopīs*, and then cast again the net of illusion and hid his form of sport (*bihāra*):

gopī āpa dikhāi eka karikai banavārī |
ūdhau ke bhare naina ḍāri vyāmohaka jārī |
apanau rūpa bihāra kau līnho bahuri durāya |[47]

The divergence of Nandadāsa from the mythological preoccupations of the *BhP.*, despite certain apparent similarities, emerges clearly from the description of Vṛndāvana in the *Rāsapañcādhyāyī.* This account contains elements which have no counterpart in the *BhP.* and which can be identified as characteristic of the symbolic description of Vṛndāvana. Among these is the description of a dais upon which a sixteen-petalled lotus, ciruclar in shape (*cakrākṛti*), is situated:

> *tahaṃ ika mani-maya-aṃka citra ko saṃkha subhaga ati* |
> *tāpara ṣodasa-dala-saroja adbhuta cakrākṛti* |13|[48]

Kṛṣṇa is said to be enthroned in the centre of this lotus on its seed-pod (*karinikā*):

> *madhi kamanīya karinikā saba sukha suṃdara-kandara* |
> *tahaṃ rājata brajarāja kuṃvarabara rasika puraṃdara* ||[49]

These motifs, i.e., a dais, a sixteen-petalled lotus, the central seed-pot of the lotus as the seat of the deity, and the circular area, all occur frequently in texts to be examined and characterize the symbolic portrayal of Vṛndāvana as opposed to the mythological.

Later in the text a connection is made between the circular area depicted as a sixteen-petalled lotus and the circular *rāsa* dance which is depicted as taking place upon the lotus:

> *ārambhita adbhuta surāsa uhi kamala-cakra para* |[50]

In this way, a link is formed between the concept of a circle already present in the *rāsamaṇḍala* of the three *Purāṇas* and the *Sūrasāgara*, and the concept of Vṛndāvana as a circular area. It is arguable that in both the symbolic element is present, but in the mythological texts it is presented as an event, while in the symbolic expression it is an image of an unchanging condition.

Though the term *rāsamaṇḍala* is not used in the *Hariv.*, the circular concept appears even here in a verse which describes Kṛṣṇa as being surrounded by a circle (*cakravāla*) of *gopīs*:

> *evaṃ sa kṛṣṇo gopīnāṃ cakravālair alaṃkṛtaḥ* |
> *śaradīṣu sacandrāsu niśāsu mumude sukhī* |[51]

In the *ViP.* and the *BhP.*, on the other hand, the term *rāsamaṇḍala* is frequently used for the formation of the *gopīs* around Kṛṣṇa in Vṛndāvana. The *ViP.* describes how Kṛṣṇa forms the *rāsamaṇḍala* taking the hands of the *gopīs*, one by one:

> *hastena gṛhya caikaikāṃ gopīnāṃ rāsamaṇḍalam* |
> *cakāra tatkarasparśanimīlitadṛśaṃ hariḥ* ||[52]

Similarly, the *BhP.* relates how the *rāsa* festival formed by the circle (*maṇḍala*) of *gopīs* was initiated by Kṛṣṇa:

> *rāsotsavaḥ saṃpravṛtto gopīmaṇḍalamaṇḍitaḥ* |
> *yogeśvareṇa kṛṣṇena tāsāṃ madhye dvayor dvayoḥ* ||[53]

A slightly more spatial element is introduced into the concept of the circular *rāsa* by Sūradāsa when he specifies the area encompassed by the *rāsamaṇḍala* as being twelve *kośa* in perimeter:

> *kosa dvādasa rāsa parimita racyau nandakumāra* |[54]

The general picture is still, however, that of a circle formed in dance.

From the above discussion it appears that the circle (*maṇḍala*) is throughout an important element in the concept of Vṛndāvana, basically disconnected from any geographical features. Whereas this element appears in the three *Purāṇas* and the *Sūrasāgara* in the form of a mythological event, it is given a more concrete symbolic form by Nandadāsa as the circular lotus within which the *rāsa* occurred. The similarity of this type of symbolic imagery with that of the *yantra* would seem to be more than coincidental. Not only the circle but also the lotus with its pericarp as the central form are basic *yāntric* images.

A text which exhibits the comparability of the conception of Vṛndāvana with a *yantra* at its most explicit is the *Brahma-saṃhitā*. Passages of this work are included in the *Laghubhāgavatāmṛta* and it also has a commentary attributed to Jīva Gosvāmī. Both these facts suggest a pre-Gosvāmī date for the text, as well as indicating its acceptability within the Gauḍīya theological framework. A comparison of the terminology of this text with that of Tāntric accounts of *yantra* show evidence of an intention to portray a *yantra*-like form. At the same time the similarity in a number of respects with the description of Vṛndāvana by Nandadāsa is noteworthy.

A first point which may be observed is that the term Gokula is used in this text very much in accordance with the Rūpa Gosvāmī interpretation, i.e., as a general term for the abode of Kṛṣṇa not distinct from Vṛndāvana. It is also clearly not meant here in the Purāṇic sense of a cowherd encampment, but instead is used as a proper name.

The description begins with the lotus imagery already observed in Nandadāsa. In this case, Gokula is said to be a thousand-petalled lotus:

> *sahasrapatraṃ kamalaṃ gokulākhyaṃ mahat padam* |[55]

Comparable uses of the thousand-petalled lotus image can be found, for example, in the *Lakṣmī-tantra*, a Pañcarātra text, which describes how the first stage of meditation upon Viṣṇu involves the visualization of a thousand-petalled lotus within which the deity has its abode:

> *tataḥ samutthitaṃ padmaṃ dhyāyet kṣīrārṇavodarāt* | . . .
> *sahasradalasaṃpannaṃ sahasrakiraṇāvṛtam* |
> *saharsraraśmi-saṃkāśaṃ tatpṛṣṭhe cāsanaṃ nyaset* ||[56]

In this case the thousand-petalled lotus is an image symbolizing the transcendental realm of the divine for the purposes of meditation. As will be seen, ritualized meditation also appears to be involved in such representation of Vṛndāvana.

The image of a thousand-petalled lotus is similarly used for the highest of the eight *cakras*, or spiritual centres within the body:

> *visargādhaḥ padmaṃ daśaśatadalaṃ pūrṇacandrātiśubhram* |[57]

Here it represents the supreme spiritual state and hence is essentially identical in its connotations with both the thousand-petalled abode of the deity and the thousand-petalled Gokula, i.e., a symbolically spatial representation of a metaphysical concept.

The similarity of the *Brahma-saṃhitā* with both Nandadāsa and *tāntric* texts is further observable in its definition of the pericarp of this lotus as the abode of Kṛṣṇa:

> *tatkarṇikāraṃ taddhāma tadanantāṃśasambhavam* |[58]

The Tāntric parallel can be found, for example, in a statement of the *Mahānirvāṇa-tantra* to the effect that the main deity is to be situated in the pericarp of the lotus drawn in the *yantra* for the purposes of worship.[59] The pericarp is thus seen as the innermost point of the lotus and in all *yāntric* diagrams, the central point represents the subtlest essence with gradually evolves into grosser forms as it moves outwards.

The Tāntric parallel continues to be observable in the second verse of the

Brahma-saṃhitā where the above described pericarp is portrayed as hexagonal in shape (*ṣaṭkoṇa*) and is specifically termed a *yantra*:

> *karṇikāraṃ mahadyantraṃ ṣaṭkoṇaṃ vajrakīlakam* |[60]

The hexagon image may again be compared with that of the *Mahānirvāṇa-tantra* which describes how in the construction of a *yantra* the sequence should be first a triangle around which is drawn a circle; around that is inscribed a hexagon and the outermost boundary is quadrilateral.[61] Even this particular sequence is more or less observed by the *Brahma-saṃhitā* when it describes the hexagon as being surrounded by a quadrangle called Śvetadvīpa, the four corners of which form the fourfold abode of the four forms (presumably the *caturvyūtha* — Vāsudeva, Sankarṣaṇa, Pradyumna and Aniruddha):

> *caturasraṃ tatparitaḥ śvetadvīpākhyam adbhutam* |
> *caturasraṃ caturmūrti caturdhāma catuṣkṛtam* ||[62]

There is thus an unmistakable resemblance between the description of a *yantra* as found in a Tāntric text and the reperesentation of Gokula in a Vaiṣṇava text.

In the *Brahma-saṃhitā* not only is the main deity situated in the pericarp of the lotus, but the filaments of the lotus are allocated to the portions of this deity, while the *śrīs*, i.e., the female energies identifiable with the *gopīs*, are situated on the petals:

> *tatkiñjalkaṃ tadaṃśānāṃ tatpatrāṇi śriyām api* |[63]

This can be compared with the way in which minor deities or aspects of *śakti* are situated on the various filaments and petals of the lotus in a *yantra*. The *Tantrarāja*, for example, describes the *śaktis* who are to be worshipped on each of the eight petals of the *cakra* of the Srī Yantra.[64] Such a placement can also be compared with the encircling of the *gopīs* around Kṛṣṇa in the *Purāṇas*, only the *yāntric* image is a static one. It again suggests, however, that a single concept is being presented in two different ways — one mythological, the other symbolic.

That the *Brahma-saṃhitā* was accepted, particularly in its view of Vṛndāvana, by the Gauḍīya sect is supported by the fact that identical images and features can be found in a Braj Bhāṣā Gauḍīya account of Vṛndāvana — the *Vṛndāvana yogapīṭha* ascribed to Gadādhara Bhaṭṭa. The use of *Yogapīṭha* in the title is in itself significant, since the term *pīṭha* is used both for the four main geographical seats of *śakti* worship as well as for the seat of the deity in a *yantra*. A homology is thus found between the geographical place (the *pīṭha*) and a symbolic formation (the *yantra*) in the Tāntric texts[65] similar to that made in the case of Vṛndāvana by the Vaiṣṇava texts.

Like the *Brahma-saṃhitā,* the *Vṛndāvana yogapīṭha* describes the *pīṭha* as a thousand-petalled lotus with filaments between each petal:

tā maṇḍapa maha yogapīṭha paṅkaja ruci lāgī|
tāke mana meṃ udaya hota jo koū baḍabhāgī| 17|
tāke patra vicitra sahasra madhya kiṃjalkai|
padmarāga kī bhāṃti agra muktā maṇi jhalakai||[66]

This is itself might not be enough to indicate direct influence, since the image of a thousand-petalled has been seen to be a common one. The *Brahma-saṃhitā* also describes however, the pericarp as being *vajrakīlakam,* an uncommon phrase meaning literally 'having a diamond wedge or pin'. Exactly the same phrase is used by Gadādhara Bhaṭṭa to describe the pericarp:

kanaka barana karnikā kīla bajrana kī sohai|[67]

The term *kīla* or *kīlaka* is apparently used for the inner syllables of a *mantra.*[68] Such syllables are inscribed on a *yantra,* thus combining a symbolism of sound and form. The connection of the *mantras* is borne out by the second half of the verse from the *Vṛndāvana yogapītha* which goes on to speak of the greatness of the ten-syllabled *mantra*:

mantradasākṣara rūpa kahana mahimāko ko hai|19|[69]

The use in both texts of the identical phrase suggests that the Braj Bhāṣā text was familiar with the images of the *Brahma-saṃhitā.* This in turn indicates the acceptance by the Gauḍīya sect of this symbolic picture of Vṛndāvana, particularly for the purposes of ritual meditation.

The *Padma Purāṇa* is another text which shows a *yāntric* symbolic representation of Vṛndāvana combined with an emphasis on the eternal and unceasing nature of the pastimes of Rādhā and Kṛṣṇa. Passages from this text are quoted by the Gauḍīya Gosvāmīs, indicating that at least parts of it predate them. The rejection of the concept of the incarnation of Kṛṣṇa as an event can be seen in the statement to the effect that the *gopīs,* the cowherd boys, Vṛndāvana and the Kṛṣṇa incarnation are all eternal:

nityaṃ me mathurāṃ viddhi vanaṃ vṛndāvanaṃ tathā|
yamunāṃ gopakanyāś ca tathā gopālabālakāḥ||
mamāvatāro nityo 'yam atra mā saṃśayaṃ kṛthāḥ|
mameṣṭā hi sadā rādhā sarvajño 'haṃ parātparaḥ|[70]

Such a concept of the eternal Kṛṣṇa incarnation is very much in accord with the Gauḍīya theology as expressed, for example, in the *Laghubhāgavagtāmṛta.*

If Nandadāsa can be said to combine the symbolic and the mythological aspects of Vṛndāvana, the *PadP*. combines the symbolic and the geographical forms of imagery. Geographical imagery will be discussed at length later in the chapter (see below p. 114); for the moment it may be noted that salient features of such imagery is the treatment of Vṛndāvana as one of twelve woods surrounding Mathurā, and the designation of the entire area as Māthuramaṇḍala. The enumeration of the twelve woods can be found in the *PadP*:

> *bhadraśrīlohabhāṇḍīramahātālakhadīrakhāḥ* |
> *bakulaṃ kumudaṃ kāmyaṃ madhu vṛndāvanaṃ tathā* |[71]

However, such a limitation of Vṛndāvana as being no more than one of twelve other woods is contradicted by other passages which treat Vṛndāvana either as encompassing the entire area or as the innermost centre of the entire area (see below p. 105). In neither of these cases is the conception of Vṛndāvana geographical in nature, it is celestial and symbolic. The inclusion of Vṛndāvana as one of twelve woods along with these other statements would therefore appear to be an attempt to incorporate the geographical picture into a basically symbolic layout.

A similar duality of interpretation can be observed in the use of the term Māhuramaṇḍala which could be seen as meaning no more than the geographical area of Mathurā with no particular connotations of a circular area. However, the *PadP*. makes the symbolic, circular connotations of the *maṇḍala* in this context clear by describing the Māthuramaṇḍala as having the form of a thousand-petalled lotus and as being encircled by the *cakra* of Viṣṇu:

> *sahasrapatrakamalākāraṃ māthuramaṇḍalam* |
> *viṣṇucakraparimāṇaṃ dhāma vaiṣṇavam adbhutam* ||[72]

The image of the Viṣṇu *cakra* not only emphasizes its circular nature but also its character as a supramundane realm. Geographical consideration are thus clearly subordinate to symbolic representation.

Other *yāntric* images used by the *PadP*. in its portrayal of Vṛndāvana include that of an eight-petalled lotus within a sixteen-petalled lotus. A similar image can be found in the Tāntric description of the Śrī Cakra, where the second *cakra* going inward is a sixteen-petalled lotus and the third *cakra* is eight-petalled.[73]

The integration of the geographical and the symbolic can be seen in the way in which the twelve *vanas* are depicted as being situated on the various petals of these lotuses, along with the various scenes of Kṛṣṇa's *līlās*. For example, the seventh petal of the outer lotus is said to be Bakulavana, while the eighth petal is Tālavana where the demon Dhenuka was killed by Kṛṣṇa:

> *saptamaṃ bakulāraṇyaṃ dalaṃ ramyaṃ prakīrtitam |*
> *tatrāṣṭamaṃ tālavanaṃ tatra dhenuvadhaḥ smṛtaḥ ||*[74]

That Vṛndāvana is on a higher level than the rest of the Māthuramaṇḍala is indicated by its being called the pericarp of the thousand-petalled lotus:

> *sahasradalapadmasya vṛndāraṇya varāṭakam |*[75]

The importance of the pericarp in *yāntric* diagrams has been discussed above and the use of this image once again shows the basically symbolic preoccupations of the *PadP*. It differs from the mythological layout insofar as Vṛndāvana becomes a central point, on a higher level from the rest of the Māthuramaṇḍala.

The description of the pericarp itself in the *PadP*. is remarkably similar to the description of Vṛndāvana in the *Rāsapañcādhyāyī* of Nandadāsa. The *PadP*. describes how an octagonal *yogapīṭha* is situated in Vṛndāvana:

> *tanmadhye mañjubhavane yogapīṭham samujjvalam |*
> *tadaṣṭakoṇanirmāṇaṃ nānādīptimanoharam ||*[76]

Upon this *yogapīṭha* is a jewelled throne:

> *tasyopari ca māṇikyaratnasiṃhāsanaṃ śubham |*[77]

This can be compared with the bejewelled dais described by Nandadāsa. The *PadP*. further describes how an eight-petalled lotus is situated upon this throne and in the pericarp of that lotus stands Kṛṣṇa:

> *tasminn aṣṭadalaṃ padmaṃ karṇikāyāṃ sukhāśrayam |*
> *govindasya paraṃ sthānaṃ kim asya mahimocyate ||*[78]

This is paralleled by the *ṣoḍasa-dala-saroja* and *madhi kamanīya karinikā* of Nandadāsa. All of these are such standard *yāntric* images, however, that it seems unnecessary to conjecture any direct relation between the two texts. It is more likely that these had become traditional images in the description of Vṛndāvana and both texts subscribed to this tradition, showing a similarity in their concept of Vṛndāvana.

Resembling the minor deities (*āvaraṇa devatās*) and *śaktis* which are placed around the main deity in a *yantra*, the *PadP*. depicts Rādhā and Kṛṣṇa as being surrounded, in the inner circle at the eight corners of the throne, by the eight foremost beloveds of Kṛṣṇa:

> *tadbāhye yogapīṭhe ca svarṇasiṃhāsanāvṛte* |
> *pratyaṅgarabhasāveśāḥ pradhānāḥ kṛṣṇavallabhāḥ* ||[79]

Proceeding outwards are then found four doorkeepers:

> *śrīdāmā paścimadvāre vasudāmā tathottare* ||
> *sudāmā ca tathā pūrve kiṅkiṇī cāpi dakṣiṇe* ||[80]

Of these two, Sudāman and Śrīdāman, correspond to childhood playmates of *sakhās* of Kṛṣṇa.[81] The other two are, in fact, puzzling since although from a previous verse which says that all four are equal in strength and prowess[82] it would seem that these were also intended as masculine names, they are actually feminine forms and can be traced as goddesses;[83] a fact which again suggests an association with *yantras*.

These doorkeepers are followed by the cowherd boys and the cows.[84] The outside the *yogapīṭha*, on each of its four sides, lies a golden *pīṭha* in which one of the four *vyūhas* is enthroned.[85] This can be compared with the description of the four forms at the four corners of Gokula in the *Brahma-saṃhitā*. Finally, as the outermost doorkeepers, are the four Viṣṇus — white, golden, red and black, each having four arms.[86]

That these represent successive stages in the apprehension of the divine can be seen much more explicitly in the Braj Bhāṣā texts to be examined in due course. Even here, however, a progression can be traced in which the lowest level is represented by the four-armed Viṣṇu doorkeepers, indicating the subordination of Viṣṇu to Kṛṣṇa, as in the Gauḍīya texts. The four *vyūhas* are envisaged as the next stage upwards and inwards, followed by the cows and cowherd boys who are associated with the Braj *līlā*. The final circle is formed by the *gopīs* or *sakhīs*, while Rādhā and Kṛṣṇa occupy the innermost point.

The use of the *PadP*. depiction of Vṛndāvana in sectarian Braj Bhāṣā texts, illustrating the compatibility of such images with sectarian views, can be seen particularly clearly in a Rādhāvallabha text attributed to one Rasikadāsa and written in A.D. 1691.[87] The actual title of the text as given in the colophon is *Rasakadaṃbacūḍāmaṇi* but it is popularly known today by the devotees of the sect as *Vṛndāvana yogapīṭha*, thus placing it in the same category as the *yogapītha* of Gadādhara Bhaṭṭa. In other words, it is a text describing Vṛndāvana for the purposes of ritual meditation.

Similarities with the *PadP.* are numerous. The same image is used of the outermost boundary being formed by the Sudarśana Cakra of Viṣṇu within which lies a thousand-petalled lotus:

sahasra sudala kau kamala kala kahyau purāna ke māṃhi |
cakrasudarasana para lasata saṃsai yāmauṃ nāṃhi |17||[88]

All of the seven successive enclosures (*āvaraṇas*) the similarly described as eight- or sixteen-petalled lotuses. As in the *PadP.* this texts describes the twelve *vanas* and the scenes of the various *līlās* as being situated on the sixteen petals of the sixth enclosure.[89] Not only the *vanas* but even the *upavanas* correspond to those mentioned in the *PadP.* They are, in fact, mentioned in the same order, the difference being that in this text they are made to number thirty-two, as in the *Brajabhaktivilāsa* discussed below (see pp. 117-18), whereas in the *PadP.* the number is left unclear. The *PadP.* says for example:

anyac copabanaṃ proktaṃ kṛṣṇakrīḍārasasthalam |[90]

This would appear to mean no more than that there are other *upavanas*, places having the essence of Kṛṣṇa's sport. The Braj Bhāṣā text, however, has taken the phrase *kṛṣṇakrīḍārasasthalam* as referring to three of the *upavanas*, i.e., *Kṛṣṇavana, Krīḍāvana* and Raha Asthala:

prathama kṛṣṇa vana guni manahi krīḍā vana dvai jāṃna |
raha asthala hai tīsarau aurau suni dai kāṃna |7|[91]

This can be seen as localizing the *līlās* further, possibly connected with the continued process of identification of *līlāsthalas,* as well as the emphasis on the unity of the symbolic and geographical Vṛndāvana.

It may be observed that the structure of Vṛndāvana in both the *PadP.* and the *Rasakadaṃbacūḍāmaṇi* is basically the same, with certain modifications. In both there is a progression from Viṣṇu-doorkeepers through cowherd boy doorkeepers to the *gopīs,* with Rādhā and Kṛṣṇa in the centre. In the *Rasakadaṃbacūḍāmaṇi* the implications of this picture, in terms of a progression towards both increasing intensity and purity of devotion and a more complete expression of the divine, and more clearly formulated.

The hierarchy among the forms of devotion represented in each surrounding enclosure (*āvaraṇa*) is expressed by dividing the seven *āvaraṇas* into five categories, i.e.,

(1) the first and second outermost *āvaraṇas* are said to consist of pure majesty (*aiśvarya*):

> *prathama dutiya āvarana maiṃ kevala guna īśvarja* |[92]

Among these two, those who perform devotion combined with observance of ritual and social practices, are entitled to the first *āvaraṇa:*

> *tahāṃ adhikārī kahauṃ nyārī rīti dikhāi* |
> *bhakti karma miśrā kareṃ tana mana je cita lāi* |5|[93]

Those who combine devotion with knowledge, on the other hand, reach the second covering:

> *bhakti gyāna miśrā karata jaba je hota prapaṃna* |
> *taba te āi ihāṃ aho pahucata haiṃ śubha dina* |8|[94]

As in the *PadP.*, the doorkeepers of the first *āvaraṇa* are four-armed Viṣṇus.[95] This is again in accordance with the theme of *aiśvarya,* since the four-armed Viṣṇu is always seen as inspiring awe, in contrast to the two-armed Kṛṣṇa who inspires pure love.

(2) The third *āvaraṇa* falls into the second category of majesty combined with sweetness (*mādhurya*).[96]

(3) Pure sweetness is found in the fourth to the sixth *āvaraṇa*, and this sweetness is connected with Braj *bhakti:*

> *suni caturtha āvarana teṃ chaṭha aiṃ lauṃ suvicāri* |
> *vrjāvarana nita hāṃ hoi gaurasa mādhurja apāra* |2|[97]

The significance of the doorkeepers assigned to each enclosure may again be noted — cowherd boys in the case of the fifth[98] and the playmates (*sakhās*) in the case of the sixth enclosure.[99] This is roughly the same sequence as the *PadP.* and again fits in with the form of devotion ascribed to these *āvaraṇas*, i.e., Braj *bhakti.*

(4) In the seventh *āvaraṇa*, sweetness is combined with love (*prema*).[100] This *prema* is evidently the term used for the devotion of the *gopīs*, since it is here that the *rāsa* is portrayed as taking place.[101] Here also the *gopīs* propitiate Kātyāyanī in order to obtain Kṛṣṇa as their husband.[102] This particular *āvaraṇa* is envisaged as forming the link between the Braj and Vṛndāvana *līlās*. Thus the eighth and last petal of this particular

enclosure is defined as being neither Vṛndāvana nor Braj, but the meeting-place of both:

> *vṛndāvana teṃ nyāre ī astama dala ye jāni* |
> *bṛjahū teṃ nyāre inahi lai ura maiṃ hīṃ māni* |53|
> *vṛndāvana vṛja hu duni kī saṃdhahi samajhi vicāri* |[103]

(5) Finally, is the pericarp, only pure love exists:

> *tāke āgeṃ karanikā niju premā suvilāsa* |[104]

It is here that the divine couple, Rādhā and Kṛṣṇa disport themselves eternally, and it is only *sakhīs* such as Lalitā that can enter this *āvaraṇa*,[105] since in the devotion of the *sakhīs* alone is love found in its purest form. The pericarp is thus the scene for the eternal *vihāra*.

Corresponding to the various forms of devotion, a progression can be traced in the expression of the divine. Thus Viṣṇu is envisaged as dwelling in the second enclosure. Here he appears in two forms, i.e., as Mahāvaikuṇṭhanātha,[106] and as Viṣṇu who lies on Śeṣa.[107] The subordination of Viṣṇu to Kṛṣṇa is this way, as well as the portrayal of two forms of Viṣṇu, is very reminiscent of the Gauḍīya texts.

The third *āvaraṇa* contains the four *vyūhas* — Vāsudeva, Sankarṣaṇa, Pradyumna and Aniruddha.[108] This can be seen as a statement about the position of the Dvārakā and Mathurā *līlās*, envisaged as superior to the Vaikuṇṭha of Viṣṇu but inferior to Braj and Vṛndāvana *līlā*.

The fourth, fifth and sixth *āvaraṇas*, above seen to be associated with *mādhurya*, are all three involved in the manifestation of Braj *līlās*. These include the tending of cows[109] as well as Kṛṣṇa's childhood sports.[110]

We have already seen how Kṛṣṇa appear as the Lord of the *gopīs* in the seventh covering, and finally in the pericarp itself the divine couple are found, eternally engaged in their divine play:

> *tāmeṃ rājata rucira ati bhrājata mithuna kiśora* |[111]

A hierarchy is thus maintained with Vṛndāvana Kṛṣṇa sporting eternally with Rādhā on the highest rung; Viṣṇu on the lowest level; and Braj Kṛṣṇa in between. A contrast is thus made between Vṛndāvana and Braj, but it is different in nature from that made in the three *Purāṇas* and the *Sūrasāgara*. Here Vṛndāvana is envisaged as purely the scene for the eternal union of Rādhā and Kṛṣṇa. All of thee *līlās* which in the *Sūrasāgara*, for example, were portrayed as taking place in Vṛndāvana, such as the *rāsa* and the grazing of cows, are here categorized as Braj *līlās.*

The above symbolic representation also differs from the mythological portrayal of events in that Vṛndāvana and Braj *līlās* are depicted as taking place simultaneously, each one in its own position in the *yāntric* layout. In this way it agrees with Rūpa's concept of unmanifest *līlā*, in which all the facets of *līlā* are eternally co-existent. In the *Purāṇas* and Sūradāsa, on the other hand, there is a sequence of events and so a movement to and fro between Vṛndāvana and Braj. This is what Rūpa calls manifest *līlā.*

The correlation of the acceptance of the concept of *nitya vihāra*, and hence rejection of the theory of incarnation, with a symbolic, *yāntric* portrayal of Vṛndāvana is again supported by the *Mahāvāṇī* of Harivyāsadeva. This text, whose concept of the eternal nature of the sport of Rādhā and Kṛṣṇa and its separateness from the process of incarnation has been discussed above (see p. 52), presents a picture of Vṛndāvana possessing many of the *yāntric* elements found in the *PadP.*, Nandadāsa and the other symbolic descriptions, though not including such specific details as to suggest direct borrowing.

The outermost boundary of Vṛndāvana in this account is said to be formed by the Yamunā river which is described as having the shape of a bracelet, i.e., as being circular:

> *kaṃkanākāra sauḍhāri saritā* |
> *bahati ati surasa siṃgāra bharitā* |9|[112]

Such a picture of the Yamunā as encircling Vṛndāvana is absent from the mythological picture where Vṛndāvana instead is situated beside the Yamunā. The encirclement here is again reminiscent of the outer circle of a *yantra*, or the Sudarśana Cakra, making Vṛndāvana circular in form.

The lotus imagery is equally in evidence here. Within the area encompassed by the Yamunā is said to be a lotus with innumerable petals:

> *aiso nijadhāma jā madhya nītibhūmi* |
> *amitadala kamala ākāra rahi jhūmi* ||[113]

This can be compared with the thousand-petalled lotus found in the *Brahma-saṃhitā*, Gadādhara's *Yogapīṭha*, the *PadP.*, and the *Rasakadaṃbacūḍāmaṇi*. Moreover, as in the above texts, the next stage inward is formed by a row of eight petals:

> *madhya maṃjula banī aṣṭadala pāṃti* |[114]

Equally familiar is the way in which each of the eight petals is described as having the bower of one of the eight main *sakhīs* situated upon it:

> *upari priya sakhini kī kuṃja sarasāṃti* |18|[115]

The *sakhīs* here are equivalent to the *śaktis* found similarly situated in Tāntric *yantras.*

From here on, the text proceeds to combine *yāntric* elements with palace imagery. That the two are basically compatible has been pointed out by Eliade in his discussion of the *maṇḍala,* in which he sees royal symbolism as playing an important part.[116] It is, of course totally absent from the *Purāṇas.* The *Mahāvāṇī* describes how a palace with eight doors stands in the centre of four lakes:

> *cahuṃ saravarana ke madhya soheṃ* |
> *mahala aṭhadvāra chavi koṃ vimoheṃ* ||[117]

The image of four lakes is also present in the *Rasakadaṃbacūḍāmaṇi* where they are said to be in the seventh *āvaraṇa.*[118] This image is, in fact, also present in the *PadP.* which says that there are four lakes in the centre of the thousand-petalled lotus:

> *sahasradalapadmasya saṃsthānaṃ madhyakorakam* |
> *catuḥsaraś caturdvāram aścaryakulasaṃkulam* |[119]

This section describes how Arjuna wished to take part in the *līlā* of Kṛṣṇa and the *gopīs,* and eventually after bathing in these lakes he assumes the form of a woman and achieves his desire.

Certain basic *yāntric* forms continue to be used by the *Mahāvāṇī* in the description of the palace. The palace is said to contain a *cauka,* which can mean courtyard but is literally a four-sided area. Within the *cauka* is said to be *maṇḍala,* again ambiguous in that it can be understood as either a circle or a platform:

> *tāju mahala ke cauka bici maṇi maṇḍala rasapuṃja* |[120]

The image here of a circle within a square is remarkably similar to the *yantra* described above from the *Mahānirvāṇa-tantra* which used the same pattern. In this way the two images of palace and *yantra* are interwoven.

The *yāntric* images continue in the description of the octagonal throne situated upon the *maṇḍala* with one of the eight *sakhīs* standing at each corner of the throne:

āṃgana mohana mahala ke mohana maṇḍala maṃju |
tā ūpara aṭha kauṃna ko sukha siṃghāsana raṃju |34|
koṃna koṃna pratyeka ika priya pramadāgana saṃga |[121]

This is obviously similar to the *PadP.*

The presence of such image in the *Mahāvāṇī,* traditionally a Nimbārkīya text, demonstrates the way in which their use is not confined to one sect. Nandadāsa of the Vallabha sect, Rasikadāsa of the Rādhāvallabha sect, Gadādhara Bhaṭṭa of the Gauḍīya sect and Harivyāsadeva of the Nimbārkīya sect, all employ to a greater or lesser extent similar images. Sūradāsa, on the other hand, who is traditionally claimed by the Vallabha sect, but whose divergence from sectarian preoccupations has been demonstrated in other contexts, does not.

If the *PadP.* and *Rasakadaṃbacūḍāmaṇi* are compared, though both are similar in many ways, the emphasis on the different levels in the expression of devotion (*rasa*) is much more pronounced in the *Rasakadaṃbacūḍāmaṇi.* It is this aspect which predominates in the poetry of authors such as Dhruvadāsa and Bihārinadāsa. Though the picture of Vṛndāvana basically corresponds to that represented in the texts above, the aim in the two cases would appear to differ. Whereas texts such as the *PadP.* are more concerned with ritual and the depiction of Vṛndāvana as an aid to the meditational aspect of such ritual, poets such as Dhruvadāsa are entirely preoccupied with the experience of *rasa.* This is reflected in the poetry through a less stylised depiction of Vṛndāvana. Nevertheless, some of the same images are used and the picture is definitely symbolic rather than mythological in nature.

The use of *yāntric* imagery in the poetry of Dhruvadāsa can be seen, for example, in his discussion of the relation between Vṛndāvana, Braj and Mathurā. This is described, as in the *Rasakadaṃbacūḍāmaṇi,* in terms of circular areas within circular areas, each progressively superior as they proceed inwards. Thus the Braj *maṇḍala* is said to be within the Mathurā *maṇḍala* and also superior to it:

baikuṇṭha hu te adhika hai mathurā maṇḍala jāni |
tāmeṃ tāhu te adhika vrajamaṇḍala sukha-khāni |32|[122]

In the centre of the Braj *maṇḍala,* in turn, lies Vṛndāvana which is compared to a jewel in a crown:

madhi rājata jyoṃ mukuṭa maṇi vṛndāvana rasakanda |[123]

The term *maṇḍala* has, of course, also the connotation of an area or district; so that the picture intended here could be a geographical one of a smaller district within a larger district rather than the symbolic circular image. The concept of a progression in circles from the innermost supreme point (*bindu*) outward, each circular area successively depicting an inferior manifestation of divine power resembles that a *yantra* too closely, however, to be a mere coincidence. Moreover, the same gradation of Mathurā, Braj and Vṛndāvana corresponding to the level of devotion as well as to the fullness of the divine manifestation, has been seen to be depicted in symbolic terms in the texts discussed above, suggesting the presence of a tradition to this effect. It may be noted that here again the contrast between Braj and Vṛndāvana is seen in terms of a contrast between the eternal sport of Rādhā and Kṛṣṇa with the *rāsa* with the *gopīs*, and not the mythological contrast between *vana* and *grāma*.

Dhruvadāsa does occasionally use *yāntric* images in other contexts as well. In his *Muktāvalī līlā* can be found the image of Vṛndāvana as a sixteen-petalled lotus upon a bejewelled circle with Kṛṣṇa and Rādhā in the very centre and a *sakhī* on each petal:

maṇḍala manimaya adhika virājai nirakhata koṭi bhāna sasi lājai |
tāpara kamala sudesa suvāsā ṣoḍasa dala rājate cahuṃ pāsā |
madhya kiśora kiśorī sohaiṃ dala dala prati sahacari chabi johaiṃ |[124]

Like Harivyāsadeva, he also describes the Yamunā as encircling Vṛndāvana. In *Premāvalī līlā*, Dhruvadāsa compares the Yamunā to liquid love itself (*sṛngāra rasa*) flowing in a circle around Vṛndāvna:

taranisutā cahūṃ disa bahai sobhā liye athāna |
manauṃ ḍharyau siṃgāra rasa kuṇḍala bāṃdhi pravāha |55|[125]

He goes on to compare the river to a necklace of blue gems worn by Vṛndāvana:

āvata upamā aura ura adbhuta parama rasāla |
vṛndāvana pahirī mano nīla manina kī māla |56|[126]

Both of these similes conjure up a circular picture compatible with that of the *yāntric* concept, but not with the imagery of the *BhP*.

Bihārinadāsa resembles Dhruvadāsa in his use of the *yāntric* images purely for the purposes of describing the different levels of devotion. This can be seen, for example, in a passage (discussed above, p. 74) which describes how Kṛṣṇa who sports eternally in Vṛndāvana is far beyond the devotion manifested in Braj, let along ordinary *bhakti*. The different levels are the same as those found in the *Rasakadaṃbacūḍāmaṇi*; ordinary *bhakti* followed by Braj *bhakti*, and finally the pure *rasa* expressed in Vṛndāvana alone.

Of particular interest is the use of the term *āvaraṇa* in this passage. This is the term used in the *Rasakadaṃbacūḍāmaṇi* for the seven areas surrounding the central paricarp, Vṛndāvana. The verse of Bihārinadāsa describes the *āvaraṇas* of Braj as being the *gopīs*, cows and cowherd boys:

tā braja ke āvarana suni gopī gāi guvāla |[127]

The description of the *gopīs*, etc., as 'coverings' is, in fact, only comprehensible in the light of the above discussion.

The order in which the *gopīs*, cows and cowherd boys are mentioned suggests a hierarchy in which the *gopīs* are on the highest level. If it is seen in terms of circular areas surrounding the central point, the *gopīs* would be situated in the innermost circle. This is again in accordance with the *Rasakadaṃbacūḍāmaṇi* and again corresponds to the different *bhāvas*, proceeding from *sakhya*, represented by the cowherd boys, through to *mādhurya* or *gopī-bhāva*. Beyond this is the pericarp, the *bindu*, where only the love manifest through the eternal sport of Kṛṣṇa with Rādhā exists — the *nitya vihāra* — which can only be entered by the *sakhīs*.

The devotion of the *sakhīs* is frequently called by Bihārinadāsa the service in the palace (*mahala kī ṭahala*). In the description of Vṛndāvana as a palace an echo can be detected of the type of imagery used by Harivyāsadeva. The descriptions in this case are, however, much less detailed and the emphasis is more on the expression of *rasa*. The actual term *mahala* is, of course, an Arabic word, suggesting possible Sufi influence. The use of the palace as a metaphor for an inner spiritual state can be seen in the description of the palace of Padmāvatī by the Sufi poet, Jāyasī. This palace is described as having seven levels and on the highest level is the bed where the union of Ratansen and Padmāvatī takes place.[128] This can be compared with the seven *āvaraṇas* surrounding the central point where Rādhā and Kṛṣṇa are united eternally, and could equally be the result of Hindu influence.

The use of Arabic terms is, however, very marked in some of Bihārinadāsa's verses, suggesting that in his case at least the influence was from the Sufi side, made possible by elements already within the *bhakti* tradition. For example, in a verse using very much the same sequence in the stages of devotion as those outlined above in the *yāntric* scheme, he first describes ordinary devotees and those follow the path of wisdom as Khāns and Sultāns who are officers of the border:

bhakta bahu jagata abhimāna gyānī ghaneṃ khāṃna sultaṃna sarahada thānai |[129]

The inhabitants of Braj are nearer than these since they have the duty of attendants (*khavāsī*) and serve in the army which, presumably, guards the palace:

brajavāsī nikati nema khavāsī kaṭaka maiṃ bahuta umarāva biradaīta bānai |[130]

Some devotees reach even as far as the door of the palace, but then turn back, for only the inmates (*mahalani*) know the true nature of the palace:

paga baṃdhā bāhirī paura daure phireṃ mahala kī bāta mahalanī jānaiṃ |[131]

The sequence is thus once again, starting from the outside, (1) ordinary *bhaktas;* (2) those who follow Braj *bhakti;* and finally (3) the *sakhīs.* It could be argued, however, that the very use of non-*yāntric* terms indicates a movement away from the ritualization of the *yantra* to a concentration on Vṛndāvana as an inner spiritual state, to be obtained by *sakhī-bhāva.*

The Geographical Representation

Both the symbolic and the mythological description of Vṛndāvana are basically non-historical and non-geographical in nature. The mythological uses apparently historico-geographical terms, but in actuality is speaking about divine space. The nearest approach to a geographical representation in which the physical situation of Vṛndāvana is in question would seem to be found in the pilgrimage text.

As early pilgrimage text of this nature describing Mathurā and the surrounding areas is the Jain *Vividhatīrthakalpa* in Prākrit. The next is assigned to between A.D. 1307 and 1332,[132] i.e., more than 150 years before the rediscovery of the Vṛndāvana area by either Vallabha or the Gauḍīya Gosvāmīs. The connection with Kṛṣṇa is, however, maintained even here. Mathurā is, for example, said to be the birthplace of Kṛṣṇa Vāsudeva:

ittha nayarīe kaṇhavāsudevassa bhāvititthaṃkarassa janmo |[133]

The place of Vṛndāvana in this account is that of one of twelve woods situated in the Mathurā area:

duvālasavanāiṃ| taṃ jahā-lohajaṃghavaṇaṃ madhuvaṇaṃ
billavaṇaṃ tālavaṇaṃ kumuavaṇaṃ kāmiavaṇam kolavaṇaṃ
bahulavaṇaṃ mahāvaṇaṃ |[134]

It may be noticed that this list is essentially the same as that of the *PadP.* with the exception of the substitution of Kola-*vana* and Bilva-*vana* for Bhadra-*vana* and Śrī-*vana.*

The account in this text contains none of the *yāntric* images seen in the texts above.

There is no suggestion, for example, of any circular shape. The dimensions of Mathurā are given as twelve *yojanas* long and nine *yojanas* wide:

> *tayā ya mahurā bārahajoaṇāiṃ dīhā navajoaṇāiṃ vitthiṇṇā . . .* |[135]

The term *maṇḍala* is not used at all; Mathurā is referred to only as Mathurāpurī, never as Mathurāmaṇḍala.

A description akin to the one above can be found in the *Māthuramāhātmya* of the *Varāha Purāṇa*. Its nature as basically a pilgrimage text is established in the opening where the earth asks which pilgrimage place is the best of all:

> *tīrthaṃ tad vada kalyāṇaṃ tīrthānām uttamottamam* |[136]

The reply of Varāha is that no place in any of the regions is as dear to him as Mathurā which is on earth:

> *na vidyate ca pātāle nāntarikṣe na mānuṣe* |
> *samānaṃ mathurāyā hi priyaṃ mama vasundhare* ||[137]

The emphasis here on Mathurā as a place on earth is in accordance with the geographical nature of the description. The orientation towards pilgrimage can also be seen in the way the text describes the various spots at which one must bathe, the appropriate rituals to be undertaken and the fruits of these actions. The description of each spot in the Mathurā area is followed by such details. It is thus very clearly speaking of a place on earth which can be visited and not of a mythological, celestial or symbolic place, though its nature as a pilgrimage place means that it again does involve sacred space.

The situation of Vṛndāvana as described by this text is the same as that in the *Vividhatīrthakalpa*, i.e., as one of the twelve woods in the Mathurā area:

> *vṛndāvanaṃ dvādaśamaṃ vṛndayā parirakṣitam* |
> *mama caiva priyaṃ bhūma mahāpātakanāśanam* |[138]

The list of the twelve woods is the same in the two texts, with the exceptions of Kunda for Kumuda, and, as in the *PadP.*, Bhadra for Kola.

In this text, however, a correspondence is made between the geographical pilgrimage centre of Vṛndāvana and the symbolic space of the *yāntric* diagram through the use of certain *yāntric* images. While the *PadP.* fitted the geographical into the symbolic scheme, here the symbolic is applied to the geographical. The difference can be seen primarily as one of emphasis.

Yāntric influence can be seen, for example, in the use of the term *maṇḍala* for the Mathurā area, a term not used in the Jain text. The circular connotation of this term is reinforced by the way in which at one point the *maṇḍala* is described as a lotus:

> *viṃśatir yojanānān tu māthuraṃ mama maṇḍalam* |
> *idaṃ padmaṃ mahābhāge sarveṣāṃ muktidāyi ca* |15|[139]

The concept of the principal deity as situated in the pericarp with lesser manifestations on surrounding petals is also found in this text, though here again the geographical nature of the text is shown in the fact that reference appears to be made here to actual images in the area. The text states that Keśava stands in the pericarp of the lotus:

> *karṇikāyāṃ sthito devi keśava keśanāśanaḥ* |[140]

To the west is the dweller in Govardhana:

> *paścimena hariṃ devaṃ govardhananivāsinam* |[141]

To the north is Govinda:

> *utterena tu govindaṃ dṛṣṭvā devaṃ paraṃ śubham* |[142]

Viśrāntideva is said to be situated on the eastern petal:

> *viśrāntisaṃjñake devaṃ pūrvapatre vyavasthitam* |[143]

Finally to the south is said to be an image resembling the Keśava form:

> *dakṣiṇena tu māṃ viddhi pratimāṃ divyarūpiṇīm* |[144]

The use of the term *pratimā* shows that reference is being made to images of deities, while the correspondence with the geographical location can be seen in the fact that the Govardhana mountain is actually said to be situated in the west.[145] There is thus an attempt to fit geographical realities into a symbolic plan.

The *Varāha Purāṇa* forms the basis for two further pilgrimage texts. These are the *Kṛtyakalpataru* of Lakṣmīdhara Bhaṭṭa which has been given the early date of the twelfth century A.D.,[146] and the later *Vīramitrodaya* of Mitramiśra,[147] assigned to the early seventeenth century, i.e., nearly a hundred years after the date given for the arrival of Rūpa and Sanātana in Vṛndāvana, and approximately contemporary with Dhruvadāsa. In both these texts, as in the Jain text discussed above, Mathurā is described as one of many pilgrimage places such as Vārāṇasī, Prayāga and Gayā. The texts deal with Dharmaśāstra in general and do not show any sectarian bias.

The older *Kṛtyakalpataru* (approximately 75 verses long) is much the shorter of the two accounts. It does not include the lotus imagery of the *Varāha Purāṇa*, but only the verse wherein the Māthuramaṇḍala is said to be twenty *yojanas* in diameter:

> *viṃśadyojanavistāre māthure mama maṇḍale* |[148]

The fact that the overtly symbolic imagery is absent from this early text suggests the possibility that it forms, in fact, a later interpolation into the *Varāha Purāṇa* itself.

The *Vīramitrodaya* gives a much longer description (approximately 250 verses)[149] includes all which is left out of the *Kṛtyakalpataru*, as well as additional passages, some attributed to other *Purāṇas* such as the *Padma* and *Skanda*.

A possible argument to the effect that the above type of description is confined to non-sectarian works where Mathurā is regarded as just one of many pilgrimage centres, is disproved by the existence of the same pattern in the work of a follower of the Gauḍīya sect, i.e., the *Brajabhaktivilāsa* of Nārāyaṇa Bhaṭṭa. This text, said to have been written in about A.D. 1553, does differ in its use of the terms Braj and Gokula, both conspicuously absent from all of the above texts. In this work Brajamaṇḍala is, in fact, used as Mathurāmaṇḍala was in the other texts. This Brajamaṇḍala is said to have a circumference of 84 *krośa:*

> *caturaṣṭakakrośena paripūrṇavirānjitam* |
> *asya pradakṣiṇīṃ kurvan dhanadhānyasukhaṃ labhet* |[150]

In another passage it is described as being a limb of the Lord:

> *atha savanacaturaṣṭakrośamaryāda vrajamaṇḍalaṃ bhagavadaṃgasvarūpaḥ* |[151]

Braj is thus evidently used as a term for the entire area and not, as in the *BhP.*, for a nomadic settlement, nor, as in the *Sūrasāgara*, for a particular town. The use of Braj in this way can be seen to be more in accordance with the picture of Braj as seen in the symbolic representations where it is a larger area surrounding Vṛndāvana. It could, therefore, be argued that in this text Nārāyaṇa Bhaṭṭa is applying to the geographical area a symbolic concept, and that the idea of Braj *bhakti* led to the use of the term Braj as designating the whole area.

Nārāyaṇa Bhaṭṭa also differs from the *Purāṇas* and other texts in the distinction he draws between Gokula and Braj. Whereas Braj is used for the entire area, Gokula is specified as one of the twelve *adhivanas* of the area (which is said in all to have twelve *vanas*, twelve *upavanas*, twelve *prativanas*, and twelve *adhivanas*):

> *saptamaṃ gokulaṃ sthānaṃ aṣṭamaṃ baladevakam* |[152]

This Gokula is further described as being the location for the abode of Nanda (*nandamandira*),[153] the place where Yaśodā lay (*yaśodāśayanasthala*),[154] and where Pūtanā suckled Kṛṣṇa.[155]

The similarity to the pilgrimage texts above can be seen in the portrayal of Vṛndāvana as one of twelve *vanas*, for like Gokula, Vṛndāvana is described as one of the *adhivanas*:

> *mukhyaṃ vṛndāvanaṃ śreṣṭham ekādaśaṃ prakīrttitam* |[156]

The other twelve *vanas* of the *Varāha Purāṇa* are put in the ordinary *vana* category.[157] Vṛndāvana is thus shown to be superior to the other *vanas*, a departure from the approach of the other texts. The basic pattern of twelve *vanas* is, however, retained.

The use of this particular layout would seem to be inextricably connected with the nature of the text as being pilgrimage orientated. The text is concerned with describing the geographical area which the pilgrim is to visit, the rites he is to perform at each place, and the fruits of such rites. It describes, for example, the prayer to be recited on entering Vṛndāvana,[158] and how one is freed from all worldly bondages and ills by the circumambulation of the five *krośa* of Vṛndāvana:

> *pañcakrośapramāṇena pradakṣiṇam athācaret* |
> *muktibhāgī bhavel loko mucyate vyādhibandhanāt* |79|[159]

The influence which the purpose of a particular text has on the way in which it describes Vṛndāvana may be seen from the fact that the twelve woods are not mentioned once in the poetry of Sūradāsa, Dhruvadāsa, Bihārinadāsa or Nandadāsa. All of these are concerned with the symbolic and mythological aspects of Vṛndāvana, not its role as a pilgrimage centre. Nārāyaṇa Bhaṭṭa, however, wishes to place Vṛndāvana in the contest of pilgrimage, therefore he uses the structure of other pilgrimages texts.

From the above discussion it is clear that not only are there three main divisions in ways of describing Vṛndāvana, i.e., the mythological, symbolic and geographical, but that these three overlap at times depending on the nature of the text. The divisions and sub-divisions can be analyzed as follows :

1. Mythological. Texts of this category include the *Hariv.*, *ViP.*, *BhP.*, and the *Sūrasāgara.*

2. Symbolic

   (a) Purely symbolic—such descriptions can be found in the *Brahma-saṃhitā* and the works of Harivyāsadeva and Gadādhara Bhaṭṭa, which portray Vṛndāvana as an object of meditation using *yāntric* images.

   (b) Combining symbolic and mythological. Descriptions of this sort can be found in the *Laghubhāgavatāmṛta* where the symbolic is equated with unmanifest *līlā* and the mythological with manifest *līlā*. Nandadāsa similarly combines the two in his *Rāsapañcādhyāyī.*

   (c) Symbolic incorporating the geographical. The *Padma Purāṇa* and the *Rasakadaṃbacūḍāmaṇi* are mainly concerned with describing Vṛndāvana in symbolic terms. Within this symbolic picture, however, they incorporate the geographical tradition.

   (d) Symbolic unconnected with ritual meditation. This can be found in the poetry of Bihārinadāsa and Dhruvadāsa where the symbolic plan is retained but the concern is with *rasa* rather than ritual meditation, so that the description is far less stylized.

3. Geographical. This resembles the mythological in that Vṛndāvana is portrayed as a place near Mathurā, but differs in the absence of any reference to a Braj or Gokula (except in type (c) below) and in its enumeration of twelve woods. A few of the *vanas,* such as Vṛndāvana itself, Tālavana and Bhāṇḍīraka are mentioned in the mythological texts but the rest are absent.

   (a) Purely geographical – as the Jain *Vividhatirthakalpa.*

   (b) Geographical incorporating symbolic, such as the *Varāha Purāṇa.*

   (c) Texts using the ancient geographical descriptions and incorporating into them many new places identifiable with present-day sites. The *Brajabhaktivilāsa* of Nārāyaṇa Bhaṭṭa is an example of this type of work.

References

1. Cf. A.A. Macdonell, *Vedic Index*, Vol. II, London, 1912, p. 340, and K.F. Geldner, *Vedische Studien*, Vol. 2, Stuttgart, 1897, p.282.
2. Cf. O. Böhtlingk, *Sanskrit Wörterbuch*, Vol. III, St. Petersburg, 1858, p. 794. (*Mbh.* 3.17179).
3. *Harivaṃśa,* P.L. Vaidya ed., Poona, 1969, 53.3. 'Before a dreadful massacre by the wolves, our entire encampment should move away.'
4. *Ibid.*, 53.7. 'Having perceived their decision to go to Vṛndāvana for the sake of the establishment of the encampment and for the well-being of the cows.'
5. *Ibid.*, 53.30. 'That place of the encampment, surrounded by the woods, looked even more beautiful.'
6. *ViP., op. cit.*, V.6.24. .'Therefore we should go from here to Vṛndāvana without delay, before a terrestrial disaster befalls the encampment.'
7. *Ibid.*, V.6.30. 'Then the whole settlement encamped in Vṛndāvana.'
8. *BhP., op. cit.*, X.11.20. 'The elder cowherds, such as Nanda, experiencing disasters in the great forest, gathered together and discussed what was to be done about the settlement.'
9. *Ibid.*, X.11.22. 'We who desire the well-being of the *gokula* should depart from here.'
10. *Ibid.*, X.11.22. 'There with the carts they established an encampment in the shape of a semi-circle.'
11. *Hariv., Op. cit.*, 52.17-18. 'The cows desire to eat grass which has not been made use of. Therefore rich encampments should move to a wood with fresh grass. Neither those surrounded by closed doors, nor those possessing house and fields are as famed in the world as the *vrajas* which move from one place to another.'
12. *BhP. op. cit.*, X.11.29. 'Each one having made ready his own *vraja*, they set off, their goods being carried.'
13. *Ibid.*, X.6.2. .'(Pūtanā) wandered in towns, villages and encampments, slaying children.'
14. *Hariv., op. cit.*, 50.1. 'Performing the duties of a cowherd in the cow-encampment of Nanda. . .'
15. *ViP., op. cit.*, V. 11.22. 'For seven nights the great clouds rained down upon the *gokula* of Nanda.'
16. *BhP., op. cit.*, X. 'From that time the encampment of Nanda, endowed with all wealth, became the place of Ramā's sport, through virtue of being the dwelling-place of Hari.'
17. Ch. Vaudeville, 'Braj, lost and found', *Indo-Iranian Journal*, 18 (1976), p.198.
18. *Hariv., op. cit.*, 65.30

    kadācit tu tadā kṛṣṇo vinā saṃkarṣaṇam gurum |
    cacāra tadvanavaraṃ kāmarūpī varānanaḥ |

    'Then once the handsome Kṛṣṇa, capable of assuming any form, wandered to that most excellent forest without the elder Sankarṣaṇa.'
19. *Ibid.*, 56.14. 'In the meantime all the cowherd boys, frightened, went weeping to the settlement, their speech indistinct with tears.'
20. *Ibid.*, 65.30. 'Keeping the *gokula* dry he held the mountain Govardhana.'
21. *ViP., op. cit.*, V. 5.7. 'When those two were living in the *gokula,* Pūtanā, the murderess of children. . .'
22. *Ibid.*, V.6.49-50. 'Those two, with happy hearts, wandered, playing in the forest. Then in the

evening, those two of mighty strength returned to the settlement with the cows, surrounded by groups of cowherd boys, having disported themselves as was fit.'

23. *BhP., op. cit.*, X.29.19. 'Return to the settlement. Women should not remain here, O beautiful ladies.'
24. *Ibid.*, X.29.21. '(You) have seen the forest in flower, moonlit, adorned with tree-twigs agitated by the sports of the Yamunā river breeze.'
25. *Ibid.*, X.29.22. 'Then return without delay to the settlement and serve your husbands, O pure women.'
26. Sūradāsa, *op. cit.*, *pada* 1090. 'Let us go to Braj; evening has come now. Take all the cows, herding them in front. Let it not fall (while we are in) the forest.'
27. *Ibid.*, *pada* 1097. 'In the evening the cowherd boy, looking beautiful, comes with the cows from the wood to Braj.'
28. *Ibid.*, *pada* 644. 'There was great joy in every home and dance in various places. Bringing gifts to the door of Nanda, the whole of Gokula village overflowed (with joy).'
29. *Ibid.*, *pada* 1621. *calī bana benu sunata jaba dhāi/*
'When they went running to the forest on hearing the flute. . . '
30. *Ibid.*, *pada* 1629. 'Why have you come running to the forest at night?'
31. *Ibid.*, *pada* 1629. 'Laughingly Śyāma says, "Or have you forgotten the way to Braj? You went to sell curds in Mathurā and there became late." '
32. *Ibid.*, *pada* 1301. 'With his words he brought Rādhā. "Come, let us go to the forest of Vṛndā", says Śyāma, with full intent.'
33. *Ibid.*, *pada* 1304. 'Youthful Gopāla and youthful Rādhā, imbued with the fresh essence of love, both disport themselves in the forest, each one full of love.'
34. *Ibid.*, *pada* 1340. *yaha vṛsabhānupurā ye braja maiṃ kahāṃ duhāvana āī* || '
Why has this girl from the city of Vṛṣabhānu come milking in Braj.'
35. *Ibid.*, *pada* 1020. 'This thought entered the minds of (his) mother and father, "Everyday there are disasters in Gokula. We should go and settle in Mathurā." '
36. *Ibid.*, *pada* 648. 'The men of Gokula city were absorbed in joy.'
37. *Ibid.*, *pada* 1145. 'Śyāma reached the city of Braj; Mohana and Bala went home.'
38. Rūpa Gosvāmī, *Laghubhāgavatāmṛta*, op. cit., p. 249, v. 175. 'His (Kṛṣṇa's) abode was said to be divided into two — Māthura and Dvāravatī; and Māthura was said to be twofold — as Gokula and the city.'
39. *Ibid.*, p. 230, v. 158. 'There, in the manifest sport, Kṛṣṇa goes to and fro between Gokula, Mathurā and Dvāravatī.'
40. *Ibid.*, p. 240, v. 167. 'In Braj there is separation from him for three months in the manifest *līlā*.'
41. *Ibid.*, p. 246, v. 172. 'With his dearest, most beloved inhabitants of Gokula, Hari always disports himself in the forest of Vṛndā.'
42. *Ibid.*, p. 254, v. 181. 'Thus in the triple abodes Hari ever disports himself; still in Gokula his sweetness is greatest.'
43. *Ibid.*, p. 256, v. 183. 'His fourfold sweetness only appears in Braj, (that is) majesty, sport, the flute and a beautiful form.'
44. Nandadāsa, *Bhramaragīta, op. cit.*, v. 55. 'Forgetting Madhubana you have come to Gokula. Here

dwell only those with love, not your customers.'

45. *Ibid.*, v. 72. '(Uddhava) said again and again to Śyāma, "Go and stay in Vṛndāvana, where you will have the company of the *gopīs* who are formed of supreme love." '

46. Nandadāsa, *Virahamañjarī*, in *Nandadāsagranthāvalī, op. cit.*, v. 6. 'He always dwells in the abode of Vṛndāvana.'

47. Nandadāsa, *Bhramaragīta, op. cit.*, v. 75. 'Banavārī showd himself and the *gopīs* to be one. Having cast a deluding net over the tear-filled eyes of Uddhava, he again caused his sportive form to disappear.'

48. Nandadāsa, *Rāsap., op. cit.*, I.31. 'There is a bejewelled dais, made of variegated shell, extremely beautiful. Upon that is a sixteen-petalled lotus, astonishing, circular in shape.'

49. *Ibid.*, I.32. 'In the centre is a lovely pericarp, the beautiful source of all happiness; there is enthroned the Lord of Braj, the best of youths, the foremost of *rasikas*.'

50. *Ibid.*, V.4. 'The extraordinary *rāsa* started on that lotus circle.'

51. *Hariv., op. cit.*, 63.45. 'Thus that joyful Kṛṣṇa adorned by circles of *gopīs*, rejoiced in the moonlit, autumn night.'

52. *ViP. op. cit.*, V.13.50. 'Having taken by the hand the *gopīs*, one by one, whose eyes closed at the touch of his hand, Hari formed the *rāsa* circle.'

53. *BhP., op. cit.*, X.33.3. 'The *rāsa* festival, formed by circles, of *gopīs*, was initiated by Kṛṣṇa, the lord of *yoga*, (who was) between every two of them.'

54. Sūradāsa, *op. cit., pada* 1752. 'Nandakumāra formed the *rāsa*, twelve *kośa* in perimeter.'

55. *Brahma-saṃhitā*, commentary by Jīva Gosvāmī, ed. by A. Avalon, Calcutta, 1928, v.2. 'The thousand-petalled lotus called Gokula, the great abode.'

56. *Lakṣmī-tantra*, ed. V. Krishnamacharya, Adyar, 1959. 36.10-12. 'Then one should meditate on the lotus which arises from the interior of the ocean of milk. . ., thousand-petalled surrounded by a thousand rays, like the sun. In the back of that should be placed the seat.'

57. *Ṣaṭcakranirūpaṇam*, ed. by A. Avalon, Calcutta, 1913, v. 40. 'Below the *visarga* is the thousand-petalled lotus, radiant as the full moon.'

58. *BrSaṃ., op. cit.*, v. 2. 'The pericarp of that (is) his (Kṛṣṇa's) abode, (and has) arisen from his infinite portions.'

59. *Mahānirvāṇa-tantra*, ed. by Arthur Avalon, Madras, 1927, 5.179. 'Having established the deities of the seats in accordance with the rites for the placing of seats, and having worshipped (them), one should worship the original deity in the centre of the pericarp.

60. *BrSaṃ., op. cit.*, v. 'The pericarp (is) a great *yantra*, a hexagon, with a diamond wedge.'

61. *MahāT., op. cit.*,

    athātmayantrayor madhye māyāgarbham trikoṇakam |
    vṛttaṃ ṣaṭkoṇam ālikhya caturasram likhed vahiḥ |

    'Then having inscribed the triangular *māyā*-interiror, a circle and a hexagon between oneself and the *yantra*, a quadrangle should be drawn outside.'

62. *BrSaṃ., op. cit.*, v. 6. 'Around it is the marvellous quadrangle called Śvetadvīpa. The four corners are the four abodes — the four forms, fourfold.'

63. *Ibid.*, v. 5. 'Its filament belongs to his portions and its petals to the *śrīs*.'

64. *Tantrarāja-tantra*, ed. by A. Avalon, London, 1918, 4.77

aṣṭasv api ca patreṣu tṛtīyāvaraṇe sthitāḥ |
'And remaining on the eight petals in the third enclosure. . . '

65. Cf. *Yoginīhṛdayadīpikā*, Benaras, 1923, commentary Amṛtananda Nātha, v. 41, p. 36.
etāś catasraḥ śaktayas tu kā pū jā o iti kramāt |
'These four *śaktis*, *Kā Pū*, *Jā*, and *O*, in this order.' According to the commentary *kā* stands for Kāmarūpa, *pū* for Pūrṇagiri, *jā* for Jālandhara and *o* for Oḍyāṇa.

66. *Gadādhara Bhaṭṭaji kī vāṇī*, Vṛndāvana, 1958, v. 17-18. 'In that is a lotus seat, liking for which arises in the heart of one who is very fortunate. Between its variegated thousand petals are filaments, and on their tips pearls gleam like rubies.'

67. *Ibid.*, v. 19. 'The golden pericarp, a wedge of diamond, looks beautiful.'

68. M. Monier-Williams, *op. cit.*, p. 285, col. 2.

69. *Gadādhara*, *op. cit.*, v. 19. 'Who can describe the glory of the ten-syllabled *mantra*.'

70. *Padma Purāṇa*, ed. by V.N. Maṇḍalika, Poona 1894. 'Know my Mathurā to be eternal and also the wood Vṛndāvana, with the Yamunā, the *gopīs*, and the cowherd boys. My incarnation is eternal; have no doubt about this. My beloved is always Rādhā, I am omniscient and supreme.'

71. *Ibid.*, 4.69.16. 'Bhadra, Śrī, Loha, Bhāṇḍīra, Mahā, Tāla, Khadīraka, Bakula, Kumuda, Kāmya, Madhu, and Vṛndāvana.'

72. *Ibid.*, 4.69.14. 'Māthuramaṇḍala, having the shape of a thousand-petalled lotus, measured by the discus of Viṣṇu, is the extraordinary Vaiṣṇava abode.'

73. Cf. Arthur Avalon's description in the introduction to *TantraT*. *op. cit.*, p. 6-7, and also *Yoginīhṛdaya*, *op. cit.*, v. 8.

74. *PadP.*, *op. cit.*, 4.69.44. 'The seventh lovely petal is famed as the Bakula forest; the eighth is the Tālavana where the destruction of Dhenu (took place) according to tradition.'

75. *Ibid.*, 4.69.70.' *Vṛndāvana is the pericarp of the thousand-petalled lotus*.'

76. *Ibid.*, 4.69.81. 'In the midst of that lovely palace is a radiant *yogapīṭha*. That eight-cornered construction shines with manifold brilliance.'

77. *Ibid.*, 4.69.82. 'Upon that is a splendid throne formed of gems and jewels.'

78. *Ibid.*, 4.69.82. 'Within that is an eight-petalled lotus having a pericarp which is the resting place of happiness. That is the supreme place of Govinda; what can be said of its glory.'

79. *Ibid.*, 4.70.3-4. 'Outside in the *yogapīṭha* which surrounds the golden throne, are the foremost beloveds of Kṛṣṇa, their every limb possessed with ardour.'

80. *Ibid.*, 4.70.20-21. 'Śrīdāmā at the western door, and Vasudāmā at the northern, Sudāmā at the eastern, and Kiṅkiṇī at the southern.'

81. Cf. *BhP.*, *op. cit.*, 10.15.20; Sūradāsa, *op. cit.*, *pada* 1028.

82. *PadP.*, *op. cit.*, 4.70.19. *samānaveṣavayasaḥ samānabalapauruṣāḥ* |
'Identical in dress and age, identical in strength and valour.'

83. Cf. M. Monier-Williams, *op. cit.*, Kinkiṇī p. 282, col. 1, and Vasudāmā, p. 931, col. 1.

84. *PadP.*, *op. cit.*, 4.70.22-25.
svarṇavedyantarasthe tu svarṇābharaṇabhūsite |
stokakṛṣṇāṃśubhadrādyair gopālair ayutāyutaiḥ |22| . . .
kṣaratpayobhir govṛndair asaṃkhyātair upāvṛtam |

'On the (*pīṭha*) in the interior of the golden altar, adorned with decorations, gather round myriads of cowherd boys, such as Stokakṛṣṇa, Aṃśu and Bhadra . . . and innumerable herds of cows, their udders dripping with milk.'

85. *Ibid.*, 4.70.26-46.

86. *Ibid.*, 4.70.59-64.

87. The text is an unpublished manuscript in the collection of a Rādhāvallabha Gosvāmī, called Choṭe Sarkār in Vṛndāvana. The colophon runs:

    likhitaṃ rasakadaṃbacūḍāmaṇi graṃtha||
    saṃvatu satraha sai varaṣa eka adhika paṃcāsa||
    agahana vadi ṣaṣṭīi sutitha dina dina mani suprakāsa||

    'The book *Rasakadaṃbacūḍāmaṇi* has been written. In the year *Saṃ*. 1751, on the auspicious date of the sixth day of the dark half of the month of Agahana, it became manifest.'

88. *Rasakadaṃba., op. cit.*, 2.7. 'It is described in the *Purāṇa* how the beautiful lotus with a thousand petals adorns the Sudarśana discus, there is no doubt about this.'

89. *Ibid.*, 13. 2-3.

    prathama bhadravana velavana puni sulohavana ehu||
    aru bhāṃḍīrabanahi nirakhi mahāvana lehu|2|
    itahi tālavana khidravana bahulāvana abhirāma||
    karahu kumudavana kāmavana madhuvana kauṃ paranāma|3|

    'First Bhadravana, then Velavana and beautiful Lohavana; and having seen Bhāṃḍiravana you reach Mahāvana. Here itself is Tālavana, Khidravana and beautiful Bahulavana. I bow to Kumudavana, Kāmavana and Madhuvana.'

90. *PadP.*, 4.69.18. 'And another minor grove was described, a place having the essence of Kṛṣṇa's sport.'

91. *Rasakadaṃba., op. cit.*, 13.7. 'Know in your heart the first to be Kṛṣṇa and the second as Krīḍāvana. The secret place is the third. Listen to the rest attentively.'

92. *Ibid.*, 2.3. 'In the first and second enclosures, the only quality is majesty.'

93. *Ibid.*, 3.5. 'I will describe those who are entitled to that place; those who, showing a unique method, practise devotion combined with performance of rites, with body, mind and consciousness.'

94. *Ibid.*, 4.8. 'Those who become suppliant, performing devotion combined with knowledge, they reach here on an auspicious day.'

95. *Ibid.*, 18.21. 'At the four doors are the doorkeepers with their *śaktis;* there all four are said to be four-armed, devoted to the great glory.'

96. *Ibid.*, 2.3.

    prathama dutiya meṃ kahyau vara ati īśvarja apāra|
    aba īśvarja mādhurja kī tṛtīyeṃ saṃdhi vicāra||

    'In the first and second has been said to be the best supreme majesty. Now consider the third — the meeting of majesty and sweetness.'

97. *Ibid.*, 2.4. 'Listen with consideration (to the description) of the fourth to the sixth enclosures. This is the enclosure of Braj, where there is always the milk of unlimited sweetness.'

98. *Ibid.*, 11.28, and 21.52-53.

99. *Ibid.*, 12.6.
100. *Ibid.*, 2.5.
    saptama jo āvarana hai tahāṃ sunau cita lāi |
    suṭhi suṭhoṃna mādhurja vara prema sahita lasāi |5|
    'In the seventh covering, listen with attention, which is very beautiful, shines the best sweetness with love.'
101. *Ibid.*, 18.36.
102. *Ibid.*, 18.45-46.
103. *Ibid.*, 18.54. 'Know this eighth petal to be distinct from Vṛndāvana. Understand consideration, realize that it is the conjunction of both Vṛndāvana and Braj.'
104. *Ibid.*, 2.6. 'Beyond that is the pericarp (where there is) the sportive expression of their own love.'
105. *Ibid.*, II.5.1-20 and II. 7.
106. *Ibid.*, 6.4.
107. *Ibid.*, 4.8.
108. *Ibid.*, 21.46.
109. *Ibid.*, 9.5.
110. *Ibid.*, 16.15.
111. *Ibid.*, II.1.27. 'In that are enthroned the most beautiful, shining youthful couple.'
112. Harivyāsadeva, *op. cit.*, *pada* 3, v.9. 'The river pours forth, bracelet-shaped. It flows with the essence of love.'
113. *Ibid.*, *pada* 3, v. 17. 'Such is their own abode in the midst of which is the eternal ground which sways with joy, shaped as a lotus of innumerable petals.'
114. *Ibid.*, *pada* 3, v. 18. 'In the midst is a lovely row of eight petals.'
115. *Ibid.*, *pada* 3, v. 18. 'Upon them flourish the bowers of the dear *sakhīs*.'
116. M. Eliade, *Yoga, immortality and freedom*, New York, 1958, pp. 220-21.
117. Harivyāsadeva, *op. cit.*, *pada* 3, v. 23. 'In the centre of the four lakes stands the eight-doored palace which enchants beauty itself.'
118. *Rasakadaṃba.*, *op. cit.*, I.18.9.
    ihi saptama āvarana kī dutiya taraṃga ke māṃjha |
    cāri sarovara aṣṭadala sumira udai dina sāṃjha ||
    'Here in the second part of the seventh enclosure are four lakes and an eight-petalled (lotus). Remember their appearance day and night.'
119. *PadP.*, *op. cit.*, 4.74.57. 'The place in the centre stalk of the thousand-petalled lotus, having four lakes and four doors, is exceedingly astonishing.'
120. Harivyāsadeva, *op. cit.*, *pada* 3, v. 28. 'In the middle of the four-sided courtyard of that palace is a circular platform of gems, formed of *rasa*.'
121. *Ibid.*, *pada* 3, vv. 34-35. 'In the midst of the palace's enchanting courtyard is an entrancing dais. Upon that is an octagonal, pleasant and pleasing. At each corner is a beloved with all her group of women.'
122. Dhruvadāsa, *Bṛhadbāvanapurāṇa*, *op. cit.*, v. 32. 'Know the circular area of Mathurā to be superior

to Vaikuṇṭha; in that and superior to that (area of Mathurā) is the circular area of Braj, a mine of happiness.'

123. *Ibid.*, v. 34. 'Vṛndāvana, the source of love, adorns the middle like a jewel in a crown.'

124. Dhruvadāsa, *Rasa muktāvalī līlā,* in *Bayālīsa līlā, op. cit.*, vv. 15-17. 'The bejewelled circular platform looks very splendid; seeing it thousands of suns and moons are put to shame. Upon it is a lotus, a lovely fragrant place, having sixteen petals on all sides. The middle is graced with the youth (Kṛṣṇa) and the young girl (Rādhā), while on each petal a *sakhī* gazes on their beauty.'

125. Dhruvadāsa, *Premāvalī līlā* in *Bayālīsa līlā, op. cit.*, v. 55. 'The Yamunā flows on all sides with an unfathomable beauty. It is as if liquid love were overflowing, its stream taking the shape of an ear-ring.'

126. *Ibid.*, v. 56. 'Another simile, astonishingly beautiful, enters the heart — it is as if Vṛndāvana had worn a necklace of blue gems.'

127. Bihārinadāsa, *op. cit.*, v. 662, p. 244. 'Hear of the coverings of that Braj — the *gopīs*, the cows and the cowherd boys.'

128. Malik Muhammad Jāyasī, *Padamāvata,* ed. V.S. Agravāla, Cirgāṃva, 1961, p. 335, v. 291.1.

    sāta khaṃḍa ūpara kabilāsū |

    taha sovanāri seja sukhavāsū |1|.

    'Above the seven sections is (the top-most part called Kailāsa. There is the bedroom, (in which) is the bed, the most pleasant place.'

129. Bihārinadāsa, *op. cit.*, p. 293, v. 30, line 1. 'In the world there are many proud devotees and many who follow the path of knowledge; (these are) Khāns and Sultāns who guard the border.'

130. *Ibid.*, p. 293, line 2. 'The dwellers in Braj (who are) closer (to the palace), have the special duty of attendants, (and are like) many chieftains famed for their brave character in the army.'

131. *Ibid.*, p. 293, line 4. 'Others are stopped outside, wandering around the doorway like doorkeepers. Only the inmates know the nature of the palace.'

132. See introduction by Jina Vijaya to Jinaprabhasūri's *Vividhatīrthakalpa,* Śāntiniketana, 1934, pp. 2-3.

133. *Ibid., Mathurāpurīkalpaḥ,* p. 18, line 28. 'In this city is the birth of the future Tīrthaṅkara, Kānha Vāsudeva.'

134. *Ibid.*, p. 18, lines 30-32. 'The twelve woods — they were said to be: Lohajaṃghavana, Madhuvana, Bilvana, Tālavana, Kumudavana, Kāmyavana, Kolavana, Bahulavana, and Mahāvana.'

135. *Ibid.*, p. 17, line 4. 'That Mathurā is twelve *yojanas* long and nine *yojanas* wide.'

136. *Varāha Purāṇa*, ed. Hṛṣīkeśa Śāstrī, Calcutta, 1893, 152.7. 'Describe that beneficial pilgrimage place which is best among pilgrimage places.'

137. *Ibid.*, 152.8. 'Neither in the nether regions, nor in the heavens, nor in the human regions is to be found anything as dear to me as Mathurā which is no earth.'

138. *Ibid.*, 153.45. 'Vṛndāvana is the twelfth, guarded by Vṛndā, my favourite, destroyer of great sins.'

139. *Ibid.*, 163.14. 'My Māthura region is of twenty *yojanas,* and this lotus bestows salvation upon all, O most fortunate one.'

140. *Ibid.*, 163.16. 'In the pericarp is situated Keśava, the destroyer of Keśa, O goddess.'

141. *Ibid.*, 163.18. 'To the west that Lord Hari, inhabitant of Govardhana . . . '
142. *Ibid.*, 163.19. 'To the north having seen Govinda, the Lord, supreme and brilliant . . . '
143. *Ibid.*, 163.20. 'The Lord remaining on the eastern petal called Viśrānti.'
144. *Ibid.*, 163.21. 'To the south know me (to be as) an image of divine form.'
145. *Ibid.*, 164.1.

    asti govardhanaṃ nāma kṣetraṃ paramadurllabham |
    mathurāpaścime bhāge adūrād yojanadvayam |1|

    'There is an area called Govardhana, very inaccessible, in a region to the west of Mathurā, not very far, only two *yojanas*.'
146. P.V. Kane, *History of Dharmaśāstra*, Poona, 1975, Vol. I, part 2, p. 699.
147. *Ibid.*, p. 953.
148. Lakṣmīdhara Bhaṭṭa, *Kṛtyakalpataru*, ed. R.V. Rangasvāmī Aiyangar, Baroda, 1942, Vol. VIII *Tīrthavivecanakāṇḍam*, chapter 9, *Mathurā-māhātmyam*, p. 193, line 7. 'In my region of Mathurā which is twenty *yojanas* in area . . . ' Cf, *VārP.*, *op. cit.*, 158.1.
149. Mitramiśra, *Vīramitrodaya*, Benares, 1971, Vol. X, *Tīrthaprakāśa*, pp. 502-28.
150. Nārāyaṇa Bhaṭṭa, *Brajabhaktivilāsa*, Kusamasarovara, 1951, I.10. 'Performing the circumambulation of this (area) which covers 84 *krośa*, one acheives the happiness of wealth and prosperity.'
151. *Ibid.*, I.92. 'Now the area of Braj, which with the wood has a boundary of 84 *krośa*, (has) the form of a part of the Lord.'
152. *Ibid.*, I.30. 'The seventh is the place Gokula, the eighth is that of Baladeva.'
153. *Ibid.*, III.73.
154. *Ibid.*, III.74.
155. *Ibid.*, III.86.
156. *Ibid.*, I.32. 'Vṛndāvana, the eleventh, is famed as the foremost and the best.'
157. *Ibid.*, I.13.
158. *Ibid.*, X.151.
159. *Ibid.*, X.79. 'Then one should perform the circumambulation which is five *krośa* in extent. People attain salvation and are freed from the bondages of suffering.'

5

The Role of Vṛndāvana in Devotional Practice and Experience

A COROLLARY to the role of Vṛndāvana in divine self-expression, discussed in chapter 3, is the part it plays in devotional experience. Since Vṛndāvana is the divine space within which the divinity reveals itself, it is this divine space itself which makes possible to the human soul participation in the divinity.

The question of the relation between the devotee and Vṛndāvana is interlinked with the understanding of Vṛndāvana as a terrestrial or extraterrestrial place. An injunction to live in Vṛndāvana immediately raises the problem as to whether a physical act or a spiritual state is involved. Insofar as residence in Vṛndāvana is a physical act, Vṛndāvana must be regarded as a place on earth. If on the other hand, it is a spiritual state, Vṛndāvana itself must be a supramundane realm.

The importance of dwelling in Vṛndāvana is not equally stressed in all the texts under consideration. An examination of these texts suggests a correlation between what has been termed the symbolic approach and the preoccupation with living in Vṛndāvana, while texts taking the mythological approach show no such emphasis.

An apparent contradiction lies in the fact that the very texts which portray Vṛndāvana the most unequivocally as a transcendent realm, are at the same time the texts which place most emphasis on dwelling in the geographical Vṛndāvana. The resolution of this problem would seem to lie in an understanding of the nature of the physical Vṛndāvana as a symbol.

It has been pointed out in chapter 4 that certain *yāntric* images are used in the symbolic representation of Vṛndāvana. This suggests that the nature of the relationship between the divine and the geographical Vṛndāvana can be compared with that between the *yantra* and the divinity which it symbolizes. That is to say, just as the *yantra* is not regarded as merely a representation of the divinity but as partaking of the divine nature itself, so too there is identity between the physical and the divine Vṛndāvana.

A parallel to this identification of divine and earthly space may also be seen in the

Vallabha notion of Kṛṣṇa's images being *svarūpas*, i.e., manifestations, instead of *mūrtis* or representations. This distinction expresses itself not only in the fact that worship of the image is regarded as *sevā* and not *pūjā*, but also in the explanation of its origin. The *svarūpa* is not constructed by human hands out of mundane material into which the divine is then invoked, but manifests itself.[1]

The Mythological Tradition

The identity between terrestrial and celestial is in a sense inherent in the concept of Vṛndāvana from the beginning and is not entirely absent even from texts which place Vṛndāvana in a mythological context. It can be seen, for example, in the constant ambiguity maintained in the imagery describing Vṛndāvana in the *ViP*. and the *Hariv*. (see chapter 2), allowing for a supramundane as well as a mundane interpretation. The fact that it is envisaged in the mythological past conceals the full symbolic implications as well as distancing it from devotional practice.

No injunction to devotees physically to dwell in Vṛndāvana as part of their spiritual practice is attested in the *ViP*., *Hariv*., or even the *BhP*. In the *BhP*. there is a passage where Uddhava expresses the desire to be made a tree or plant of Vṛndāvana:

> *āsām aho caraṇareṇujuṣām ahaṃ syām*
> *vṛndāvane kim api gulmalatauṣadhīnām* |
> *yā dustyajam svajanam āryapathaṃ ca hitvā*
> *bhejur mukundapadavīṃ śrutibhir vimṛgyām* |61|[2]

This particular verse is referred to in later texts as an example of praise of Vṛndāvana. Prabodhānanda, for example, in his *Vṛndāvanamahimāmṛta* asks to be born again and again in Vṛndāvana even as grass or shrub:

> *janmani janmani vṛndāvanabhuvi vṛndārakendra-vandyāyām* |
> *api tṛṇagulmakabhāve bhavatu mamāśāsamullāsa* |9|[3]

It is evident that the inspiration for this verse lies in the *BhP*. passage. The *api tṛṇagulmakabhāve* here echoes the *kim api gulmalatauṣadhīnām* of the *BhP*. The connection between the two is made explicit in the next verse of the *Vṛndāvanamahimāmṛta*. Where Prabodhānanda specifically refers to Uddhava, saying that he himself makes salutation to that forest of Rādhā where Uddhava, though fulfilled through the experience of the *rasa* of massaging Hari, desires to become grass:

> *haripadapaṅkajasaṃvāhanarasam anubhūya pūrṇo 'pi* |
> *yatroddhava āśāste tṛṇatāṃ tan naumi rādhikāvipinam* |10|[4]

Prabodhānanda thus sees in the utterance of Uddhava in the *BhP.* an affirmation of the greatness of Vṛndāvana, similar in nature to that expressed by Prabodhānanda himself.

Viewed in its context, however, the *BhP.* verse can be seen as an affirmation of the greatness of the devotion typified by the *gopīs,* rather than an injunction to live in Vṛndāvana. The aim of Uddhava in becoming a plant of Vṛndāvana is to receive the dust of the *gopīs'* feet. The emphasis of the passage is on the apparent lowliness of the *gopīs* which nevertheless enables them to have an experience of the divine which is impossible even for Lakṣmī. Once again, therefore, immanence is being contrasted with transcendence, and incarnation is shown to be an expression of divine grace (*anugraha*) with Vṛndāvana as the scene for this expression in the mythological past.

The *BhP.* does not include any mention of living in Vṛndāvana in its discussions of religious practice. Such spiritual practices as are mentioned consist, on a mental level, of the remembrance of the activities of Kṛṣṇa and, on a physical level, of image worship. The most well-known account of devotional practice in the *BhP.* is the 'nine-fold' path (*navadhā bhakti*) expounded by Prahlāda:

> *śravaṇaṃ kīrtanaṃ viṣṇoḥ smaraṇaṃ pādasevanam* |
> *arcanaṃ vandanaṃ dāsyaṃ sakhyam ātmanivedanam* |23|[5]

Of these nine, the first three are forms of meditation of the activities of Kṛṣṇa — hearing them, reciting them and mentally remembering them. The next three have connotations of worship — serving the feet, worshipping and making obeisance. Reference may be made here either to mental or to image worship. The final three suggest entering into a relationship with the divine (*bhāva*) — the result of the two first stages.

The way in which the *gopīs* are portrayed as remembering the *līlās* of Kṛṣṇa and imitating them after his disappearance during the *rāsa* would seem to exemplify the path of devotion as envisaged by *BhP.* The *gopīs* whose hearts are disturbed by the enchanting smiles, glances and playful activities of Kṛṣṇa are said to have assumed identity with him (*tadātmikā*) performing those same activities:

> *gatyanurāgasmitavibhramekṣitair manoramālāpavihāravibhramaiḥ* |
> *ākṣiptacittāḥ pramadā ramāpates tās ta vicestā jagṛhus tadātmikāḥ* |[6]

Here, as well, the *BhP.* sees remembrance of the divine sport of Kṛṣṇa as leading to union with him.

The *Sūrasāgara* resembles the *BhP.* insofar as residence in Vṛndāvana is not depicted as an integral part of devotional practice. There are indications that the few *padas* which do explicitly advocate residence in Vṛndāvana belong to a very late stratum of the *Sūrasāgara.*

In *pada* 1792, for example, the poet says that through the grace of Rādhā he will obtain residence in Braj:

śrī rādhikā syāma kī pyārī kṛpā bāsa braja pāuṃ ||[7]

An even more specific reference to physically living in the place is made in a further line where he speaks of building a hut near the forest abode of Rādhā and Kṛṣṇa:

nava nikuṃja bana dhāma nikaṭa ika ānandakuṭī racāūṃ |[8]

According to Hawley, in his article on the *Sūrasāgara,* this *pada* is found only in later manuscripts.[9] Other features suggesting that it belongs to a tradition different from the majority of *padas* in the *Sūrasāgara,* and possibly closer to that of the Rādhāvallabha texts can be seen in the emphasis on the grace of Rādhā. The *pada* also refers to the grace of *guru* through which the poet says he will make known the glory of *bhajana*:

bhajana pratāpa carana mahimā taiṃ guru kī kṛpā dikhāūṃ |[10]

Such references are uncommon in the *Sūrasāgara* and suggest sectarian affiliations.

Another *pada* which appears to advocate physical residence in Vṛndāvana is *pada* 1108. It opens by using the imperative with regard to living in Braj:

aisaiṃ basie braj kī bīthini |[11]

It goes on to describe the physical means of livelihood — how, for example, one should subsist on grains of rice taken from the leaf-plates of the cowherds:

gvāranai ke panavāre cuni cuni udara bharījai sīthini |[12]

It describes how one should roll in the ground of every bower and cover one's body with the dust of Braj:

kuṃja kuṃja prati loṭi loṭi braja raja lāgai raṃga rītani |[13]

All of these images suggest an acceptance of the importance of physically living in Braj.

That this *pada* is also a later addition, probably originating from a Rādhāvallabha source, is suggested by the fact that an almost identical *pada* is found in a collection attributed to the Rādhāvallaba author, Harirāmavyāsa. It is, of course, not possible to come to a firm conclusion as to the source of the *pada* without more information about the results of Hawley's investigations into the *Sūrasāgara* as well as a critical study of the Harirāmavyāsa *padas.* Nevertheless, Hawley's conclusion based on his findings regarding *padas* common to the *Sūrasāgara* as well as Hita Harivaṃśa and Paramānandadāsa that '. . . poems whose authorship was attributed to Sūr and another poet turn out to have been drawn into the Sūr corpus from elsewhere rather than dissipated from the *Sūrasāgara* into other collections.' would suggest the probability that this is a further example of a *pada* originating outside the *Sūrasāgara.*

It is interesting to notice the way in which the differences in wording between the Sūradāsa *pada* and the Harirāmavyāsa *pada* would seem to reflect differences in outlook. Whereas, for example, Sūradāsa speaks of eating from the plates of cowherds, Harirāma describes the plates as belonging to *sādhus*:

> *sādhuna ke panavāre cuna cuna udara poṣiyata sīthini* |[14]

The difference is significant, since by speaking of *sādhus* Harirāma places the actions much more clearly in the present-day Vṛndāvana. Sūradāsa, on the other hand, is speaking in terms of the mythological Braj inhabited by the cowherd companions of Kṛṣṇa.

The divergence of the *Sūrasāgara* from the Rādhāvallabha images of the Harirāma *pada* can also be seen in the way that Sūradāsa speaks of seeing the darling of Nanda everyday:

> *nisidina nirakhi jasodānandana aru jamunā jala pītani* |[5]

Harirāma, on the other hand, speaks of Rādhā and Kṛṣna:

> *nita prati darasa syāma syāmā kau. . .* |[16]

This reflects the Rādhāvallabha concentration on the sport of Rādhā and Kṛṣṇa to the exclusion of all other *līlās.*

A final difference can be seen in the last line where Sūradāsa says that through touching and seeing the divine the body becomes pure:

> *parasata sūra hota tana pāvana darasana karata atītani* ||[17]

Harirāma, on the other hand, says that in this way the body becomes pure and through this method one obtains the divine:

aisehiṃ vyāsa hota tana pāvana ihiṃ bidhi milata atītini ||[18]

Here once again there is an impression that whereas Sūradāsa is speaking of the experience of the devotees in the mythological past, at the time of the incarnation of Kṛṣṇa, Harirāma is speaking in terms of dwelling in Vṛndāvana as a spiritual practice to be followed at the present time.

If, therefore, *pada* 1108 was introduced into the *Sūrasāgara* from another source, it is clear that changes were incorporated into it, making the *pada* more in accord with the sentiments and concepts of the rest of the *Sūrasāgara.*

The third *pada* of the *Sūrasāgara* which includes the expression of a personal desire to live in Vṛndāvana, i.e., as the wish of the poet himself, is extremely long — 121 verses. This in itself, according to the findings of Hawley, suggests lateness.[19] Most of the *pada* is an account of the *rāsa* along the lines of the *BhP.* The last six lines (three verses) coming after the Sūradāsa signature (*chāpa*), introduce a number of terms much more characteristic of Rādhāvallabha poetry than of the rest of the *Sūrasāgara.*

The verse asking for residence in Vṛndāvana runs:

sūra āsa kari varanyau rāsa |
cāhata hau bṛmdābana bāsa ||
rādhā(bara) itani kari kṛpā |[20]

If the *bara,* which is in brackets in the published text, were omitted, Sūradāsa would be requesting Rādhā for the favour of being allowed to live in Vṛndāvana, a request similar to that *pada* 1792 discussed above and very frequently found in Rādhāvallabha poetry. The significance of the brackets is unexplained in the text. Presumably the word in brackets is included in some manuscripts and not in others. The test of scanning the metre suggests that the *bara* is redundant, since without it we have a thirteen *mātrā* line, and the rest of the *pada* consists of two fifteen *mātrā* lines alternating with one thirteen *mātrā* line. At this point the possibility of Rādhāvallabha influence may be noted.

The suggestion of influence from outside the main body of the *Sūrasāgara* tradition becomes even stronger in the next few lines of the *pada,* where the poet asks Hari to keep him there where *harivaṃsī* and *haridāsīare,* and to grant him participation in the eternal sport — *nita bihāra*:

harivaṃsī haridāsī jahāṃ |
hari karunā kari rākhahu tahāṃ ||
nita bihāra ābhāra dai |[21]

Though the first line could be understood as referring to the flute and servant-maids of Hari, the placing of the two names together in such a context would seem to be too much of a coincidence, particularly in view of the reference to *nita bihāra*, which is such an important term in the poetry of the Rādhāvallabha and Haridāsī sects, while rare in the *Sūrasāgara*. Moreover, a further Rādhāvallabha/Haridāsī term, *rasa rīti*, is used in the following line which says that reciting and listening enhances the way of *rasa*:

kahata sunata bāḍhata rasa rīti |[22]

A final point which may be made about this *pada* is that the eight lines incorporating the Rādhāvallabha/Haridāsī elements all occur after the Sūradāsa signature. It is unusual for the signature to be anywhere but in the last or second to last line. The fact that these last eight lines occur after the signature could well indicate that they are later additions to the *pada*.

The three *padas* discussed above contain the main references in the *Sūrasāgara* which can be construed as referring to physical residence in Vṛndāvana along the lines of Rādhāvallabha and Haridāsī poetry. The fact that all three show distinct features suggesting that they are later additions, differing in outlook from the mainstream of the *Sūrasāgara* tradition, would seem to prove that such a concept was not a part of that tradition.

There are, however, a number of *padas* which refer to the blessedness of living in Braj-Vṛndāvana, and yet still do fit into the *Sūrasāgara* tradition. This is because they are speaking in mythological terms. An example of this can be seen in *pada* 689, which says that Nanda, the father of Kṛṣṇa, is blessed; the *gopīs* are blessed; blessed it is to live in Braj and blessed is the birth of Kṛṣṇa which purifies the earth:

dhanya naṃda dhani dhanya gopī dhanya braja kau bāsa |
dhanya dharanikaranapāvana janma sūrajadāsa ||[23]

The reference to the *gopīs* and Nanda in the same line as to living in Braj indicates that they are to be understood as examples of people who enjoyed such an experience. The activity of living in Braj is thus placed in the mythological past, at the time of the birth of Kṛṣṇa, the incarnation. In other words, Braj-Vṛndāvana as the scene of incarnation is being glorified, but no connection is made with a particular geographical locality. The devotee involves himself in the experience, first through memory of it and finally realization of that event within himself. It may be noted that this presentation is in line with the differences found in *pada* 1108 in contrast to the Harirāma *pada* 97.

One means employed to place the desire to live in Vṛndāvana in a mythological context is that of expressing this sentiment in the words of characters who form part of the mythological framework, rather than in the words of the poet himself. *Pada* 1107, for example, begins with the line, 'O Mādhava, make me the dust of Vṛndāvana':

mādhau mohiṃ karau vṛndāvana renu।[24]

At first sight the sentiment appears to be close in tone to those found in Rādhāvallabha literature. The rest of the *pada* makes it clear, however, that these words are being attributed to Brahmā. The third line speaks of the worthlessness of his divine body and high position:

kahā bhayau yaha deva deha dhari aru ūṃcaiṃ pada pāeṃ ainu।[25]

These are both obviously attributes of Brahmā and not of a devotee.

Moreover, here again the emphasis is on the presence of Kṛṣṇa, the incarnation, in Vṛndāvana, not on physical inhabitation of Vṛndāvana as a spiritual practice. Brahmā desires to be made the dust of Vṛndāvana because the feet of Kṛṣṇa touch it everyday:

jihiṃ caranani ḍolata naṃdanandana dina prati bana bana cārata dhenu।[26]

The mythological structure implicit in the above *pada* is made explicit in a further long *pada* which describes the Brahmā episode at length. Here again Brahmā is depicted as asking to be allowed to live in Vṛndāvana in any form — whether creeper, stone or tree:

karahu mohiṃ braja renu dehu vṛndāvana bāsā।
māṃgauṃ yahai prasāda aura meraiṃ nahiṃ āsā।
joi bhāvai soi karahu tuma latā silā druma gehu।[27]

Again the contrast is made between the dust of Vṛndāvana and the celestial realm of Brahmā which is said no longer to please him:

bṛṃdābana raja hvai rahauṃ brahma loka na suhāi।[28]

The other context in which desire to live in Vṛndāvana is expressed by the *Sūrasāgara* — that of the goddesses watching the *rāsa* — resembles the above, both in its contrast of a celestial region with Vṛndāvana and in the way the utterances are put in words of a mythological character. In *pada* 1664, for example, the goddesses ask why the creator did not make them women of Braj, why he made them live in heaven:

hamakauṃ bidhi brajabadhū na kīṃhī
kahā amarapura vāsa bhaeṃ |[29]

They, like Brahmā, ask to be made trees and creepers of Vṛndāvana:

bṛṃdāvana druma latā hūjiyai karata sauṃ māṃgiyau calau |[30]

Here again it is the nature of Vṛndāvana as the realm in which the divine becomes immanent which is emphasized.

The Symbolic Approach

The concept of living in Vṛndāvana as a devotional practice as well as a spiritual state emerges distinctly from the writings of the Gauḍīya Gosvāmīs. The *Bhaktirasāmṛtasindhu* of Rūpa Gosvāmī, for example, describes the *sādhanā* to be practised by a devotee. The five main practices advised are: (1) worship of an image; (2) listening to the *BhP.* as a means of remembering the activities of the divine; (3) keeping company with other devotees; (4) repeating the divine name; and, finally (5) residing in the Mathurā area. The first four are all advised by the *BhP.* as well. This means that the idea of living in Vṛndāvana is one in which the Gosvāmīs display most clearly their difference from the *BhP.*

It does not seem sufficient to explain this difference purely on the grounds of the establishment of the area as a sectarian centre by the Gosvāmīs. Rather it is arguable that the impulse to re-discover Vṛndāvana arose from the religious doctrines themselves; i.e., in particular the concept of *līlā* as being an eternal, unceasing fact. The geographical Vṛndāvana was not important to the *BhP.* tradition because it was concerned with the mythological expression of a metaphysical concept. The Gauḍīya Gosvāmīs, on the other hand, were concerned with its symbolic expression.

The lack of distinction between physical practice and spiritual state owing to the identification of the geographical with the symbolic Vṛndāvana is evident in the writings of the Gauḍīya Gosvāmīs. This can be seen in the way that the *Bhaktirasāmṛtasindhu* describes the importance of living in Vṛndāvana both as a part of *sādhanā-bhakti,* i.e., physical practice, and *bhāva-bhakti,* i.e., the state of devotion itself.

The paradox of the divine and earthly nature of Mathurāmaṇḍala is evident in the description in the *sādhanā-bhakti* section. Salvation is said to be the fruit obtained in other pilgrimage centres, while in Mathurā that devotion to Hari which is sought by salvation itself is obtained:

> *anyeṣu puṇyatīrtheṣu muktir eva mahāphalam* |
> *muktaiḥ prārthyā harer bhaktir mathurāyām tu labhyate* ||[31]

The comparison of Mathurāmaṇḍala with other pilgrimage centre places it in a similar category of a place on earth which is to be physically visited, though the difference in the objects obtained in each — one devotion, the other salvation — is already apparent.

The transcendental nature of the realm is illustrated by the fact that Mathurā is said to be greater than Vaikuṇṭha, the celestial region:

> *aho madhupurī dhanyā vaikunṭhāc ca garīyasī* |[32]

The very next line indicates its geographical nature by saying that through dwelling there for one day devotion to Hari is born:

> *dinam ekaṃ nivāsena harau bhakti prajayate* |[33]

This again affirms the importance of physical inhabitation of Vṛndāvana leading to a spiritual state — devotion.

The mythological aspect of Vṛndāvana is undoubtedly drawn upon in the Gauḍīya texts far more than in the Rādhāvallabha and Haridāsī. This can be seen, for example, in the description of love for the dwelling-place of Kṛṣṇa found in the *bhāva* section of the above text. The devotee is depicted as desiring to visit Vṛndāvana where once Kṛṣṇa performed certain acts, and in this context refers to a number of *BhP*. *līlās* such as the destruction of the cart and binding of Kṛṣṇa by Yaśodā:

> *atrāsīt kila nandasadma śakaṭasyātrābhavad bhañjanam*
> *bandhacchedakaro 'pi dāmabhir abhūd baddho 'tra dāmodaraḥ* |
> *itthaṃ māthuravṛddhavaktravigalatpīyūṣadhārāṃ pivann*
> *ānandāśrudharaḥ kadā madhupurīṃ dhanyaś cariṣyāmy aham* ||[34]

Here the use of the past tense, e.g., *āsīt*, *abhavad*, and *abhūt*, is noteworthy, suggesting a reference to the incarnation of Kṛṣṇa in the mythological past, and at the same time a geographical Vṛndāvana in the present. In this it differs from both the *Sūrasāgara* tradition where all references to living in Vṛndāvana are in terms of the mythological past itself, as well as from the Rādhāvallabha texts where Kṛṣṇa and Vṛndāvana are eternally inseparable — Kṛṣṇa is always present in Vṛndāvana.

The paradox of identity and difference between the transcendental Goloka and the immanent Gokula is expressed in the *Laghubhāgavatāmṛta* of Rūpa in the context of discussing the different abodes of Kṛṣṇa. These are said to be basically threefold — i.e., Gokula, Mathurā and Dvāravatī. The apparent existence of a fourth abode — Goloka — is explained by saying that if a Goloka is postulated, that is also derived from the power (*vaibhava*) of Gokula:

yat tu golokanāma syāt tac ca gokulavaibhavam |[35]

In other words Gokula and Goloka are not in reality two separate *dhāmans*. By analogy, however, with the concept of manifestations of the divine as *vaibhavas* (discussed in Chapter 2), it would follow that Gokula is the original source of Goloka and so superior. This interpretation is substantiated by the next verse which states that the fact of Goloka's derivation from the power of Gokula results from the immenseness of the glory of Gokula:

tadātmakavaibhavatvaṃ ca tasya tanmahimonnateḥ |[36]

In other words the transcendent is a reflection of the immanent. This basically fits in with the way in which the Kṛṣṇa aspect of the divine is regarded as superior to the Viṣṇu aspect.

The relation between the divine and the earthly Vṛndāvana, as well as the role of living in Vṛndāvana as a part of devotional practice, is also discussed in the *Bṛhadbhāgavatāmṛta* of Sanātana Gosvāmī with conclusions similar to those discussed above.

The principles of religious practice outlined in the *Bhaktirasāmṛtasindhu* are here put into the context of a narrative dealing with devotees within historical time. These devotees are depicted performing the type of *sādhanā* advocated in the above text. For example, after the Brāhman in the story has repeated the *mantra* given to him, he is told in a dream not to take *sannyāsa* but to go to Vṛndāvana:

mā mūrkha kuru sannyāsaṃ drutam śrīmathurāṃ vraja |
tatra vṛndāvane 'vaśyaṃ pūrṇārthas tvaṃ bhaviṣyasi ||[37]

Thus the repetition of the divine name eventually leads one to residence in Vṛndāvana. That going to Vṛndāvana usurps the place of *sannyāsa* is also interesting, as such a concept is echoed in the Braj Bhāṣā texts as well.

The concept of the simultaneous identity and difference between Goloka and Gokula is expressed in this text in a verse which says that Kṛṣṇa sports in the land of Braj just as he does in Goloka. The only difference is that one is below and the other above, i.e., one is immanent, the other transcendent:

yathā krīḍati tadbhūmau goloke 'pi tathaiva saḥ |
adhaūrddhyatayā bhedo 'nayoḥ kalpyeta kevalam ||[38]

The text goes on to say that in Braj, i.e., the earthly region, Kṛṣṇa is not always seen by all, though he is sporting tirelessly with Nanda and others:.

kintu tadbrajabhūmau sa na sarvair dṛśyate sadā |
taiḥ śrīnandādibhiḥ sārddham aśrāntaṃ vilasann api ||[39]

This corresponds to the concept of manifest and unmanifest *līlā* discussed above (see pp. 35-36). Goloka is the scene of unmanifest *līlā,* Gokula of manifest *līlā.*

The essential identity of the two abodes comes across most explicitly in a further verse according to which the same means through which aspirants can reach Goloka will also enable them to see the same Lord and his sport here in the world of mortals:

śrīgolokaṃ gantum arhanty upāyair yadṛgbhis taṃ sādhakās tādṛśaiḥ syuḥ |
draṣṭum śaktā martyaloke 'pi tasmiṃs tādṛk krīḍaṃ suprasannaṃ prabhuṃ tam |[40]

Thus, living in the terrestrial Vṛndāvana is not only a spiritual practice but also the goal achieved through such practice.

The concept of identity between the transcendent and the immanent, the symbolic and the geographical, is echoed in a statement of one of the characters, Gopa, who describes how after he had reached Goloka he realized that it was identical with the Mathurāmaṇḍala situated in the mortal world. It had all the same features — cowherds, cows, *gopīs,* mountains, rivers and so forth:

evaṃ tatra ciraṃ tisṭhan martyalokasthitam tv idam |
mathurāmaṇḍalaṃ śrīmad apaśyaṃ khalu tādṛśam |
tattacchrīgopagopībhis tābhir gobhiś ca tādṛśaiḥ |
paśupakṣikṛmikṣābhṛtsarittarvādibhir vṛtam ||[41]

The transcendental abode is thus conceived as being modelled in the image of the terrestrial. The emphasis is upon the way in which the divine reflects the earthly, rather than *vice versa*. This is similar to the concept of the Goloka as a *vaibhava* of Gokula found in the *Laghubhāgavatāmṛta*.

In the Braj Bhāṣā texts of the Rādhāvallabha and Haridāsī sects the ambiguity between the divine and earthly nature of Vṛndāvana is as marked as in the Gauḍīya texts. The concept of Goloka is, however, utterly ignored. The texts in question do not mention Goloka even once. The explanation for this may be seen in the fact that these texts make no attempt to incorporate the Purāṇic mythological structure. There is no manifest and unmanifest *līlā*, there is only *nitya vihāra*. There is no divine and terrestrial Vṛndāvana — the terrestrial is the divine.

The identity between the earthly and the divine Vṛndāvana is made clear by Dhruvadāsa in his *Vṛndāvana sata*. He says that though in the world, Vṛndāvana is supernatural:

> *vipina alaukika loka meṃ ati abhūta rasakanda*|[42]

The paradox between *alaukika* and *loka meṃ* reflects the paradox in the nature of Vṛndāvana. This paradoxical situation is similarly inherent in a verse which says that though Vṛndāvana is on earth, it is higher than all other regions:

> *yadyapi rājata avani para saba taiṃ ūṃcau āhi*|[43]

The nearest that Dhruvadāsa comes to giving an explanation of the situation is in the statement that though the forest of Vṛndāvana shines forth in the world, ordinary eyes cannot see it due to the influence of *māyā*:

> *pragaṭa jagata meṃ jagamagai vṛndāvipina anūpa*|
> *naina achata dīsata nahīṃ yaha māyā kau rūpa*||[44]

It is, therefore, only illusion which conceals the real nature of Vṛndāvana, just as it is illusion which prevents the soul from participating in the eternal sport.

As in the Gauḍīya texts, the act of living in Vṛndāvana is described both as a physical practice and as a spiritual state. Because Vṛndāvana is deemed to be both in the world and not of it, any differentiation between the two conditions is almost undetectable. Certainly there are frequent references to apparently physical acts. Dhruvadāsa describes how when living in Vṛndāvana one should be satisfied with leaves and vegetables gathered on the first and second day of the month:

dūje tīje jo jurai sāka patra kachu āya |
tāhī soṃ saṃtoṣa kari rahai adhika sukha pāya ||[45]

A further verse describes how the devotee wanders in the forest, clad in old clothes, his hair dishevelled, his heart filled with love, singing of the divine couple's happiness:

jīrana paṭa ati dīna laṭa hiye sarasa anurāga |
vivasa saghana bana meṃ phirai gāvata yugala suhāga ||[46]

Such a description of spiritual practice is reminiscent of the instructions of the *Bhaktirasāmṛtasindhu.*

Also apparently in support of a physical understanding of the need to live in Vṛndāvana, is a comparison of such residence with visiting a pilgrimage place. Dhruvadāsa compares leaving Vṛndāvana for another pilgrimage place with abandoning a philosopher's stone for the sake of a cowrie:

taji kai vṛndā vipina kauṃ aura tīrtha je jāta |
chāṃḍi vimala ciṃtāmaṇī kauḍī kauṃ lalacāta ||[47]

The equivalence of Vṛndāvana with a pilgrimage place is more apparent than real in this verse, since an important distinction is drawn between the two. Though a wish-yielding stone and a cowrie are apparently both stones, in actuality they are not of the same substance. Whereas one is mundane, the other is supernatural. In other words, Vṛndāvana appears like any other pilgrimage place only to those who cannot perceive its real nature.

Bihārinadāsa resembles Dhruvadāsa closely with regard to his portrayal of living in Vṛndāvana, as he does in other respects, i.e., the concept of *nitya vihāra* and his description of Vṛndāvana. This can be seen in the way a number of Bihārinadāsa's verses describe living inVṛndāvana in unmistakably physical terms. One verse says one should live in Braj carying a clay-pot and a small blanket and be satisfied with whatever rice one gets from the inhabitants of Braj:

śrībihāridāsa braja yauṃ basau karuvo kāmari khyātu |
jathā lābha saṃtoṣa gahi brajabāsina kau bhātu ||[48]

Despite verses such as the above, it is arguable that the mental and spiritual aspect of living in Vṛndāvana is emphasized even more strongly in the poetry of Bihārinadāsa than in that of Dhruvadāsa. It is certainly made clear that the physical act in itself is not enough. One verse points out that there are as many ways of living in Vṛndāvana as there are of worship, and while some are true, others are false, practised merely out of greed:

> *jeto aṃtara bāsa meṃ tetau jāni upāsa* I
> *śrībihārīdāsa kachu sāṃca hai kachu kachu lobha libāsa* II[49]

The equivalence made betwen a spiritual state and living in Vṛndāvana is apparent from the way in which never moving from Vṛndāvana is equated with the state of one-pointed devotion (*ananyabhāva*). One verse says that those who are *ananya* can never be tempted by supernatural powers, wealth or salvation itself to move a step from Vṛndāvana:

> *aṣṭasidhi nava nidhi mukti pada dai baurāvata dīkha* I
> *śrībihārīdāsa ananya na ṭari haiṃ taji vṛndāvana bīkha* II[50]

The act of living in Vṛndāvana as a spiritual state can also be seen expressed in the concept of service in the palace (*mahala kī ṭahala*). The palace has been seen to represent Vṛndāvana (see above p. 113), therefore service in the palace is synonymous with *Vṛndāvana vāsa*. It is through the service in the palace that the soul can participate in the eternal divine sport and so experience the *rasa*, which is the essence of the divine. The devotee, the soul, becomes a *sakhī* in the palace and thus one of the four essential elements of the divine sport itself. The subtle nature of the service in the palace, as well as the role of the *sakhī* in the sport, can be seen from a verse which describes how the Vedas searched the whole world and could not find the Lord. The only way of finding him is through service in the palace. The Vedas can never enter the sport where the *sakhī* keeps the divine sport alive with love, putting even *madhura-rasa* through a sieve:

> *veda ḍhamḍhorā loka kau ṭerata ḍhola bajāi* I
> *bihārīdāsa tā mahala kī ṭahala karau dularāi* I
> *śrībihārīdāsa bihāra meṃ veda na pāvaiṃ jāṃni* I
> *sakhī jivāvaiṃ prema sauṃ mahā madhura rasa chāṃni* II[51]

Thus to live in Vṛndāvana, according to poets such as Bihārinadāsa and Dhruvadāsa, essentially denotes a spiritual state, i.e., participation in the eternal divine activity which finds its expression in the divine, symbolic Vṛndāvana. At the same time, because of its nature as a symbol, and the identification of the symbol with that which it represents, the earthly Vṛndāvana is identified with the symbolic. The entire concept is linked with that of *rasa* through which the real dwelling in Vṛndāvana takes place, when *māyā* drops away, and the divine reality which in actuality was always there is at last perceived.

References

1. For further discussion on *svarūpa* see R. Barz, *The Bhakti sect of Vallabhācārya*, Faridabad, 1976, p. 48. See also P.D. Mītala, *Braj ke dharmasaṃpradāyoṃ kā itihāsa, op. cit.*, p. 237.
2. *BhP., op. cit.*, X.47.61. 'Or let me become one of the shrubs, creepers and herbs in Vṛndāvana, enjoying the dust of the feet of those girls who abandoned their own relatives, so difficult to abandon, and the noble path, and followed the path of Mukunda which the Vedas seek.'
3. Prabodhānanda, *op. cit.*, 17.9. 'Let me be inspired with desire to be born again and again even in the condition of grass or shrub in the land of Vṛndāvana which is hailed as best of groves.'
4. *Ibid.*, v.10. 'I bow to that forest of Rādhā, where Uddhava, though fulfilled through the experience of the delight of massaging Hari's feet, desires to become grass.'
5. *BhP., op. cit.*, VII. 5.23. 'Listening, glorifying, remembering Viṣṇu, serving (his) feet, worshipping, bowing down in front of, servitude, friendship, self-surrender.'
6. *Ibid.*, X.30.2. 'The women whose hearts were disturbed by the gait, smiles of love, and wandering glances, by the sweet words and sportive movements of the Lord of Ramā, assumed those actions, having identity with him.'
7. Sūradāsa, *op. cit.*, *pada* 1792. 'Through the grace of Rādhā, the beloved of Śyāma, I will obtain residence in Braj.'
8. *Ibid.*, *pada* 1792. 'Near the forest abode formed by a fresh bower, I will build a hut, full of happiness.'
9. J.S. Hawley, *op. cit.*, p. 70, footnote 5.
10. Sūradāsa, *op. cit.*, *pada* 1792. 'I will show the glory of *bhajana* through the grace of *guru* and the greatness of his feet.'
11. *Ibid.*, *pada* 1108. 'Dwell thus on the pathways of Braj.'
12. *Ibid.*, *pada* 1108. 'Fill your stomach with grains of rice taken from the leaf-plates of the cowherds.'
13. *Ibid.*, *pada* 1108. 'Rolling on the ground in every bower, cover yourself with dust, happily.'
14. Harirāmavyāsa. *Bhaktakavi vyāsajī*, Mathurā 1952, *pada* 97. 'Sustain yourself with grains of rice taken from the leaf-plates of holy men.'
15. Sūradāsa, *op. cit.*, *pada* 1108. 'Seeing the darling of Nanda everyday and drinking the water of Yamunā.'
16. Harirāma *op. cit.*, *pada* 97. 'Having every the vision of Kṛṣṇa and Rādhā. . .'
17. Sūradāsa, *op. cit.*, *pada* 1108. 'The body of Sūra becomes pure by touching and looking upon the divine.'
18. Harirāma, *op. cit.*, *pada* 97. 'In this way the body of Vyāsa becomes pure and through this method one obtains the divine.'
19. J.S. Hawley, *op. cit.*, p. 66.
20. Sūradāsa, *op. cit.*, *pada* 1798. 'Sūra with this desire describes the *rāsa* — I long to live in Vṛndāvana, O Rādhā('s husband) have this much grace upon me.'

21. *Ibid., pada* 1798. 'Hari, have compassion and keep me there, where Harivaṃśa and Haridāsa are. Grant me (participation in) the eternal sport.'

22. *Ibid., pada* 1798. 'Reciting and listening enhances the way of *rasa*.'

23. *Ibid., pada* 689. 'Blessed is Nanda; blessed, most blessed, is the *gopī*; blessed is (their) dwelling in Braj; blessed is the birth (of Kṛṣṇa) which purifies the earth, (says) Sūrajadāsa.'

24. *Ibid., pada* 1107.

25. *Ibid., pada* 1107. 'What is the use of bearing this divine body and of obtaining such a high position.'

26. *Ibid., pada* 1107. 'Which is scattered by the feet of the son of Nanda everyday as he takes the cows to graze from wood to wood.'

27. *Ibid., pada* 492. 'Make me the dust of Braj; give me dwelling in Vṛndāvana. I ask for only this blessing and have no other desire. Make me whatsoever you like — a creeper, rock, tree or house.'

28. *Ibid., pada* 492. 'I will become the dust of Vṛndāvana; I do not like Brahmaloka.'

29. *Ibid., pada* 1664. 'Why did the creator not make us women of Braj; what's the use of living in heaven.'

30. *Ibid., pada* 1664. 'Let us go and ask the creator to make us trees and creepers of Vṛndāvana.'

31. Rūpa Gosvāmī, *Bhaktirasāmṛtasindhuḥ*, ed. by Bon Mahārāja, Vṛndāvana, 1965, p. 233, I. 235. 'In other holy pilgrimage places, salvation alone is the supreme fruit. In Mathurā, however, devotion to Hari, which is sought by salvation itself, is obtained.'

32. *Ibid.*, p. 233, I.237. 'Blessed is Madhupurī, greater than Vaikuṇṭha.'

33. *Ibid.*, p. 233, I.237. 'Through dwelling there for one day devotion to Hari is born.'

34. *Ibid.*, p. 356, II.40. 'Here indeed was the abode of Nanda; here was the breaking of the cart; here Dāmodara, the cutter of bondages, was bound by a rope — drinking the flow of nectar from the mouths of the elders of Mathurā, with tears of joy flowing, blessed, when will I wander in Mathurā?'

35. Rūpa Gosvāmī, *Laghubhāgavatāmṛta, op. cit.*, p. 49. 'But the "Goloka" realm is derived from the power of Gokula.' For the use of the term *vaibhava* as manifestation of power, cf. *MārkP. śaktivaibhāvika.*

36. *Ibid.*, p. 250. 'Goloka's derivation from the power of Gokula results from the immenseness of the greatness of Gokula.'

37. Sanātana Gosvāmī, *Bṛhadbhāgavatāmṛta*, Vṛndāvana, 1975, 2.1.53. 'O fool, do not take *sannyāsa.* Quickly go to Mathurā. There in Vṛndāvana you will undoubtedly have your desires fulfilled.'

38. *Ibid.*, 2.5.168. 'As he sports in that region (of Braj), so (he sports) in Goloka. The difference between the two is only through lowness and highness.'

39. *Ibid.*, 2.5.169. 'In that Braj region, however, he is not always seen by all, though sporting with Nanda, etc., tirelessly.'

40. *Ibid.*, 2.5.172. 'By the same means through which aspirants are able to go to Goloka, they can see in that mortal world the same playful, well-pleased Lord.'

41. *Ibid.*, 2.6.371-72. 'Thus remaining there for a long time, I saw that this Mathurāmaṇḍala in the mortal world is just like that one (Goloka), having the same cowherd boys, *gopīs*, cows, animals, birds, insects, mountains, rivers, trees and so forth.'

42. Dhruvadāsa, *Vṛndāvana sata, op. cit.*, v. 35. 'The supernatural forest is in the world; a unique source of *rasa*.'
43. *Ibid.*, v. 74. 'Though it is on earth, it is higher than all else.'
44. *Ibid.*, v. 83. 'The unparalleled forest of Vṛndā shines forth, manifest in the world. Though one has eyes one cannot see it, such is the form of *māyā*.'
45. *Ibid.*, v. 89. 'Being satisfied with whatever vegetables or leaves you may gather on the second or third (day), live, having great happiness.'
46. *Ibid.*, v. 93. 'With old clothes and dishevelled hair, heart overcome, he wanders in the dense forest, singing of the couple's joy.'
47. *Ibid.*, v. 81. 'He who leaves Vṛndāvana and goes to another pilgrimage centre, (is like one who) giving up a pure wish-yielding stone, covets a cowrie.'
48. Bihārinadāsa, *op. cit.*, p. 202, v. 486. 'Bihārinadāsa says live thus in Braj, with the famous pot and blanket. Be content with whatever you get of rice from the inhabitants of Braj.'
49. *Ibid.*, p. 230, v. 603. 'As many differences as there are in dwelling, so many know there to be in worship. Bihārinadāsa says, some are true, others are (practised) through greed.'
50. *Ibid.*, p. 389, v. 69. 'The eight supernatural powers, the nine types of wealth and salvation may tempt him, but he who is one-pointed will not move a step from Vṛndāvana.'
51. *Ibid.*, p. 184, v. 420. 'The Vedas searched the world beating a drum, but Bihārīdāsa performs service in the palace with love. Bihārīdāsa says, the Vedas cannot enter the sport. The *sakhī* keeps alive the divine sport with love, putting *madhura-rasa* through a sieve.'

6

Conclusion

VṚNDĀVANA is presented in the literature in two distinct ways — mythic and symbolic. In both cases, Vṛndāvana is to be understood as an aspect of the divintiy itself, essential for its self-manifestation (*līlā*). It is a means whereby the worshipper can envisage the self-manifestation by imputing to it a time and a place.

By mythic may be understood the presentation of Vṛndāvana as the fairy-tale setting of primordial myth. The symbolic representation, on the other hand, involves a manifest Vṛndāvana which, for the worshipper, symbolizes a transcendent and yet a eternally present Vṛndāvana.

The concept of a mythic 'paradise' as an imaginary stage-setting for the ineffable process of self-manifestation and of a symbolic 'Goloka' can readily be recognized in the most ancient literature of India and Iran. The former may be seen in the wooded setting enjoyed by various primordial pairs of creatures; the latter in the *yávasa* 'cattle pasture' or *gávyūti*, Avestan *gaoyaoiti*.

In the Vedic literature an ambiguity is maintained in respect of distinctions between the unmanifest and the manifest. Neither the mythic scenes that might be taken to be prototypes of Vṛndāvana nor the 'Goloka' concept as a temporal and spiritual reward is explicitly of this world or not of this world. If anything, the divine (e.g., *tád ékam*) is more real (*sát*) than the manifest (*māyā*).

The relevant Vaiṣṇava *Purāṇas* maintain the myth, but abandon the symbolism : new symbols of eternal bliss emerge — e.g., Vaikuṇṭha. Given the notion of a mythic Vṛndāvana in the *Purāṇas*, a quasi-historical and -geographical appreciation of concept inevitably gathered strength. Nevertheless, the basic elements of Vedic symbolism (cows, cowherds, pastures etc.) subsist in the Purāṇic Vṛndāvana, conceived as a divine enviroment. Indeed in the *BhP*. there is a considerable development towards both geographical verisimilitude and symbolic metaphysical interpretations of geographical features

The *Purāṇas* postulate an ultimate reality including both the manifest, that which is related to Kṛṣṇa, and the unmanifest, that which is related to Viṣṇu. Such a duality in the nature of the divine, as well as its specific expression in terms of Viṣṇu and Kṛṣṇa, has also been seen to have its roots in the Vedic tradition.

In the Purāṇic texts, creation and incarnation are seen as both being equally forms of divine self-expression and hence of *līlā*. In fact, still no basic difference is being made between creation and incarnation: *līlā* is synonymous with any form of divine acitivity. Since Vṛndāvana is the space within which *līlā* takes place, it is as much the scene of creation as of incarnation.

In the Gauḍīya texts Vṛndāvana as the realm of divine manifestation remains a symbol of the totally transcendent world. No less than in the Vedic literature, the symbolism of cows and pastures is to the worshipper a guarantee of eternal reward; the subordination of these concepts to classical notions of Viṣṇu's divintiy as seen in the *Purāṇas* is not so much rejected as ignored.

The Gauḍīya texts, even more than the *BhP.*, envisage the manifest Kṛṣṇa as being more real than the unmanifest Viṣṇu. This is compatible with the acceptance of *līlā* as the ultimate expression of the divine. In these texts, *līlā* as divine self-manifestation is seen as being outside of creation (which is essentially a product of *māyā* and so a form of divine self-concealment rather than self-expression). Vṛndāvana is therefore equally disconnected from creation: all interest is focused on its role in relation to *līlā*, i.e., its role as concrete symbol of the divine world. However, the retention of the mythological framework of the *Purāṇas* results in Vṛndāvana being endowed with two forms — the mythic Vṛndāvana and the transcendent Goloka — which are said to be identical in reality.

The sectarian poets of Braj Bhāṣā such as Bihārinadāsa and Dhruvadāsa utterly reject all mythological elements in the expression of *līlā*, with the consequence of Vṛndāvana retaining purely its symbolic role. These poets, however, resemble the Gauḍīya texts in their total dissociation of the eternal divine sport from the process of creation. Here again unceasing divine activity is viewed as the ultimate self-expression of the divine, a concept which necessitates the maintaining of Vṛndāvana as a transcendental entity in its role as divine space without which such activity is an impossibility.

The *Sūrasāgara* appears to be the result of an attempt to modernize the actual subject-matter of the *Purāṇas*. Where the Gauḍīya Gosvāmīs interpret casuistically the actual wording of Purāṇic texts and other sectarian authors ignore them, the *Sūrasāgara* incorporates elements of symbolic development into the Purāṇic mythological structure itself, much along the lines of the *BhP*.

As regards the historical development in the conceptualization of Vṛndāvana, the mythic expression found in the Purāṇic literature clearly represents the ideas of the classical period. The symbolic role of Vṛndāvana that is, on the other hand, stressed in Braj Bhāṣā and Sanskrit commentatorial literature might therefore be taken to reflect a purely medieval development. Since however a Vedic prototype of both aspects can be traced, the possibility cannot be ruled out that at any given historical period the two concepts were developing simultaneously, the choice of emphasis depending more on the nature of the text in question than on its chronological position. The relative lateness of the *Hariv.* and the *BhP.*, for example, has not been proved by any objective criteria, but rather on the basis of one particular view of the history of ideas.

Appendix A

In the following appendix, the full text of relevant *RV.* hymns is given, with translations of extracts most important for the present purposes as well as a minimum of necessary critical discussion.

The text used is Aufrecht's transliterated edition of the RV. It must be noted that his system of transliteration differs from the standard system otherwise used in this thesis in the following way:

Aufrecht	*Standard*
â, î, û	*ā, ī, ū*
ṛi	*ṛ*
ñ	*ṅ*
ç	*ś*
sh	*ṣ*

On the upper left hand side of each section of the appendix can be found the hymn reference number — the *RV.* Maṇḍala number followed by the hymn number. Next to this, important terms or concepts of the hymn or group of hymns in question are cited. On the upper right hand side the name of the author appears in brackets followed by the deity to whom the hymn is addressed. This information is obtained from the *Anukr.* Below is the Sanskrit text in which the translated verses and phrases are **bold type**. This is followed by the translation and finally the critical notes.

Appendix A.1

6.9. *kṛṣṇám áhar, árjunam áhar* (*ṛṣi*: Bārhaspatya Bharadvāja; *devatā:* Vaiśvānara Agni)

áhaś ca kṛṣṇám áhar árjunaṃ ca   ví vartete rájasī vedyā́bhiḥ |
vaiśvānaró jā́yamāno ná rā́jā   (á)vātiraj jyótiṣāgnís támāṃsi ||1||
nā́háṃ tántuṃ ná ví jānāmy ótuṃ   ná yáṃ váyanti samaré 'tamānāḥ |
kásya svit putrá ihá váktvāni   paró vadāty ávareṇa pitrā́ ||2||
sá ít tántuṃ sá ví jānāty ótuṃ   sá váktvāny ṛtuthā́ vadāti |
yá īṃ cíketad amṛ́tasya gopā́   aváś cáran paró anyéna páśyan |3| |
ayáṃ hótā prathamáḥ páśyatemám   idáṃ jyótir amṛ́taṃ mártyeṣu |
ayáṃ sá jajñe dhruvá ā́ níṣatto   (á)martyas tan(ú)vā várdhamānaḥ ||4||
dhruváṃ jyótir níhitaṃ dṛśáye káṃ   máno jáviṣṭhaṃ patáyatsv antáḥ |
víśve devā́ḥ sámanasaḥ sáketā   ékaṃ krátum abhí ví yanti sādhú ||5||
ví me kárṇā patayato ví cákṣur   v(í) idáṃ jyótir hṛ́daya ā́hitaṃ yát |
ví me mánaś carati dūráādhīḥ   kíṃ svid vakṣyā́mi kím u nū́ maniṣye ||6||
víśve devā́ anamasyan bhiyānā́s   tvā́m agne támasi tasthivā́ṃsam |
vaiśvānaró (á)vatūtáye no   (á)martyo (a)vatūtáye naḥ ||7||

1. *kṛṣṇá áhar* and *árjuna áhar* alternate according to the *vedyā́s*[1] (what is to be known, must be determined? cf. 8.96.10-12 *kuvíd angá vedat* 'he (Indra) will surely know/understand', like v. 2 ab here, a type of phrase used to introduce important conundrums). Agni Vaiśvānara, as a new-born king, overcame the darkness with *jyótis.*

2. . . . Whose son is it will speak *váktvas* (what is to be said cf. *vedyā́bhiḥ* in v. 1.) here (that are) superior to his inferior father('s)?

3. . . . He who is the *amṛ́tasya gopā́ḥ* will perceive this, wandering below and seeing (what is) above the Other.

4. He is the first *hótṛ*, behold him, this *amṛ́tam jyótis* among men; he has been forn placed in the *dhruvá*, the immortal, *tanvā́ várdhamānaḥ*. . .

7. Vīśve Devā́ḥ worshipped Thee in fear, Agni, as Thou stoodest in the darkness. . .

Geldner sees here a 'Sängerstreit, i.e., competition between singers, but doe some violence to the text to maintain his view. Significant for the present purpose is that there is speculation as to Agni's form when he stands in the dark. The dark and light forms are named as *kṛṣṇá* and *árjuna* respectively, and the dichotomy is associated with the of *pára* and *ávara* which are identified as Viṣṇu and Agni respectively in *AitBr.* 1.1. The *RV.* evidently associated the matter with the higher and lower 'birds on a tree' motif (cf. especially the use of the term *anyá* in both contexts).[2] From this it would follow that Kṛṣṇa is already envisaged in a *vana,* and is designated a *gopāḥ* (v. 3.).

Important also is the fact of this being an Agni hymn, as this confirms the connection between Kṛṣṇa and Agni.

Appendix A.2

8.85[3] *kṛ́ṣṇaḥ* (*ṛṣi*: Kṛṣṇa Āngirasa: *devatā*: Aśvins)

ā́ me hávaṃ nāsatyā́śvinā gácchataṃ yuvám |
mádhvaḥ sómasya pītáye ||1|
imáṃ me stómam aśvinemáṃ me śṛṇutaṃ hávam |
mádhvaḥ sómasya pītáye ||2|
ayáṃ vāṃ kṛ́ṣṇo aśvinā hávate vājinīvasū |
mádhvaḥ sómasya pītáye ||3|
śṛṇutáṃ jaritúr hávaṃ kṛ́ṣṇasya stuvató narā |
mádhvaḥ sómasya pītáye ||4|
chardír yantam ádābhyaṃ víprāya stuvaté narā |
mádhvaḥ sómasya pītáye ||5|
gáchataṃ dāśúṣo gṛhám itthā́ stuvató aśvinā |
mádhvaḥ sómasya pītáye ||6|
yuñjā́thāṃ rā́sabhaṃ ráthe vīḍvàṅge vṛṣaṇvasū |
mádhvaḥ sómasya pītáye ||7|
trivandhuréṇa trivṛ́tā ráthenā́ yātam aśvinā |
mádhvaḥ sómasya pītáye ||8|
nū́ me gíro nāsatyā́śvinā prā́vataṃ yuvám |
mádhvaḥ sómasya pītáye ||9|

3. I, Kṛ́ṣṇa, call upon you, the Aśvins, rich in mares, so that sweet Soma may be drunk.
4. Listen to the invocation of the singer Kṛ́ṣṇa as he offers praise, O heroes, so that sweet Soma may be drunk.

There is no explicit suggestion that this Kṛ́ṣṇa is in difficulties, but this is usually the basic idea of such passages and the presumable prototype, the adjacent passage 8.96.13ff refers to the help of Indra, while the ritual exhortation to the *jaritṛ́* forms a part of the other framework of the story. Transfer to the Aśvins has involved drastic simplification *vis-à-vis* 8.96.

Appendix A.3

10.39 f.	*(doṣā́ — vástor āyātam madhupéyam)*	(*ṛṣi*: Kākṣīvatī Ghoṣā; *devatā*: Aśvins)
10.41	appeal to Aśvins for offspring, with list of ancients helped by Aśvins	(*ṛṣi*: Suhastya Ghauṣeya; *devatā*: Aśvins)

A.3a
10.39

yó vāṃ párijmā suvṛ́d aśvinā rátho ***doṣā́m uṣā́so*** *hávyo havíṣmatā |*
śaśvattamā́sas tám u vām idáṃ vayáṃ pitúr ná nā́ma suhávaṃ havāmahe ||1|
codáyataṃ sūnṛ́tāḥ pínvataṃ dhíya út púraṃdhīr īrayataṃ tád uśmasi |
yaśásaṃ bhāgáṃ kṛṇutaṃ no aśvinā sómaṃ ná cā́ruṃ maghávatsu nas kṛtam ||2|
amājúraś cid bhavatho yuváṃ bhágo (a)nāśóś cid avitā́rāpamásya cit |
andhásya cin nāsatyā kṛśásya cid yuvā́m íd āhur bhiṣájā rutásya cit ||3|
yuváṃ cyávānaṃ sanáyaṃ yáthā ráthaṃ púnar yúvānaṃ caráthāya takṣathuḥ |
níṣ ṭaugryám ūhathur adbhyás pári víśvét tā́ vāṃ sávaneṣu pravā́cyā ||4|
purāṇā́ vāṃ vīry\ā prá bravā jáne (á)tho hāsathur bhiṣájā mayobhúvā |
tā́ vāṃ nú návyāv ávase karāmahe (a)yáṃ nāsatyā śrád arír yáthā dádhat ||5|
iyáṃ vām ahve śṛṇutáṃ me aśvinā putrā́yeva pitárā máhyaṃ śikṣatam |
ánāpir ájñā asajātyā́matiḥ purā́ tásyā abhíśaster áva spṛtam ||6|
yuváṃ ráthena vimadā́ya śundhyúvaṃ n(í)y ūhathuḥ purumitrásya yóṣaṇām |
yuváṃ hávaṃ vadhrimatyā́ agacchataṃ yuváṃ súṣutiṃ cakrathuḥ púraṃdhaye ||7|
yuváṃ víprasya jaraṇā́m upeyúṣaḥ púnaḥ kalér akṛṇutaṃ yúvad váyaḥ |
yuváṃ vándanam ṛśyadā́d úd ūpathur yuváṃ sadyó viśpálām étave kṛthaḥ ||8|
yuváṃ ha rebháṃ vṛṣaṇā gúhā hitám úd airayataṃ mamṛvā́ṃsam aśvinā |
yuvám ṛbī́sam utá taptám átraya ómanvantaṃ cakrathuḥ saptávadhraye ||9|
yuváṃ śvetáṃ pedáve 'śvinā́śvaṃ navábhir vā́jair navatī́ ca vājínam |
carkṛ́tyaṃ dadathur drāvayátsakhaṃ bhágaṃ ná nṛ́bhyo hávyaṃ mayobhúvam ||10|
ná táṃ rājānāv adite kútaś caná nā́ṃho aśnoti duritáṃ nákir bhayám |
yám aśvinā suhavā rudravartanī purorathā́ṃ kṛṇutháḥ pátnyā sahá ||11|
ā́ téna yātaṃ mánaso jávīyasā ráthaṃ yáṃ vām ṛbhávaś cakrúr aśvinā *|*
yásya yóge duhitā́ jā́yate divá ubhé áhanī sudíne vivásvataḥ *||12|*

tā́ vartír yātaṃ jayúṣā ví párvatam ápinvataṃ śayáve dhenúm aśvinā |
vṛ́kasya cid vártikām antár ās(i)yād yuváṃ śácībhir grasitā́m amuñcatam ||13|
etáṃ vāṃ stómam aśvināv akarma átakṣāma bhṛ́gavo ná rátham |
ny àmṛkṣāma yóṣaṇāṃ ná márye nítyaṃ ná sūnúṃ tánayaṃ dádhānāḥ ||14|

10.39.12 With the chariot faster than thought, which the Ṛbhus made for you, at whose yoking the Daughter of Heaven is born, O Aśvins, come at the two auspicious days of Vivasvat.

In fact the Aśvins come night and morning — 10.39.1. *doṣā́m uṣā́saḥ*, 1040.4. *doṣā́ vástoḥ;* so there is a clear allusion here to *kṛṣṇám áhar árjunam áhar.*

A.3b
10.40

ráthaṃ yā́ntaṃ *kúha kó ha vāṃ narā práti dyumántaṃ suvitā́ya bhūṣati |*
prātaryā́vāṇaṃ *vibhvàṃ viśé-viśe* ***vástor-vastor*** *váhamānaṃ dhiyā́ śámi ||1|*
kúha svid doṣā́ kúha ***vástor*** *aśvínā kúhābhipitváṃ karataḥ* ***kúhoṣatuḥ*** *|*
kó vāṃ śayutrā́ vidháveva devárаṃ máryaṃ ná yóṣā kṛṇute sadhástha ā́ ||2|
prātár jarethe *jaraṇéva kā́payā* ***vástor-vastor*** *yajatā́* ***gacchatho gṛhám*** *|*
kásya dhvasrā́ bhavathaḥ kásya vā narā rājaputréva sávanā́va gacchathaḥ ||3|
yuvā́ṃ mṛgéva vāraṇā́ mṛgaṇyávo doṣā́ vástor havíṣā ní hvayāmahe |
yuváṃ hótrām ṛtuthā́ júhvate narā íṣaṃ jánāya vahathaḥ śubhas patī ||4|
yuvā́ṃ ha ghóṣā páry aśvinā yatí rā́jña ūce duhitā́ pṛché vāṃ narā |
bhūtáṃ me áhna utá bhūtam aktáve (á)śvāvate rathíne śaktam árvate *||5|*
yuváṃ kavī́ ṣṭhaḥ páry aśvinā rátham víśo ná kútso jaritúr naśāyathaḥ |
yuvór ha mákṣā páry aśvinā mádhv āsā́ bharata niṣkṛtáṃ ná yóṣaṇā ||6|
yuváṃ ha bhujyúṃ yuváṃ aśvinā váśaṃ yuváṃ śiñjā́ram uśánām úpārathuḥ |
yuvó rárāvā pári sakhyám āsate yuvór ahám ávasā sumnám ā́ cake ||7|

yuváṃ ha kṛśáṃ yuvám aśvinā śayúṃ yuváṃ vidhántaṃ vidhávām uruṣyathaḥ |
yuváṃ saníbhya stanáyantam aśvinā (á)pa vrajám ūrṇuthaḥ saptā́syam ||8|
jániṣṭa yóṣā patáyat kanīnakó ví cā́ruhan vīrúdho daṃsánā ánu |
***ā́smai rīyante nivanéva síndhavo (a)smā́ áhne bhavati tát patitvanám** ||9|*
jīváṃ rudanti ví mayante adhvaré dīrghā́m ánu prásitiṃ dīdhiyur náraḥ |
vāmáṃ pitṛ́bhyo yá idáṃ sameriré máyaḥ pátibhyo jánayaḥ pariṣváje ||10|
ná tásya vidma tád u ṣú prá vocata yúvā ha yád yuvatyā́ḥ kṣéti yóniṣu |
priyósriyasya vṛṣabhásya retíno gṛháṃ gamemā́śvinā tád uśmasi ||11|
ā́ vām agant sumatír vājinīvasū ny àśvinā hṛtsú kā́mā ayaṃsata |
ábhūtaṃ gopā́ mithunā́ śubhas patī priyā́ aryamṇó dúryān aśīmahi ||12|
tā́ mandasānā́ mánuṣo duroṇá ā́ dhattáṃ rayíṃ sahávīraṃ vacasyáve |
kṛtáṃ tīrtháṃ suprapāṇáṃ śubhas patī sthāṇúṃ patheṣṭhā́m ápa durmatíṃ hatam ||13|
kvà svid adyá katamā́sv aśvínā vikṣú dasrā́ mādayete śubhás pátī |
ká īṃ ní yeme katamásya jagmatur víprasya vā yájamānasya vā gṛhám ||14|

10.40.1. . . . chariot which leaves at dawn . . . drives at dawn . . .

2. . . . at eve . . . at dawn . . . they turn in . . . they have spent the night . . . in bed . . . in the assembly.

3. . . . you woke at dawn . . . you go home at dawn . . . like princes.

4. . . . at eve and at dawn . . .

5. Ghóṣā, the king's daughter, approached the Aśvins and said, 'I ask you, my Lords, be with me for the day and for the night; be helpful for a hero with horses and chariot.'

9. A maiden was born, a young boy took flight, and plants came forth wondrously; to him rivers came running as if downstream, to him is vouchsafed the status of husband for the day.

A. 3c
10.41

samānám u tyáṃ puruhūtám ukthyàṃ ráthaṃ *tricakráṃ sávanā gánigmatam |*
párijmānaṃ vidathyàṃ suvṛktíbhir vayáṃ v(i)yuṣṭā ***uṣáso*** *havāmahe ||1|*
prātaryújaṃ nāsatyā́dhi tiṣṭhathaḥ prātaryā́vāṇaṃ madhuvā́hanaṃ rátham |
víśo yéna gácchatho yájvarīr narā kīréś cid yajñáṃ hótṛmantam aśvinā ||2|
adhvaryúṃ vā mádhupāṇiṃ suhástyam agnídhaṃ vā dhṛtádakṣaṃ dámūnasam |
víprasya vā yát sávanani gácchatho ***(á)ta ā́ yātaṃ madhupéyam aśvinā*** *||3|*

10.41.2. The chariot which is yoked at dawn . . . leaves at dawn.

3. Come, Aśvins, to the sweet (Soma-)drinking.

This 3-verse hymn thus combines a version of the 6.9.1. motif (day/night) and of the 8.85 motif (refrain: sweet Soma).

Appendix A.4

10.42-44 (*ṛṣi:* Kṛṣṇa Āngirasa; *devatā:* Indra)

A.4a
10.42

ásteva sú pratarám lā́yam ásyan bhū́ṣann iva prá bharā stómam asmai |
vācā́ viprā́s tarata vā́cam aryó ***ní rāmaya jaritaḥ sóma índram*** *||1|*
dóhena gā́m úpa śikṣā sákhāyam prá bodhaya jaritar jārám índram *|*
kóśaṃ ná pūrṇáṃ vásunā n(í)yṛṣṭam ā́ cyāvaya maghadéyāya śū́ram ||2|
kím aṅgá tvā maghavan bhojám āhuḥ śiśīhí mā śiśayáṃ tvā śṛṇomi |
ápnasvatī máma dhī́r astu śakra vasuvídaṃ bhágam indrā́ bharā naḥ ||3|
tvā́ṃ jánā mamasatyéṣv indra saṃtasthānā́ ví hvayante samīké |
átrā yújaṃ kṛṇute yó havíṣmān nā́sunvatā sakhyáṃ vaṣṭi śū́raḥ ||4|
dhánaṃ ná ***syandráṃ*** *bahuláṃ yó asmai tīvrā́n sómān āsunóti práyasvān |*
tásmai śátrūnt sutúkān prātár áhno ní sváṣṭrān yuváti hánti vṛtrám *||5|*
yásmin vayáṃ dadhimā́ śáṃsam índre yáḥ śiśrā́ya maghávā kā́mam asmé |
ārā́c cit sán bhayatām asya śátrur ny àsmai dyumnā́ jányā namantām ||6|
ārā́c chátrum ápa bādhasva dūrám ugró yáḥ śámbaḥ puruhūta téna |
asmé dhehi ***yávamad gómad*** *indra kṛdhí dhíyaṃ jaritré vā́jaratnām ||7|*
prá yám antár ***vṛṣasavā́so*** *ágman tīvrā́ḥ* ***sómā*** *bahulā́ntāsa índram |*
nā́ha dāmā́naṃ maghávā ní yaṃsan ní sunvaté vahati bhū́ri vāmám ||8|
utá prahā́m atidī́vyā jayāti kṛtáṃ yác chvaghnī́ vicinóti kālé |
yó devákāmo ná dhánā ruṇaddhi sám ít táṃ rāyā́ sṛjati svadhā́vān ||9|
góbhiṣ ṭaremā́matiṃ durévāṃ yávena kṣúdhaṃ puruhūta víśvām |
vayáṃ rā́jabhiḥ prathamā́ dhánāny asmā́kena vṛjánenā jayema ||10|
bṛ́haspátir naḥ pári pātu paścā́d utóttarasmād ádharād aghāyóḥ |
índraḥ purástād utá madhyató naḥ sákhā sákhibhyo várivaḥ kṛṇotu ||11|

10.42.1. . . . make Indra halt at the Soma.

2. . . . bring hither the *sákhī* (like a) cow with milking, wake Indra (like a) lover.

5. . . . breaks his enemies to the yoke in the dawn of the day.

10-11. May we overcome ruinous poverty of thought with herds (of ideas), hunger with corn . . . May we be first to win wealth with our nation and our rulers. Let Bṛhaspati protect us from the enemy behind and from the one above and below; let Indra (protect) us from the one in front and in the midst, let the ally make space for the allies.

(References to cows, etc.: v. 5 *syandrám*; 7 *yávamad gómat*; 8 *vṛṣasavā́saḥ. . . sómāḥ*)

There appears to be here, at the outset (vv. 1, 2, 5) a vestige of the night/day motif. At the end, there is an insistence on nationhood and military power (suggestive, perhaps, of Dvārakeśa Kṛṣna); note the parallel syntax of the second verse and the second last verse. The concepts of *sákhi* and cows are prominent in the intervening standard accumulation of praise of Indra.

A.4b
10.43.

ácchā ma índraṃ matáyaḥ *svarvídaḥ sadhrī́cīr víśvā uśatī́r anūṣata |*
pári ṣvajante jánayo yáthā pátiṃ
máryaṃ ná śundhyúṃ maghávānam ūtáye ||1||
ná ghā tvadríg ápa veti me mánas tvé ít kā́maṃ puruhūta śiśraya |
rā́jeva dasma ní ṣadó 'dhi barhíṣy
asmínt sú sóme 'vapā́nam astu te ||2||
viṣūvṛ́d índro ámater utá kṣudháḥ sá íd rāyó maghávā vásva īśate |
tásyéd imé pravaṇé saptá síndhavo
váyo vardhanti vṛṣabhásya śuṣmíṇaḥ ||3||
váyo ná vṛkṣáṃ supalāśám ā́sadant
sómāsa índraṃ mandínaś camūṣádaḥ |
praíṣām ánīkaṃ śávasā dávidyutad vidát svàr mánave jyótir ā́ryam ||4||
kṛtáṃ ná ***śvaghnī́*** *ví cinoti* ***dévane*** *saṃvárgaṃ yán maghávā sū́ryaṃ jáyat |*
ná tát te anyó ánu vīryàṃ śakan ná purāṇó maghavan nótá nū́tanaḥ ||5||
víśaṃ-viśaṃ maghávā páry aśāyata jánānāṃ dhénā avacā́kaśad ***vṛ́ṣā*** *|*
yásyā́ha śakráḥ sávaneṣu ráṇyati sá tīvraíḥ sómaiḥ sahate pṛtanyatáḥ ||6||
ā́po ná síndhum abhí yát samákṣarant sómāsa índraṃ kulyā́ iva hradám |
várdhanti víprā máho asya sā́dane yávaṃ ná vṛṣṭír divyéna dā́nunā ||7||

***vṛ́ṣā** ná kruddháḥ patayad rájaḥsv ā́ yó aryápatnīr ákṛṇod imā́ apáḥ |*

sá sunvaté maghávā jīrádānave (á)vindaj jyótir mánave havíṣmate ||8|

*új jāyatāṃ paraśúr jyótiṣā sahá bhūyā́ **ṛtásya sudúghā** purāṇavát |*

ví rocatām aruṣó bhānúnā śúciḥ svàr ṇá śukrám̐ śuśucīta sátpatiḥ ||9|

góbhiṣ ṭaremā́matiṃ ... (= 10.42.10) ||10|

bṛ́haspátir naḥ pári ... (= 10.42.11) ||11|

10.43.1-2. Let my thoughts . . . full of desire, shout forth to Indra; let them embrace the lord for favour, like wives the husband, or like (fathers) the splendid youth. My mind set on Thee cannot tear itself away, I have fixed my desire on Thee alone, Puruhūta sit down, Dasma, on the strew, like a king. Let the refreshment be thine at this very Soma.

3. Indra is the driver away of poverty and hunger. He, the Lord, rules over riches and goods; these seven rivers in their descent increase the strength of that mighty bull.

4. As birds to the leafy tree, let the cheering vats of Soma flock to Indra.

Reference to *dyu* : v.5 *śvaghnī́. . . dévane.* Reference to cows etc: v.6 *vṛ́ṣā*, v.8 *vṛ́ṣā*, v.9 *tásyua sudúghāḥ*; vv. 10-11=10.42.10-11.

The romantic beginning (i.e., Vṛndāvana?) here contrasts even more starkly than in the preceding hymn with the military flavour (Dvārakā?) of the close. The mentions of *sákhi* and cows in 10.42 here gives way to a fairly detailed description of a landscape, admittedly on a grander scale than is eventually envisaged for Vṛndāvana, and developing into a piece of standard Indra hymnography.

If an etymology from the adverb *ví*(s) — is postulated for the epithet Viṣṇu (and the characteristic activity of Viṣṇu is *vikramaṇa*, not *veśana*), then a link is acknowledged in v.3 between Viṣṇu and Indra, and so a link is established between Viṣṇu and this hymn. Similarly, 8.89.14 *víṣuṇe.*

Thus just as the *kṛṣṇám áhar* inspiration of 10.39ff is petering out, we may observe the accumulation of *gopā́*, Vṛndāvana, and Viṣṇu motifs accruing under the wide age is of Indra and the tenuous leitmotif of Kṛṣṇa.

At the level of the *Anukr.*, we may note that 10.43f may be deemed to contain allusions to the curious names of *ṛṣis* who are coupled with 'Kṛṣṇa Āngiras' at 8.80ff., viz. Ekadyu Naudhasa and Nodhā Gotama: 10.43.5 contributes *dévane,* and 10.44 contributes *nā́vam.* Of more significance is the possibility of registering the presence of a *'līlā'* motif here in the guise of *dévana* 'gambling'.

10.44 is dedicated to the stupendous exploits of the powerful gigantic Indra, with the intention of stimulating him to produce cows and vegetation. The motifs at the close could be associated with the Govardhanadhara and demon destroying aspects of the eventual Kṛṣṇa story:

A.4c
10.44

ā́ yātv índraḥ svápatir mádāya yó dhármaṇā tūtujānás túviṣmān |
pratvakṣāṇó áti víśvā sáhāṃsy apāréṇa mahatā́ vŕṣṇyena ||1|
suṣṭhā́mā ráthaḥ suyámā hárī te mimyákṣa vájro nṛpate gábhastau |
śī́bhaṃ rājan supáthā́ yāhy arvā́ṅ várdhāma te papúṣo vŕṣṇyāni ||2|
éndravā́ho nṛpátiṃ vájrabāhum ugrám ugrā́sas taviṣā́sa enam |
prátvakṣasaṃ vṛṣabháṃ satyáśuṣmam ém asmatrā́ sadhamā́do vahantu ||3|
evā́ pátiṃ droṇasā́caṃ sácetasam ūrjá skambháṃ dharúṇa ā́ vṛṣāyase |
ójaḥ kṛṣva sáṃ gṛbhāya tvé ápy áso yáthā kenipā́nām inó vṛdhé ||4|
gámann asmé vásūny ā́ hí śáṃsiṣaṃ svāśíṣaṃ bháram ā́ yāhi somínaḥ |
tvám īśiṣe sā́sminn ā́ satsi barhíṣy anādhṛṣyā́ táva pā́trāṇi dhármaṇā ||5|
pṛ́thak prā́yan prathamā́ deváhūtayo (á)kṛṇvata śravas(i)yāni duṣṭárā |
ná yé śekúr yajñíyāṃ nā́vam ārúham īrmaívá té ny àviśanta képayaḥ ||6|
evaívā́pāg ápare santu dūḍhyó (á)śvā yéṣāṃ duryúja āyuyujré |
itthā́ yé prā́g úpare sánti dāváne purū́ṇi yátra vayúnāni bhójanā ||7|
girī́ṁr ájrān réjamānān adhārayad dyaúḥ krandad antárikṣāṇi kopayat |
samīcīné dhiṣáṇe ví ṣkabhāyati vŕṣṇaḥ pītvā́ máda ukthā́ni śaṃsati ||8|
imáṃ bibharmi súkṛtaṃ te aṅkuśáṃ yénārujāsi maghavañ chaphārújaḥ |
asmín sú te sávane astv okyàṃ sutá iṣṭaú maghavan bodhy ā́bhagaḥ ||9|
góbhiṣ ṭaremā́matiṃ ... (= 10.42.10) ||10|
bṛ́haspátir naḥ pári ... (= 10.42.11) ||11|

Appendix A.5

8.96[4]	*drapsá kṛṣṇá*	(*ṛṣi*: Tiraścī Āngiras
	aṃśumáti nadī́	or Dyutāna Māruta;
	dhámantam (kṛṣnám)	*devatā*: Indra/Indra-Mārutaḥ/
	viṣuṇe	Indra-Bṛhaspati)

asmā́ ***uṣā́sa ā́tiranta yā́mam*** *índrāya* ***náktam ū́rmyāḥ*** *suvā́caḥ |*
asmā́ ā́po mātáraḥ saptá ***tasthur*** *nṛ́bhyas* ***tárāya síndhavaḥ supārā́ḥ*** *||1|*
átividdhā vithurénā cid ástrā tríḥ saptá sā́nu sáṃhitā girīṇā́m |
ná tád devó ná mártyas tuturyād yā́ni právṛddho vṛṣabháś cakā́ra ||2|
índrasya vájra āyasó nímiśla índrasya bāhvór bhū́yiṣṭham ójaḥ |
śīrṣánn índrasya krátavo nireká āsánn éṣanta śrútyā upāké ||3|
mánye tvā yajñíyaṃ yajñíyānāṃ mánye tvā cyávanam ácyutānām |
mánye tvā sátvanām indra ketúṃ mánye tvā vṛṣabháṃ carṣaṇīnā́m ||4|
ā́ yád vájraṃ bāhvór indra dhátse madacyútam áhaye hántavā́ u |
prá párvatā ánavanta prá gā́vaḥ prá brahmā́ṇo abhinákṣanta índram ||5|
tám u ṣṭavāma yá imā́ jajā́na víśvā jātā́ny ávarāṇy asmāt |
índreṇa ***mitráṃ*** *didhiṣema gīrbhír úpo námobhir vṛṣabháṃ viśema ||6|*
vṛtrásya tvā śvasáthād ī́ṣamāṇā víśve devā́ ajahur ***yé sákhāyaḥ*** *|*
marúdbhir *indra sakhyáṃ* ***te astv*** *áthemā́ víśvāḥ pṛ́tanā jayāsi ||7|*
tríḥ ṣaṣṭís tvā ***marúto*** *vāvṛdhānā́* ***usrā́ iva*** *rāśáyo yajñíyāsaḥ |*
úpa tvémaḥ kṛdhí no bhāgadhéyaṃ śúṣmaṃ ta enā́ havíṣā vidhema ||8|
tigmám ā́yudhaṃ marútām ánīkaṃ kás ta indra práti vájraṃ dadharṣa |
anāyudhā́so ásurā ***adevā́ś cakréṇa tā́n ápa vapa ṛjīṣin*** *||9|*
mahá ugrā́ya taváse suvṛktíṃ préraya śivátamāya paśváḥ |
gírvāhase gíra índrāya pūrvír dhehí tan(ú)ve kuvíd aṅgá védat *||10|*
ukthávāhase vibh(ú)ve manīṣā́ṃ drúṇā ná pārám īrayā nadī́nām *|*
ní spṛśa dhiyā́ tan(ú)vi śrutásya júṣṭatarasya ***kuvíd aṅgá védat*** *||11|*
tád viviḍḍhi yát ta índro jújoṣat stuhí suṣṭutíṃ námasā́ vivāsa |
úpa bhūṣa jaritar mā́ ruvaṇyaḥ śrāváyā vā́caṃ ***kuvíd aṅgá védat*** *||12|*

áva drapsó aṃśumátīm atiṣṭhad iyānáḥ kṛṣṇó daśábhiḥ sahásraiḥ |
ā́vat tám índraḥ śácyā dhámantam ápa snéhitīr nṛmáṇā adhatta ||13|
drapsám apaśyaṃ víṣuṇe cárantam upahvaré nadyò aṃśumátyāḥ |
nábho ná kṛṣṇám avatasthivā́ṃsam íṣyāmi vo vṛṣaṇo yúdhyatājaú ||14|
ádha drapsó aṃśumátyā upásthe (á)dhārayat tanvàṃ titviṣāṇáḥ |
víśo ádevīr abhy ācárantīr bṛ́haspátinā yujéndraḥ sasāhe ||15|
tvā́ṃ ha tyát saptábhyo jā́yamāno (a)śatrúbhyo abhavaḥ śátrur indra |
gūḷhé dyā́vāpṛthivī́ ánv avindo vibhumádbhyo bhúvanebhyo ráṇaṃ dhāḥ ||16|
tvā́ṃ ha tyád apratimānám ójo vájreṇa vajrin dhṛṣitó jaghantha |
tvā́ṃ śúṣṇasyā́vātiro vádhatrais tvā́ṃ gā́ indra śácyéd avindaḥ ||17|
tvā́ṃ ha tyád vṛṣabha carṣaṇīnā́ṃ ghanó vṛtrā́nāṃ taviṣó babhūtha |
tvā́ṃ síndhūṁr asṛjas tastabhānā́n tvám apó ajayo dāsápatnīḥ ||18|
sá sukrátū ráṇitā yáḥ sutéṣv ánuttamanyur yó áheva revā́n |
yá éka ín náry ápāṃsi kártā sá vṛtrahā́ prátíd anyám āhuḥ ||19|
sá vṛtrahéndraś carṣaṇīdhṛ́t tám suṣṭutyā́ hávyaṃ huvema |
***sá prāvitā́ maghávā no 'dhivaktā́** sá vā́jasya śravasyàsya dātā́ ||20|*
sá vṛtrahéndra ṛbhukṣā́ḥ sadyó jajñānó hávyo babhūva |
kṛṇvánn ápāṃsi náryā purū́ṇi sómo ná pītó hávyaḥ sákhibhyaḥ ||21|

8.96.1. The dawns traversed their stages, the nights by night. . . rivers stopped for crossing . . .

6f. We would make friendship . . . the gods who are your allies. Let there be alliance between Thee and the Maruts.

8. Maruts like herds of cattle.

9. Cast aside those godless Asuras with thy disc.

10. Make many speeches for Indra in person, who is most gracious to the victim; he will surely know.

11. Drive the devotion as with a boat to the far side of the river . . . he will surely know.

12. Perform this service (*viṣ-*) . . . he will surely know.

13. Drapsá Kṛṣṇá came down to (the river) Aṃśumati marching with ten

thousand, Indra helped him as he blew mightily and in heroic fashion plucked out those who were drowning.

14. I beheld Drapsá Kṛṣṇá moving away having come down black as a cloud into the lap of the river Aṃśumáti; I send you, (Marut) bulls, fight in the conflict.

15. So Drapsá in the lap of Aṃśumati shone forth and preserved his person. Indra joined with Bṛhaspati defeated the attacking godless hordes.

16. As soon as Thou wert born, Indra, Thou didst become the opponent of the seven unopposed.

20. . . . The Maghávan is our helper, our advocate . . . the giver . . .

21. Indra, the slayer of Vṛtra, leader of ṛbhus as soon as he was born, he became worthy to be called upon, doing many heroic (*nárya*) deeds, (he became) worthy to be called upon by his allies (*sákhi*).

The text can be deemed to be in principle a discussion between the Maruts and Indra, with another speaker as first person narrator (according to *Anukr.* the narrator is Dyutāna Māruta, cf. v.15 suggest that *Anukr.* sees Drapsá as the offspring or foster child of the Maruts).

One important necessary correction is the identification of a single individual or entity, *drapsá kṛṣṇá*. As Geldner[5] observes, the tradition offers two separate stories by way of background explanation, one with reference to *drapsá* only (=Soma) and the other with reference to *kṛṣṇá* (=Asura) only. Both mistakenly represent Indra as defeating Soma or Asura. Sāyana[6] rejects the Soma story as without scriptural authority; it is probable that he sees *RV.* 1.130.8 as the authority for a *kṛṣna asura* (Geldner refers to 1.130.8, but understands there a reference to Dravidian autochthons, which certainly does not seem plausible in view of the tenor of 8.96). This connection (*índraḥ. . .prā́vat . . .svàrmīḍheṣu ājíṣu . . .śā́sad avratā́n, tvácaṃ kṛṣṇā́m arandhayat*) relates Drapsá Kṛṣṇá here then presumably with the *kṛṣṇá/árjuna* of 6.9, the basic idea being made explicit at the outset of 8.96.1 (*suśā́sah. . .naktam. . .*) Geldner correctly sees that Drapsá is aided by Indra. Against Sāyaṇa, Ludwig and Oldenberg, he takes Kṛṣna to be a separate individual, but must then supply separate verbs, e.g. 'Kṛṣṇa (ist) im Anzug mit zehntausend'. It is in fact quite clear that Indra saves Drapsá Kṛṣṇá who as the Soma drop in the river is destined to emerge as a Kārttikeya saviour.

Having established a link between this 'Kṛṣṇa' hymn and the *kṛṣṇám áhar* concept, it is of considerable importance to the argument that the hymn shows a distinct intention of connecting the Kṛṣṇá Drapsá (or inchoate form of Agni-Soma) with Viṣṇu (or Indra-Viṣṇu), reflected in the inclusion of two etymologies of the name Viṣṇu. The name of the person addressed by the Maruts in the *tṛca* 10-12 is not given, but it contains the first reference to the root *viṣ* (*viviḍḍhi*) as the action which is demanded of that person.

It follows that the person addressed here is the same as the one who gives the eye-witness account of the rescue/birth of 'Kṛṣṇa' in 13-15.

The alternative 'etymology' *víṣuṇe* (i.e., adverbial form of a derivative from *vi-*) is used with reference to Kṛṣṇá's plight in the river: Geldner translates 'in schlemine lage', but the sense of *viṣu* — is literally 'in all directions, various'.

Viṣṇu explicitly has the Maruts as his attendants in 5.87, for example, so the connection with Maruts in this hymn is not unusual.

What is important is the *RV.* attestation of Viṣṇu and Kṛṣṇa, the latter realizing his potential for expression and performance of action thanks to Viṣṇu's faculties of cognition and speech. The usual conception that Viṣṇu belongs ultimately to *parama vyoman* and Indra-Kṛṣṇa to the lower regions is evidently significant; so also is the intermediary role of *sakhis* (Maruts), associated with cattle (*usrā iva rāśáyaḥ*).

The flute of Kṛṣṇa must surely be connected with the *dhámantam kṛṣṇám* here where the blowing conception is an etymologizing idea based on the form *drapsá* (i.e., bubble or drop) that Indra assumes (see Geldner, *ad. loc.*). Drapsá is explicitly Soma and therefore one might conclude that Yamunā is connected with the Aṃśumatī (*soma* plant) matrix that *drapsá* (*soma*) naturally evokes.

References

1. Translated by K.F. Geldner, *Der Rig-Veda*, Vol. 2, Harvard, 1951, p.101, as 'mit Vorbedacht'; by H. Grassman, *Wörterbuch zum Rig Veda*, Leipzig, 1873, p. 1353, as 'absichtlich' i.e., 'intentionally'.
2. *RV.*, *op. cit.*, I.164.20.
3. Aufrecht, *op. cit.*, 8.74.
4. Aufrecht, *op. cit.*, 8.85.
5. Geldner, *op. cit.*, pp. 422-23.
6. Sāyana, in *Rigveda Sanhita*, ed. M. Müller, vol. 4, London, 1962, p. 871.

Glossary

Ādhibhautika : Relating to material living beings.

Ādhidaivika : Relating to the deity

Ādhyātmika : Relating to the supreme spirit

Ādi Parvan : The first section of the *Mahābhārata.*

Agni : The god of fire.

Akṣara brahman : The indestructible spirit

Aṃśa : A portion or part.

Aṃśāvatāra : The incarnation of a portion of the divine

Ānanda : Bliss, one of the three qualities making up the nature of the divine, the other two, being sat, existence, and cid, existence.

Andhakas : The descendants of Andhaka, who was an *Asura,* or demon.

Ātmarati : Expression of the essential being of the divine through delight.

Ātmavihāra : Self-sport or play intrinsic to the divine.

Avama : The lower.

Āvaraṇa : Enclosure or covering.

Avatāra : 'Descent' or incarnation, usually of Viṣṇu.

Balarāma : The brother of Kṛṣṇa.

Banayātrā : Pilgrimage to the various sites of Braja

Bhāndīra tree : The Indian fig tree.

Brajayātrā : Pilgrimage to the various sites of Braja.

Cakra : A wheel or disc.

Devaloka : The realm of the gods.

Dohā : a couplet verse

Gauḍīya : Relating to a Vaiṣṇava sect founded in the sixteenth century in Bengal by Caitanya and his disciples.

Goloka : The celestial abode of Kṛṣṇa.

Gopīs : Cowherd girls of Braja who were devoted to Kṛṣṇa

Goswami : A title used by the founders of the Gauḍīya q.v. sect.

Govardhana mountain : A mountain near Vṛndāvana.

Grāma: : A village.

Guṇa : A quality of property of a substance. Can be used in the sense of one of the three properties belonging to all created things.

Hari : Another name for Viṣṇu.

Icchā : Literally, desire.

Jasodā : Another form of the name Yaśodā, foster mother of Kṛṣṇa.

Krosa : A measure of distance equal to a fourth of a yojana.

Kṛṣṇa : As an adjective this word means 'dark'. As a noun it is the name of the eighth incarnation of Viṣṇu.

Kṛṣṇadhāman : The abode of Kṛṣṇa.

Kṛṣṇaite : Believing in Kṛṣṇa as the supreme being.

Lakṣitah : Characterised or marked.

Lakṣmī : The wife of Viṣṇu and goddess of wealth and good fortune.

Lalitā : One of the female companions of Rādhā.

Līlā : The divine play or sport.

Līlādhaman : The abode within which divine play occurs. The aspect of the divinity which forms the space for the performance of divine self-manifestation.

Līlāsthala : The various places identified with different events in the life of Kṛṣṇa.

Madhura rasa : The devotional sentiment of love expressed in terms of the relationship between a lover and beloved.

Madhusūdana : A name of Kṛṣṇa.

Mandara : The divine mountain used by gods and demons as a churning stick when they churned the ocean for nectar.

Mathurā : The city in which Kṛṣṇa was born.

Māyā : The illusion whereby one considers the unreal universe as really existent and as distinct from the Supreme Spirit.

Nanda : The foster-father of Kṛṣṇa

Nara : A term meaning 'man'

Nārāyaṇa : Another name for Viṣṇu.

Nyagrodha tree : The Indian figtree

Pada : A devotional song

Pāṇḍavas : The five sons of pāṇḍu who are the heros of the *Mahābhārata*.

Parama : The highest, best or supreme.

Paramātma : The supreme spirit

Parāśara : The name of a sage

Prakṛti : Nature or the original source of the material world.

Pratīka : A symbol

Pūja : Ritual worship

Purāṇa : Literally 'Old' 'Handed down from the past' texts containing myths and teachings of the major sects of medieval Hinduism

Puruṣa : A term meaning both 'man' and the Supreme Being.

Puruṣasūkta : A hymn in the *Ṛg Veda* describing the process of creation

Pūtanā : A demoness killed by the child Kṛṣṇa.

Rasa : A word with a range of meanings including 'juice', 'taste', 'vital essence', 'feeling of love', 'aesthetic experience'. In devotional literature, it is used for the experience of the sacred.

Rasika : Literally 'a person of taste or *rasa* q.v.' More specifically followers of the devotional sects which proclaimed the supreme nature of the eternal play of Rādhā and Kṛṣṇa.

Sādhanā : Spiritual practices to be followed by a devotee.

Sakhī : A female companion. In particular one of the companions of Rādhā.

Sakhya bhāva : The expression of devotion to the divine through a relationship such as that of a friend.

Śakti : The active power of the divine often identified with the female aspect.

Sattva guṇa : Consciousness, an elementary substance, as well as the quality of purity regarded as the highest of the *guṇas* qv.

Sevā : Service of or attendance on.

Siddhānta : A principle or teaching

Swarūpa : The true constitution or form.

Swayamrūpa : The self-form

Uddhava : A friend of Kṛṣṇa, who is described as having visited Braja.

Upaniṣadic : The *Upaniṣads* were early philosophical, mystic Hindu texts

Upavana : A grove, one of the minor woods of Vṛndāvana.

Vaikuṇṭha : The celestial dwelling place of Viṣṇu.

Vallabhāite : Following the teachings of Vallabhāchārya the founder of a medieval devotional sect of Hinduism.

Vana : A grove or wood

Vāsudeva : A name both for Kṛṣṇa, son of Vasudeva, and for Viṣṇu, the supreme being.

Vāyu : The god of air.

Vilāsa : This can mean both play and a flash. In this context it has the sense of an appearance for the sake of play

Viraha : Separation from a loved one in this context the pain the *gopīs* qv experienced when separated from Kṛṣṇa.

Viṣṇu : The divine as preserver, who is often regarded as the supreme being. He traditionally the source of incarnations such as Kṛṣṇa.

Viṣṇudhāman : The abode of Viṣṇu.

Vrṣabhāna : The father of Rādhā

Vṛṣṇis : The descendants of Vṛṣṇi, an ancestor of Kṛṣṇa.

Yyūha : A part or portion of the divine.

Yamunā : The river which runs through the land of Braja. One of the major rivers in North India.

Yātrā : Pilgrimage to holy sites.

Yojana : A measure of distance equal to eight or nine miles.

Bibliography

Sanskrit and Prakrit Sources

Ahirbudhnya-saṃhitā, ed. by M.D. Rāmānujācārya, Adyar, 1966.

Aitareya-brāhmaṇa, ed. by Kāśinātha Sāstrī Āgāśe, Ānanda Āśrama, Vol. 1. 1896.

Bālakṛṣṇa Bhaṭṭa, *Prameyaratnārṇava,* Benares, 1971.

Bhagavadgītā, ed. by W.D.P. Hill, London, 1928.

Bhāgavata Purāṇa, Bombay, 1905. Tenth Canto, Bombay, 1867.

Bilhaṇa, *Vikramāṅkadevacaritam,* ed. with intro. by Georg Bühler, Bombay, 1875.

Brahma-saṃhitā, ed. by A. Avalon, commentary by Jīva Gosvāmī, Calcutta, 1928.

Bṛhadāraṇyaka-upaniṣad, in *Aṣṭādaśa-Upaniṣadaḥ,* ed. by V.P. Limaye and R.D. Vaḍekara, Poona, 1958.

Harivaṃśa, ed. by P.L. Vaidya, Poona, 1969. by ed. Rāmacandraśāstrī Kiṃjavaḍekara, Poona, 1936.

Jinaprabhasūri, *Vividhatīrthakalpa,* Santiniketan, 1934.

Kapiṣṭhala-kaṭha-saṃhitā, ed. by Raghu Vira, Delhi, 1968.

Kauṣītaki-upaniṣad, ed. by E.B. Cowell, Benares, 1968.

Lakṣmīdhara Bhaṭṭa, *Kṛtyakalpataru,* Vol. VIII, ed. by R.V. Rangasvāmī Aiyangar, Baroda, 1942.

Lakṣmī-tantra, ed. by V. Krishnamacharya, Adyar 1959.

Mahābhārata, ed. by V.S. Sukthankar, Poona, 1936.

Mitramiśra, *Vīramitrodaya,* Vol. X, Benares, 1971.

Nārāyaṇa Bhaṭṭa, *Brajabhakitvilāsa,* Kusumasarovara, 1951.

Padma Purāṇa, ed. by V.N. Maṇḍalika, Poona, 1894.

Prabodhānanda, *Vṛndāvanamahimāmṛta,* Vols. 1-4, Vṛndāvana, 1961-64.

Ṛg Veda, ed. by Th. Aufrecht, *Die Hymnen des Ṛigveda,* Berlin, 1861. ed. by M. Müller, *Rigveda Sanhita,* Vol. IV, London, 1962. tr. by K.F. Geldner, *Der Rig Veda,* Vol. 2, Harvard, 1951.

Rūpa Gosvāmī, *Bhaktirasāmṛtasindhu*, ed. and tr. by Bon Mahārāja, Vṛndāvana, 1965.

Rūpa Gosvāmī, *Laghubhāgavatāmṛta*, Bombay, 1902.

Sanātana Gosvāmī, *Bṛhadbhāgavatāmṛta*, ed. by Śyāmadāsa, Vṛndāvana, 1975.

Ṣaṭacakranirūpaṇam, ed. by A. Avalon, Calcutta, 1913.

Śatapatha-brāhmaṇa, Ajmere, 1902.

Tantrarāja-tantra, ed. by A. Avalon, London, 1918.

Vallabhācārya, *Aṇubhāṣyam*, ed. by S.T. Pāṭhaka, Poona, 1921.

Vallabhācārya, *Rāsapañcādhyāyī-śrīsubodhinī*, ed. by J. Casturvedī, Benares, 1971.

Vallabhācārya, *Siddhāntamuktāvalī*, Bombay, 1918.

Vallabhācārya, *Tattvārthadīpanibandha*, ed. by K.N. Miśra, Benares, 1971.

Varāha Purāṇa, ed. by Hṛṣīkeśa Sāstrī, Calcutta, 1893.

Viṣṇu Purāṇa, ed. by Jivānanda Vidyāsāgara, Calcutta, 1882.

Yoginīhṛdayadīpikā, commentary by Amṛtānanda Nātha, Benares, 1923.

Braj Bhāṣā Sources

Bihārinadāsa, *[illegible]īgurudevajī kī bānī*, in *Sarvopari-nityavihāriṇi-rasa-sāgar*, Vṛndāvana, 1969.

Dhruvadāsa, *Bayālīsa līlā*, ed. by Lalitācaraṇa Gosvāmī, Vṛndāvana, 1971.

Gadādhara Bhaṭṭa, *Gadādhara bhaṭṭajī kī vānī*, Vṛndāvana, 1958.

Harirāmavyāsa, *Bhaktakavi vyāsajī*, Mathurā, 1952.

Harivyāsadeva, *Mahāvānī*, ed. by Kuñjabihārīśaraṇa, Vṛndāvana, 1976.

Malika Muhammad Jāyasī, *Padamāvata*, Cirgāṃva, 1961.

Nandadāsa, *Nandadāsagraṃthāvalī*, ed. by Brajaratnadāsa, Kāśī, 1949.

Rasikadāsa, *Rasakadaṃbacūḍāmaṇi*, unpublished manuscript, Vṛndāvana.

Sūradāsa, *Sūrasāgara*, ed. by Nandadulāre Vājapeyī, 2 Vols., Benares, 1953.

Secondary Sources

Barz, R., *The Bhakti sect of Vallabhācārya*, Faridabad, 1976.

Bhandarkar, R.G., *Vaiṣṇavism, Śaivism and minor religious systems*, Strassburg, 1913.

Bryant, K.E., *Poems to the Child-God — structures and strategies in the poetry of Sūrdās*, Berkeley, 1978.

Dasgupta, S.N., *A history of Indian philosophy*, Vol. IV, Cambridge, 1949.

De, S.K., *Early history of the Vaiṣṇava faith and movement in Bengal*, Calcutta, 1942.

Dumezil, G., *Mythe et épopée*, Vol. I, Paris, 1968.

Eliade, M., *Patterns in comparative religion*. New York, 1958.

Eliade, M., *The sacred and profane*, New York, 1959.

Eliade, M., *Yoga, immortality and freedom*, New York, 1958.

Geldner, K.F., *Vedische Studien*, Vol. II, Stuttgart, 1897.

Gonda, J., *Die Religionen Indiens*, Vol. I, Stuttgart, 1960.

Grassman, H., *Wörterbuch zum Rig Veda*, Leipzig, 1873.

Growse, F.S., *Mathurā: a district memoir*, NWP and Oudh Gov. Press, 1883.

Hawley, J.S., 'The early *Sūr Sāgar* and the growth of the Sūr tradition', In *JAOS*, 99.1. (1979), pp. 64-72.

Hazra, R.C., *Studies in the Purāṇic records*, Dacca, 1940.

Hopkins, T.J., 'The social teaching of the *Bhāgavata Purāṇa*', In *Kṛṣṇa : myths, rites and attitudes*, Honolulu, 1966.

Ingalls, D.H.H., 'The *Harivaṃśa* as *mahākāvya*', In *Mélanges d'Indianisme á la mémoire de Louis Renou*, Paris, 1968.

Kane, P.V., *History of Dharmaśāstra*, Vol. I, pt. 2, Poona, 1975.

Kinsley, D.R., *The divine player*, Delhi, 1979.

Macdonell, A.A., *Vedic index*, 2 Vols., London, 1912.

Marfatia, M.I., *The philosophy of Vallabhācārya*, Delhi, 1967.

Mayerhofer, M., *A concise etymological Sanskrit dictionary*, Heidelberg, 1963.

McGregor, R.S., *Nanddas — The round dance of Krishna and Uddhava's message*, London, 1973.

Mītala, P.D., *Braja kā sāṃskṛtika itihāsa*, Delhi, 1966.

Mītala, P.D., *Braja Ke dharmasaṃpradāyoṃ kā itihāsa*, Delhi, 1968.

Monier-Williams, M., *A Sanskrit English dictionary*, Oxford, 1899.

Radhakrishnan, S., *The principle Upaniṣads*, London, 1953.

Schrader, F.O., *Introduction to the Pāñcarātra and the Ahirbudhnya Saṃhitā*, Adyar, 1916.

Vājapeyī, K.D., *Braja kā itihāsa*, Mathurā, 1955.

Vaudeville, Ch., 'Braj, lost and found', In *Indo-Iranian Journal*, 18 (1976), pp. 195-213.

Vaudeville, Ch., *Soûr-Das — Pastorales*, Paris, 1971.

Wright, J.C., 'Purūravas and Urvaśī', In *BSOAS*, XXX (1967), pp. 526-47.

Index